The Poetics of Sensibility

The Poetics of Sensibility

A REVOLUTION IN LITERARY STYLE

JEROME McGANN

CLARENDON PRESS · OXFORD

Oxford University Press, Great Clarendon Street, Oxford OX2 6DP

Oxford New York

Athens Auckland Bangkok Bogota Bombay Buenos Aires
Calcutta Cape Town Dar es Salaam Delhi Florence Hong Kong
Istanbul Karachi Kuala Lumpur Madras Madrid Melbourne
Mexico City Nairobi Paris Singapore Taipei Tokyo Toronto Warsaw
and associated companies in
Berlin Ibadan

Oxford is a registered trade mark of Oxford University Press

Published in the United States
by Oxford University Press Inc., New York

© Jerome McGann, 1996

First published 1996
First published as a Clarendon Paperback 1998

British Library Cataloguing in Publication Data
Data available

Library of Congress Cataloging in Publication Data
Data available
ISBN 0–19–818370–4
ISBN 0–19–818478–6 (Pbk.)

3 5 7 9 10 8 6 4 2

Printed in Great Britain
on acid-free paper by
Bookcraft (Bath) Ltd,
Midsomer Norton, Somerset

*This book is Dedicated
to My Mother,*

MARIE V. McGANN

Her ears th' enchanting strains with pleasure greet,
She asks, who sang so early, and so sweet?
           Ann Batten Cristall, 'Before Twilight. Eyezion'

Preface

This book has been a long time coming. It documents an ignorance that has pervaded my life and that I don't imagine I shall ever escape. True, it was an acquired vice. But it flourished unresisted for too long. It gained thereby what my religious teachers used to call 'the temporal punishment due to sin'.

The academic form of that larger vice is my subject here. I first glimpsed that form almost thirty years ago when I read Susan Sontag's *Against Interpretation*, where she called us to an 'erotics of reading'. For no fault of her own, Barthes—her acknowledged mentor—became a stumbling block in my case, since his work was mediated for me through venues that studiously avoided the crucial (affective) issues.

But the whole story would be tedious to recapitulate. We all have our own version of it in any case. Here I want simply to acknowledge those people who came to my assistance in more personal and immediate ways—who helped me to see that something was wrong and that something might be done.

Two people I want to single out. First is Randall McLeod (otherwise known under several witty signs) and his insistence that we learn to 'thingk'. Second is Patricia Spacks, whose passion for conversation might just possibly be greater than my own. Other friends of my enlightenment are many, but especially—so far as this book is concerned—Libby Fay, Nick Frankel, Michael Franklin, Derek Furr, Cheryl Giuliano, Terry Hoagwood, Marjorie Levinson, Marjorie Perloff, Lisa Samuels, Jeffrey Skoblow.

Finally I recall the person to whom this book is dedicated. The first poems I recollect hearing came from her lips. And one of those that ran in my mind for years began 'The boy stood on the burning deck.' It wasn't until I was far gone as a scholar that I learned the author of the poem was Felicia Hemans.

Many more years went by before I started to realize how many worlds were not well lost because I hadn't known that poet's name. The fault wasn't my mother's. She had the poem by heart and didn't think I needed the name. But I was bookish and grew more so with time, and the books I read—they weren't my mother's books—had all banished that name so that I could not see to see.

Later I found the name in the due course of my pedantry. It was a *felix culpa*, an amazing grace.

Contents

Introduction

Fraser's account of the magical and religious views of mankind is unsatisfactory; it makes these views look like errors. . . . But it will never be plausible to say that mankind does all that out of sheer stupidity.

Ludwig Wittgenstein, *Philosophical Occasions*

The words 'sensibility' and 'sentiment' name a momentous cultural shift whose terms were defined in the eighteenth century. The event all but founded the novel, and it produced an upheaval in the way poetry was conceived and written. Both romanticism and modernism organized themselves in relation to the traditions of sensibility and sentiment.

So far as high culture is concerned, however, these traditions remain something of an embarrassment—at best a topic of academic interest, at worst a perceived threat to the practice of art.

The understanding of poetry has suffered most from the situation. This happened because the twentieth-century critique of the sentimental tradition focused on poetry. The scholastic success of this critique not only disappeared a large corpus of vital and important poetry, it obscured the conventions that supported such poetry. The twentieth-century reader's access to this kind of writing was short-circuited from the start.

This book is therefore an attempt to recover a somewhat lost world. My point of departure is institutional modernism, which ordered the academic horizon of writing for most of the twentieth-century and spent much of its energy fighting against the poetic styles I will be examining. The central figure in that campaign was T. S. Eliot, whose defence of a classical tradition, as he saw it, entailed a corresponding assault upon the new and decidedly anti-classical styles of poetry founded in the eighteenth century.

But Eliot was not alone. The antipathy to 'sentimental' styles went broadcast. Of the imposing modernist writers, only Gertrude Stein kept perfect faith with this line of work.

Literary history has represented this story as the struggle of modernism against romanticism. The latter was viewed—in some respects correctly—as an advanced state of sentimentalism. That version of events quickly proved intolerable, however, and today it is a scholastic commonplace that modernism draws upon romanticism in fundamental ways.

Which of course it does. But when later twentieth-century scholars reconstructed that relationship, they also worked to preserve the classicist approach to reading and writing. To the extent that criticism has managed to incorporate romanticism into the (classicist) idea of 'tradition', it has continued to obscure the naïve-and-sentimental heritage bequeathed to all later culture by the eighteenth century. The acts of incorporation were executed by reading romanticism through its most conservative venues, where 'the balance and reconciliation of opposite and discordant qualities' would be emphasized. Roads of excess were roads not taken, and that has made all the difference.

Along with this selective reading of the past went a carefully censored version of modernism itself. Because the moving spirit remained classical, the literary histories that emerged tended to emphasize the continuities pursued by a classicist ideology rather than the contradictions it generated. So we were directed by works that bore titles like *Modern Poetry and the Tradition*. This general approach to reading and writing established its authority in the schools, which continue to rediscover, or reconstruct, new orderly (conceptualized) arrangements for our imaginative inheritance. And all this takes place even though we know very well, or profess to know, that writing—if it is alive— always resists such arrangements. (To appreciate the vitality of modernist writing—including the writing of Eliot—we do best to approach it through its internal conflicts and contradictions. In this way writing has a chance to survive the critical abstractions we bring to elucidate it.)

The poetry of sentiment and sensibility is relevant here for two reasons. First, it was (paradoxically) 'the deepest if not the most attractive legacy of the Age of Reason' (Hagstrum, 1980: 277). Second, the resistance to such writing was raised from the beginning by eighteenth-century classicist figures, and the hostility grew as the resources of sensibility developed and spread.

'Sensibility' was an equivocal condition even for those who gave their hearts to it. Eliot, like Pope in the eighteenth century, was both a great poet and a commanding cultural presence. He was also, like Pope and Johnson, a reactionary figure haunted with premonitory dreams of cultural Armageddon. This dark future cast its shadow across the presence of Pope and Johnson, on one hand, and of Eliot and Pound on the other. In the eighteenth century the shadows were legion—its names are Gray, Macpherson, the Della Cruscans, and a mob of scribbling women.

Eliot named the shadow Gertrude Stein, as we see from the review he wrote in January 1927 for *The Nation & Athenaeum*. The four books under review include Stein's *Composition as Explanation*, recently published (November 1926) by Hogarth Press. The books provoke Eliot to comment upon 'the future' of writing, of language, of art; in particular, the future (or futures) that may be thought to lie within the cultural upheaval that had begun some fifteen or twenty years earlier.

Eliot is not happy with the future he sees forecast in the books he is reviewing. One of them, John Rodker's *The Future of Futurism* (1926), imagines an epoch dominated by two kinds of writing: on one hand, 'a pantheon of super-Mallarmés for a smaller and smaller public', and on the other 'a completely Americanized' and 'popular literature' (Eliot, 1927: 595). Confronted with the example of Stein, however, Eliot sees no 'warrant for believing [with Rodker] that our sensibility will become more "complex" and "refined"' when that new day comes. For Eliot, the future according to Stein is 'precisely *ominous*' of 'a future ... more simple and ... more crude than that of the present'. Eliot ends his review in no uncertain terms:

her work is not improving, it is not amusing, it is not interesting, it is not good for one's mind. But its rhythms have a peculiar hypnotic power not met with before. It has a kinship with the saxaphone. If this is of the future, then the future is, as it very likely is, of the barbarians. But this is the future in which we ought not to be interested. (Eliot, 1927: 595)

In fact, Stein's hypnotic rhythms trace themselves back to the eighteenth century, when poetic writing began to explore the languages of the 'feelings' and the 'heart'—languages that sought to expand their expressive range by developing their non-semantic and transconceptual resources. Eliot understood this kind of writing—witness his essay on Swinburne—but he deplored it and the future it promised.[1] As it turned out, institutional modernism managed to exorcise its most demonic spirit. Swept out of the schools, Stein and seven other devils went elsewhere, and perhaps 'the last state of that man became worse than the first'. We now call that state 'postmodernism'.

The internal conflicts of modernism, the many (celebrated or deplored) postmodernisms, and the 'future' of poetic writing in which we might be interested: these subjects call us to return to the eighteenth century, and in particular to reconsider carefully the poetry of the 'feeling heart', the *cœur sensible*. We tend not to 'read' this poetry, we have tended not to do so for almost one hundred years. But it seems to me that we don't 'read' it because we think we already know it. So we pre-read it instead, if we turn to it at all, or we mine it for information. But the writing as such remains largely unencountered.

My approach here is different. I take it for granted that the poetries of sentiment and sensibility—not, as we shall see, *exactly* the same thing—operate within determinate rhetorical conventions. In this respect they function like any poetic style—like *stil novisti* writing, for example, or metaphysical verse. I also assume that adequate reading begins (though it will not end) by entering into those conventions, by reading in the same spirit that the author writ. To do this requires a considerable effort of sympathetic identification: considerable, because (a) we have been taught for so long to *un*read this kind of writing, and (b) because the writing itself is difficult, often in fact a kind of anti-writing. Its touchstone moments involve failure as well as a discourse of apparently non-articulate (or at any rate non-rational) communication.

My judgement (or my guess) is that recent work in 'Cultural Studies' and especially feminist criticism has called for a work of this kind. That scholarship helped to acquaint us with the nightwood of lost or forgotten writing and has been a salutary event. A less happy consequence of such work, as I read it, is a

[1] It is important to remember that Eliot wrote this essay in 1920, and that he included it in his *Selected Essays* (1932). The essay is one of the central documents in his argument for literary and cultural change.

tendency to evade the question of the aesthetic character and value of the obscured texts; or, if those questions are addressed, to look for value in the moral qualities that can be found in the works. But the power and value of art may have nothing as such to do with morality. Art functions as representation—reflection—and as revelation. Its office is to show and tell, nothing more is required. Part of what it may show and tell are moral realities, but in so far as these come in the form of art, they come as representations and revelations, not as ethical standards or even models. Not many would (now) regard Dante's *Inferno* as an ethical standard. It is a vision of hell through and through, a work far more terrible (and wonderful) than the notorious demonic visions of our contemporary Kathy Acker. And it is worse (and better), we now would probably say, exactly because its horrors are a function of its ethics (as one sees from the *Purgatorio* and *Paradiso*, which are also engendered by those ethics).

But we custodians of culture are continually, *professionally* inclined to imagine that art ought to deliver the best that has been known and thought in the world, and—what is worse—to think of this 'best' as a moral category. The tendency produces grotesque results for anyone interested in promoting the practice of art and imagination. Of course there will aways be a waxing and waning of readers' interests, however much other readers at the same time may deplore those fluctuations. The problem that concerns me, however, and that led me to write this book, is not change or stasis in the canon of what we read. It is the tendency to approach all art, canonical or non-canonical, in rational—in theoretical and philosophical—terms. Theory and method are essential to criticism, but they must be secondary frames of reference: tools picked up to help clarify (for readers) less mediated perceptual encounters (affect at all levels); and to help organize (for writers) the rhetoric of their works.

The poetries of sensibility and sentiment are especially apt for the purposes I am sketching here. They brought a revolution to poetic style exactly by arguing—by 'showing and telling'—that the traditional view of mind and reason would no longer serve a truly reasonable—in eighteenth-century terms, a *sensible*—mind. These poetries, along with the other literatures of sensibility and sentiment, worked their revolution by developing new and non-traditional modes of expression—styles that were the dress of their new thoughts. These new thoughts, whose (western) roots are in ancient sceptical philosophy, assume that no human action of any consequence is possible—including 'mental' action—that is not led and driven by feeling, affect, emotion. Rationalist philosophies, which neglect these matters, incline to treat language as a conceptual vehicle and semantic structure. The new Lockean approach to 'ideas', which saw them as (literally) sensational forms, radically altered the entire cultural terrain. The revolution in philosophy that ensued was accompanied by a revolution in linguistic practice and theory. True to the character of the change involved here, this linguistic revolution was carried out *as a rhetorical and stylistic event*, as a set of writing practices and conventions.

We know these best—that is, they have been most thoroughly studied—in the novels and plays of the period. The specifically poetical styles of sensibility and the sentimental, however, have been neglected. There are historical reasons for this neglect, as I have already suggested. However that may be, special needs urge one to study the poetry (rather than, say, the fiction) of sensibility, and in particular the lyric poetry, or those verse forms that emphasize expressive structure. One is tactical: twentieth-century pedagogy set the lyric as the model of poetic form, and in so doing directed its polemic squarely against the new styles founded in the eighteenth century. Our loss of reading skills is a direct function of this situation. The other reason is strategic. Poetry (unlike fiction) forces one to attend to 'the word as such'. It foregrounds the physique of lexical and grammatical fields, it approaches all aspects of the language, including the signifieds and the referents, as if they were signifying forms. Consequently, studying the poetries of sensibility and sentiment gives one a specially clear view of how a language of affective meanings—of how language *as* affective thought—functions.

Such, at any rate, is the conviction driving this study.

* * *

I die because I cannot die.

St Teresa

As we know, tears are the proper emblem of the literatures of sensibility and sentiment. They mark out a special population who live and move and have their being by affect, through sympathy: men and women of sorrow who are acquainted with grief—responding to it in others, suffering it themselves. Other emblems—blushes, involuntary sighs, swooning, a rapid pulse—expand one's sense of the experience being explored through these literatures. The expansion is a dominantly erotic one, as the touchstone fictions produced by this movement show: *Clarissa, A Sentimental Journey, La nouvelle Heloise, Werther, Paul et Virginie*. In this kind of writing, the body's elementary and spontaneous mechanisms come to measure persons themselves as well as their social relations.

To mete that measure, the 'Age of Reason' brought forth a new, a complex, and a decidedly non-rational constellation of artistic styles. Through it all, tears and a mode of elegiac lament recur and dominate. The wisdom of Ecclesiastes, that Knowledge increaseth Sorrow, centres the imaginations of sensibility and sentiment, which made an important addition to that wisdom by reversing its terms.

But the theme of loss dominates, it does not exhaust, this body of writing, as we shall see. The logic and grammar of its discourse are by no means grounded in elegy or an elegiac style, however characteristic they may be of the poetries of sentiment and sensibility. I therefore postpone the topic of elegiac writing—it comes in Part III—in order to open my subject along a rather more traditional literary-historical line.

Part I recuperates some of the basic terms needed for a study of this kind, both intellectual and stylistic. Parts II and III then consider the poetries of sensibility and of sentiment, respectively. Although the two styles bleed into each other and cannot always be clearly distinguished, we want to try to see their differences. This book argues that the discourse of sensibility is the ground on which the discourse of sentiment gets built. In terms of the crucial mind/body diad that shaped the originary philosophical discussions, sensibility emphasizes the mind in the body, sentimentality the body in the mind. The distinction is a rough one, but it corresponds to discernible features of writing and cultural attitude. The fact that sentimental writing overtakes and subsumes the discourse of sensibility between

1740 and 1840 is important to remember, as are the gender issues that come to structure much of this writing. Lockean thought materialized various spectres for 'the culture of sensibility',[2] 'Unsex'd Females' being the worst of all.[3] As the discourse of sentimentality evolved, it re-established at least the appearance of traditional hierarchies of thought (religious v. secular) and social relations (male v. female).

Those large cultural issues move at the periphery of this book, however, which is, as I have said, a book about writing and poetry, not a book about culture and ideas. (Or it is the latter only to the extent that the (mis)understanding of poetry might be judged, in our contemporary frame of reference, a serious moral and cultural problem.) All three parts of the study focus on particular writers and particular texts. Parts II and III begin with readings that sketch out the basic moves of a poetry of sensibility and a poetry of sentiment. They conclude with specific, self-contained studies of certain salient writers or bodies of writing.

I should explain that my decision to develop critical 'readings' of specific texts comprises an integral part of my critique of the academic legacy of modernism. New Criticism founded itself in a pedagogy of poetic interpretation whose centre-piece was the focused 'reading' of poems. The method explicitly dissociated the interpretable content of a poem from the (subjective) sensibility that engendered the work. Famous New Critical protocols like the Intentional and the Affective Fallacies in effect forbade the critical deployment of the stylistic conventions of sensibility and sentimentality. As a consequence, entire orders of poetical writing went virtually unread; or when certain texts from those orders *were* engaged—Keats is here the exemplary case—their most characteristic features slipped in a moment out of their poetic life. In this book, then, I have felt it important to show that 'close reading' can escape the myopias suffered and promoted by the movement most responsible for the evanishment of the poetries of sensibility and sentiment.

---

[2] The phrase alludes to G. J. Barker-Benfield's useful study *The Culture of Sensibility: Sex and Society in Eighteenth-century Britain* (Chicago: University of Chicago Press, 1992).

[3] This is the title of Richard Polwhele's 1798 poetical critique of contemporary women writers, especially those associated with 'liberal' thought (what the critics of such thought called 'jacobin').

None the less, the book relegates its conceptually 'finished' forms of presentation to subordinate critical positions. There are integral studies of particular writers, or groups of writers, or individual works, and there are also highly structured presentations of certain intellectual and stylistic 'lines'. Most of these critical units focus on individual works and their local stylistic features: they are what Walter Pater would have called 'appreciations'. They are also loosely organized in relation to each other in order to mitigate the appearance of general completion. In this case my own knowledge could not pretend to such, but—in any case—I disbelieve in that kind of completeness, which finally encourages a conceptual and abstract approach to poetic materials.

It is not just that knowledge and understanding undergo constant change. More particularly, our knowledge and understanding of *poetry* ought to hold itself in a condition of fear and trembling. The mind's will to intellectual adequacy is irresistible: hence the need, in studying works of imagination, to resist final representations of that will. A rule of incommensurability must somehow be built into every critical approach to poetry if the criticism has any hope of meeting the work on its own terms.

Such, at any rate, is another conviction driving this study.

PART I

Roads of Excess

Il prévoyait d'étonnantes révolutions de l'amour,
et soupçonnait ses femmes de pouvoir mieux que cette
complaisance agrémentée de ciel et de luxe. Il voulait
voir la vérité, l'heure du désir et de la satisfaction essentiels.
Que ce fut ou non une aberration de piété, il voulut.

Arthur Rimbaud, 'Conte' (Les Illuminations)

I

A Disordering of the Senses

'Women, Fire, and Dangerous Things': the 'natural' association of the three in the Dyirbal language, wonderfully explored by George Lakoff, recalls a similar set of categorial associations that were commonplace in eighteenth-century Europe. Idiots, children, peasants, primitive people, women—all are the 'sentimental' *figurae* of a 'naïve' order. They are imagined as sharing similar qualities, variously seen along a broad spectrum of emotions, feelings, sensations. More specifically, as the word sentimental itself shows, they are imagined as creatures who 'think' through their feelings. That imagination, so deplorable to so many even to this day, is deeply grounded in ancient ideas about mind and body, thinking and feeling, reason and sensation. In its crudest (and clearest) form this imagining represents itself in the difference between men and women, man being the image of the higher powers of mind and reason, woman of the lower orders of body and sensation.

That traditional figuration and philosophy was shaken to its core with the emergence of Locke and the rich body of thought and writing that developed from his work. The issue centres in the relation of thought to materiality. In the *Essay* Locke considers their relation (see especially 4.10.10–17) and rejects the strict materialist position that all is matter and that cogitation—like motion—is one of its dispositions. But he does not revert to the traditional spiritualist view either: for we can't know whether 'Omnipotency has not given to some system of matter, fitly disposed, a power to perceive and think, or else joined and fixed to matter, so disposed, a thinking immaterial substance' (1965: 4.3.6). We can't know this because of human reason's inherent limits.

These limits are not a function of materiality as such but of the difference between a divine and a human intelligence, according to Locke. He doesn't object to the materialist notion of 'the eternal existence of matter' (1965: 4.10.13) because his thought is fundamentally theistic; but his theism also makes him reject the idea of matter as primary generative source. On the question of whether brute matter can possess thought and consciousness, then, Locke proposes a way between the spiritualist and the materialist positions: that 'it is *some certain system of matter*, duly put together, that is this thinking eternal being' (1965: 4.10.16). For Locke, while matter is not inherently energetic, it may be powerfully disposed to thought and action by omnipotent intelligence. Nor are the priorities here temporal—as if matter's power of thought would have to evolve, or be added by God at some 'later time'. The question is strictly metaphysical. Indeed, it appears that Locke arrived at his views by reflecting on the logic of omnipotence in relation to materiality. For Locke, the philosophical disposition of matter (to thinking) must have been established from eternity.

There is no need to rehearse the vigorous discussion that Locke's essay inspired. His general line of thought had an immense effect on European culture, not least because of its congruence with Newton's work, especially the theory of gravitation. Newton's universe was clearly '*some certain system of matter*, duly put together', that possessed self-organizing powers. We want to recall Newton here because his cosmological vantage clarifies the radical shift of focus involved in Locke's philosophical psychology. Because Newton's work organized itself in a study of the non-animate order, the discussion of the vitality of matter was regularly focused at the most primitive levels. The case for or against 'thinking matter' revolved around 'insensate dust' and the 'lower' senses, especially touch.

The Lockean shift is most dramatic in Socinian ideas, especially the thought of Priestley, whose *Disquisitions Relating to Matter and Spirit* (1777) collapses the distinction between matter and spirit and argues the inherent materiality of consciousness. Priestley's position follows upon his view that 'matter is not *impenetrable*' but that it is 'endued with powers of attraction and repulsion, taking place at different distances' (1777: 19). The passage explicitly appeals to the ideas of Rudjer Boscovitch, but the figural terms are clearly Newtonian. Once matter is no longer seen as solid and impervious, it becomes no more 'incompatible with sensation and thought, than that substance . . . we have been used to call *immaterial*' (1777: 18).

Pope was no Socinian, least of all a friend to enlightened women, but even so traditional a work as *An Essay on Man* shows the upheaval that Locke's ideas were diffusing through culture. The poem celebrates established order and the general conception of a great chain of being: 'The gen'ral ORDER, since the whole began,/ Is kept in Nature, and is kept in Man' (I.171–2). Pope everywhere affirms that '*There is an universal* ORDER *and* GRADATION, *thro' the whole visible world, of the* sensible *and* mental *faculties*' (I.207 n.). But in presenting that orderliness, Pope is far more interested in the wondrous perfection of each part of the system than he is in the hierarchy of the parts. When he presents 'The scale of sensual, mental pow'rs' (I.208) in section VII, for example, he does not proceed in a strict progression from the lowest to the highest (e.g., from a consideration of the lower senses, to the higher, and then to the powers of mind, with the latter equally considered in their own ordered hierarchy). What captures his attention is 'how exquisitely fine' (I.217) each power operates, and 'What thin partitions Sense from Thought divide' (I.226). For Pope is struck by the wonder of each part and moment of the whole he is considering, including that part which is 'th' amazing whole' (I.248) itself, the set of all the sets.

> All are but parts of one stupendous whole,
> Whose body Nature is, and God the soul;
> That, chang'd through all, and yet in all the same,
> Great in the earth, as in the aethereal frame,
> Warms in the sun, refreshes in the breeze,
> Glows in the stars, and blossoms in the breeze,
> Lives through all life, extends through all extent,
> Spreads undivided, operates unspent,
> Breathes in our soul, informs our mortal part,
> As full, as perfect, in a hair as heart.
>
> (I.267–76)

This great and justly famous passage measures the presence of Locke's thought exactly because it lies open to the most disparate readings. An exquisite set of figures articulate and embody those 'thin partitions' through which sense and thought, matter and spirit, reflect and communicate with each other. Most important, the celebrated perfection is complete at every level of 'The scale of sensual, mental pow'rs'. Indeed, the diffusion of such perfection opens the lines to a pantheist reading, on one hand, or an orthodox one on the other.

The natural perfections that Pope celebrates, however, all rest in his adherence to the rules of moderation and propriety. Not that he cannot imagine, for instance, a tactile system that would be 'tremblingly alive all o'er' (I.197); indeed, this is the arachnid system, which 'Feels at each thread, and lives along the line' (I.218). 'The bliss of Man', however, 'Is not to act or think beyond mankind' (I.189–90). For Pope, human bliss should avoid the 'effluvia' of Epicurus on one hand and angelic fire on the other (I.199, 278).

But Pope's extraordinary renderings of the perfections and vitalities transacting all the spheres of creation are as tempting to the poetic imagination as Locke's and Newton's ideas were to Priestley. The figure of the spider working through (her) feelings will become traditional for the poet, as Emily Dickinson shows, and the image of the microscope is equally suggestive. If people are not born with microscopic eyes, like the fly, human nature supplies the deficiency. The trope for a 'finer optics' (I.193–6) recovers, in a distinctively enlightenment idiom, the ancient idea of the power of art as the special privilege of human *nature*.

Thus the ambiguity between mind and matter, art and nature that Locke's *Essay* fosters, affects even a conservative poet like Pope, and it multiplies its appearances through the eighteenth century. When Akenside describes the pleasant interchanges between nature and imagination, he establishes a model that will culminate in Wordsworth:

> for th' attentive mind
> By this harmonious action on her pow'rs,
> Becomes herself harmonious; wont so long
> In outward things to meditate the charm
> Of sacred order, soon she seeks at home
> To find a kindred order, to exert
> Within herself this elegance of love,
> This fair-inspir'd delight . . .
>
> (III.599–606)

This is a *locus classicus* of the aesthetics of the Beautiful. For all its modesty, the force driving the text is Eros. It sketches the figure of a woman soon to be named Clarissa Harlowe, whose fair-inspired and harmonious delights of person and mind will so inflame and unbalance the incompetently attentive mind of Lovelace.

Akenside has a Sublime that corresponds to his Beautiful. Drawn (unsurprisingly) from the Bible, it replicates 'the eternal majesty that weigh'd/ The world's foundations' (612–13). But it is an inward majesty, ultimately a social and an ethical sense and sensibility:

> all declare
> For what th' eternal maker has ordain'd
> The pow'rs of man: we feel within ourselves
> His energy divine: he tells the heart
> He meant, he made us to behold and love
> What he beholds and loves, the general orb
> Of life and being.
>
> (622–8)

These deeply correspondent passages express a core experience of sensibility. The sublime gesture essayed in the second shows very clearly that the entire experience is here gendered masculine. But its masculinity is of a special kind, as a comparison with Wordsworth makes plain. Wordsworth follows Akenside closely and he will not take his precursor to any further conceptual level. But he will develop a style for persuading us that he has encountered this same experience in an overwhelming personal way.

The continuity between Akenside and Wordsworth needs elaboration, however, for the differences are as significant as the similarities—especially if we wish to understand the styles of sensibility and sentiment (as opposed to their romantic variants). Consider more closely the first of the pair of texts from Akenside. From grammar to figure through rhetorical form, it is troped in deliberately feminine terms: the gender of 'mind', the images ('charm', 'home', 'kindred', 'elegance', 'love', etc.), the modest, distinctly un-Miltonic blank verse. One has only to compare the style with, for example, the equivalent text in Wordsworth to see what Akenside is doing:

> Imagination—here the Power so called
> Through sad incompetence of human speech,
> That awful Power rose from the mind's abyss
> Like an unfathered vapour . . .
>   (*The Prelude* VI.592–5 [1850 text])

Even when Wordsworth's thought comes most clearly out of Akenside, the manner stays aggressively Miltonic:

> Under such banners militant, the soul
> Seeks for no trophies, struggles for no spoils
> That may attest her prowess, blest in thoughts
> That are their own perfection and reward . . .
>   (VI.609–12)

The recollection of Napoleon's alpine exploits defines Wordsworth's equivalent, equally theatrical grandeurs. The text is romantic drama, what Keats rightly called the egotistical sublime. In such verse 'th' attentive mind' is to be overthrown by an unevadable 'Power'. But in Akenside, the presence of imagination is 'temper'd' and 'wears/ A chaster, milder, more attractive mien' (606–8). The mind that registers such an imagination does not ascend a mountain to be stunned by its God. Indeed, so undemonstrative is Akenside's mind (like his verse), that it will appear only to a reciprocally '*attentive* mind'. So if the philosophical aspects of Akenside's work forecast Wordsworth, as they do, his erotic civility is equally the father of the man of feeling.

Akenside imagines an erotic environment that can be kept 'harmonious' because it should. Excess brings derangement: the rape of Clarissa and her sisters, on one hand; on the other Ambrosio Furioso (whose name is legion: Lovelace, St Prieux, Werther, Sade). These histories all define both the necessity and the danger of every move toward cleansing the doors of perception, or what Blake also called 'an improvement of sensual enjoyment'. The distance in time between Locke and Priestley, Lady Mary Montagu and Mary ('Perdita') Robinson, measures the stakes involved in overturning the traditional understanding of the relations of mind and body.

2

Coleridge's 'Eolian Harp' and the Motion of Thought

No one grasped the issues more clearly than Coleridge. His earliest cultural sympathies drew him to the Socinians, to radically sensationalist philosophers like Hartley, to Della Cruscan poetry.[1] His career would shape itself and evolve as a complex reaction against those early attachments, which he came to regard as a network of materialist errors he would call, broadly and politically, 'jacobin'. We want to consider Coleridge here in order to complete the context within which the poetry of sensibility and sentiment emerged. To the extent that Coleridge's ideas about poetry became the norm of romantic thinking in England, his critique of sensibility supplies a nice differential for marking what distinguishes the various poetries of sensibility.

The pivotal text is 'The Eolian Harp', where Coleridge uses the genre of the conversation poem to enact an immediate experience and critical analysis of sensibility. In the poem sensibility appears as a dialectical condition, a continuous interchange of eroticized sensations and loose philosophical speculations. The 'pensive Sara' stands as Coleridge's emanation, a projection of his self-corrected thoughtfulness. She comes to comprehend and judge the idle and flitting fantasies of her exquisite and philosophical poet-lover.

Two key conventional features of the conversation poem genre—spontaneity and a continuity of mental action—serve Coleridge's purposes extremely well. Both are fundamental to the experience of sensibility, which is the experience Coleridge sought to represent in his poem. His purposes are clearly defined

[1] The best account of Coleridge's early intellectual involvements is John Beer's *Coleridge's Poetic Intelligence* (London and Basingstoke: Macmillan, 1977), esp. chs. 1–4.

in the work's initial textual condition, when the poem was cast in a generic form that had not yet evolved into a conversation poem proper. At that point it was what Coleridge called an 'Effusion', one of thirty-six he published as a group in his 1796 volume *Poems on Various Subjects*. In his preface Coleridge specifically characterized the effusion as a work lacking *'oneness of thought'*. Instead, the effusion tries to represent a variety of more primal experiences—sensations and emotions that are frankly erotic and often tied specifically to the feelings of the child and the affective relations of mothers and children. As *figurae* constructed by Coleridge's highly self-conscious poem, the effusion's surface actions emerge as figures of sensibility. Within that charged affective field, the central figure of the eolian harp becomes an emblem of the poem (and poet) of sensibility, and 'The Eolian Harp' becomes in its turn a higher-order poetical move upon and against the materials it takes up.[2] Coleridge would subsequently assume an unequivocally critical view of these kinds of sensibilious equations:

The mind does not resemble an Aeolian harp, nor even a barrel-organ turned by a stream of water, conceive as many tunes mechanized in it as you like, but rather as far as objects are concerned a violin or other instrument of few strings yet vast compass, played on by a musician of Genius.[3]

As the work evolved from effusion to conversation poem, Coleridge worked to distinguish the flitting fantasy (the effusion) of poet and/or poem as eolian harp from the more substantial idea of a poetical work—*this* poetical work—that reflects upon the experience of such a fantasy. In becoming a conversation poem, 'The Eolian Harp' evolved a critique of its initial enactment: a critique of the ideas of sensibility and, more crucially, of the poetic practice (the effusion) licensed by those ideas. The final conversation poem was to have achieved that *'oneness* of thought' Coleridge mentioned in his preface. Perhaps more important, the achievement would be gained in classic Coleridgean fashion: it would come as an evolution

---

[2] Paul Magnuson's ' "The Eolian Harp" in Context', *Studies in Romanticism* 24 (1985), 3–20 is an extremely useful treatment of the textual development of the poem. Magnuson's 'context' is biographically focused.

[3] This is one of Coleridge's annotations to Kant, quoted in Rene Wellek's *Kant in England, 1793–1838* (Princeton: Princeton University Press, 1931), 83.

of thought and practice, a gradual extrapolation of what was already taken to be implicit in the earliest state of the work.

In what, then, does the work's critique consist? The answer is twofold. First, the pensive Sara disapproves the pantheist and Socinian bent that Coleridge's ideas have taken. Not only are the ideas dangerous in themselves, in particular to orthodox religion, they suggest an intellectual pride needing modest correction. All this is explicit in the poem.

Less explicit is the poem's troubled critique of poetry itself. Eighteenth-century discourse of sensibility seized the eolian harp as a non-conscious tool for revealing the vital correspondences that pour through the material world.[4] Coleridge's poem goes a step further when it entertains the idea that poetry—this very poem—functions like a wind-harp. Not that Coleridge at any point fully assented to the truth of such an idea. But the comparison of wind-harp and poem can prove illuminating because it urges one to think of poems in a new way: as engines consciously made to develop an experience of non-conscious orders, both phenomenal and psychic. In this sense 'The Eolian Harp', both as effusion and as conversation poem, is an act of imaginative exploration.

What the work explores at all its stages of development are ideas associated with the sensationalist controversy initiated by Locke's *Essay*. In December 1794, shortly before he wrote the first version of the poem, Coleridge (famously) declared himself a 'compleat Necessitarian': 'but I go farther than Hartley and believe the corporeality of *thought*, namely, that it is motion' (*Letters* I: 137). The effusion published in 1796 shows that Coleridge had not yet abandoned this way of thinking when he wrote his poem. Indeed, the poem may usefully be seen as an effort to explore the adequacy of that way of thinking in a medium where the 'truth' of sensationalist philosophy would have such marked consequences. Coleridge's conversation poem is an explicit critique of the aesthetics of the effusion, that is to say, of an aesthetics of sensibility.

It is also, however, an implicit critique of the philosophic grounds of an effusive aesthetics. As we know, 'The Eolian

---

[4] See Erika von Erhardt-Siebold's 'Some Inventions of the Pre-Romantic Period and their Influence upon Literature', *Englische Studien* 66 (1931–2), 347–63 (esp. 357–63).

Harp' advances the thought that nature is 'animated' with spirit, even at its non-animate levels. In the wake of Locke's *Essay* this idea gets taken up by various parties. In itself the idea is by no means novel or heterodox, least of all 'dim and unhallowed', and it cannot be the object of the self-reproof that Coleridge displaces on the 'pensive Sara' at the end of the poem. The later revisions clarify the poem's philosophical (self-)critique.

As the first version of the poem suggests, the issue centres in free will, necessity, and an ethics of volition. In the conversation poem Coleridge tries to clarify how a philosophy of sensibility (necessarily?) involves a kind of illusion of volition. The addition of lines 26–33 come to dramatize a kind of persistence in Coleridge's 'aye-babbling spring' (57) of speculative and sensational ideas. The poem thus comes to represent Coleridge soliciting these experiences by a (paradoxically) deliberate induction of 'indolent and passive' (41) reveries—as if he were determined to fashion himself into an eolian lyre. That the early state of the poem enacts an anxiety about such a cultivation of sensations and sensational ideas is clear from the startling eroticism exposed toward the beginning (12–25). In those moments Coleridge shows himself indulging not a 'Faith that inly *feels*' (60) but a physical *voluptas*.

But the poem doesn't make this eroticism the principal object of its critique. Coleridge directs his negative judgement to the 'unregenerate mind' that cultivates various 'shapings' and 'Bubbles' (lines 55–6). The criticism falls on the presumptuousness of this mind, as if the spiritual order of 'The Incomprehensible' (59) could be summoned and comprehended by human agency. That presumptuousness appears specifically in the analogies set up between wind-harp, poem, and human being. In so far as the poet might indulge those analogies and even construct unregenerate machines—poems—for their further generation, Coleridge is laying the ground for rethinking his own thoughts, and ultimately for imagining a kind of poem that will work against its own enginery.

'The Eolian Harp' is therefore written to criticize the identification of poem and wind-harp, as well as any poetical practice that would be based on that identification. The critique is needed because such an identification would implicitly imagine the poet as a literal magician, a technician of the sacred with the power to command theophany and open access to the spiritual orders of the world. In following this faustian temptation to magical power, Coleridge represents himself in an act of (re)discovering his proper relation to God. The poem therefore comes to rest in a theism very like Locke's. In following the temptations of Socinian and Hartleyan thought, Coleridge sees that he must go back to the *fons et origo* of sensationalist philosophy—i.e., to Locke and Locke's God. For Locke, if matter is vitally organized, as logic suggests, it is an organization the human person cannot experience let alone understand, since it rests in a divine consciousness.

Coleridge's poem thus recapitulates the philosophical and poetic legacy of enlightenment culture of sensation and sensibility. Its polemical effectiveness, which is remarkable, depends upon the way it fully represents both its sympathy with, and its critique of, that legacy. Indeed, the critique evolves—in excellent Coleridgean fashion—from within, as a process of organic exfoliation. However, the best fruit of the critique is not '*what* Coleridge's thought'—at least if one means by 'thought', as did Owen Barfield, Coleridge's abstract and philosophical ideas. The best fruit is the small body of innovative poetical writing where—to borrow an apt phrase from a contemporary poet—'A Thought is the Bride of What Thinking'.[5] This is a fruit, moreover, that grew from the blossom of sensibility, where thought began to imagine itself not as a set of concepts or ideas but as a cognitive process. Correlatively, writers who worked through an aesthetics of sensibility were led to rethink the structure and resources of language, in particular poetical language. If the activity of thought can be seen as the object of thought, then the physique of language (the eighteenth century called it 'the aesthetic') would begin to appear as in itself a cognitive field. In this context, as we shall see, poetry began to treat its language not as a vehicle for carrying something else but as a kind of *Ding an Sich*.

[5] This is the title of one of Lyn Hejinian's early books of poetry (Tuumba no. 1: Berkeley, 1977).

3

Thomas Gray's 'Thoughts, that breathe, and words, that burn'

Although Johnson thought him 'dull in company, dull in his closet, dull everywhere' and a mere 'mechanical poet',[1] Gray's work survives the judgement. As with our contemporary James Merrill, Gray's learning and verbal fastidiousness can obscure the adventurousness of his poetical practice. Coleridge seconded Johnson's view, but one may fairly dissent from both, and even fairly think that Gray was in certain respects the 'daring Spirit' he dared to name himself in 'The Progress of Poesy' (line 112). An index of his boldness appears in the fact that he pursued his study of Northern Antiquities exactly as he pursued his classical studies: in the mode that Keats would later call 'negative capability'. Pindar, Lucretius, the Sagas: it was their perfect and pagan integrity that attracted Gray's Christian, enlightened mind.

The entire shape of his work is already articulate in his 'Ode on the Spring', where he learnedly contemplates 'the untaught harmony' (line 7) of the season. It is a familiar tale of the mindless vitalities of youth and energy, whose end 'Contemplation's sober eye' easily foresees:

> Brush'd by the hand of rough Mischance,
> Or chill'd by age, their airy dance
> They leave, in dust to rest.
>
> (38–40)

Rough, chill'd, dance, dust: the terms are all tactile. Gray's apprehension of mortality is fixed, quite traditionally, on the body.

---

[1] *Boswell's Life of Johnson*, ed. G. Birkbeck Hill, rev. L. F. Powell (Oxford: Oxford University Press, 1934–50), II. 327.

But in this poem it is the mind of the body that, literally, speaks the final word. Gray's first four stanzas come, in the fifth, to their dryasdust end:

> Methinks I hear in accents low
> The sportive kind reply:
> Poor moralist! and what art thou?
> A solitary fly!
> Thy joys no glittering female meets,
> No hive hast thou of hoarded sweets,
> No painted plumage to display:
> On hasty wings thy youth is flown;
> Thy sun is set, thy spring is gone—
> We frolick, while 'tis May.
>
> (41–50)

These are indeed thoughts, that breathe, and words, that burn. The ethical meditation of stanzas 1–4 dies of its own terms. Here the reflections return as literally dead and deadening thoughts. Here, like ghosts fleeing their enchanter, they are redeemed to life again (thoughts that breathe) exactly by being forced to confront and embrace their own deathliness (words that burn). Fifty years later Blake read and rewrote Gray's poem as 'The Fly':

> If thought is life
> And strength and breath
> And the want
> Of thought is death
> Then am I
> A happy fly
> If I live
> Or if I die.

Life is for the living, and so is death: that is the message of Gray's, and later Blake's, 'sportive kind'. Gray's poem works, however, because it suggests that Gray himself, like most of his fellow creatures, does not possess that wisdom 'naturally'. Gray's 'natural' knowledge comes as his post-pagan European inheritance, the contemplative and transcendental judgement of stanzas 1–4. Stanza 5 brings 'a voice unheard', with its disturbing wisdom of the body.

Several aspects of the poem's final stanza should be noted.

First, it implicitly sets up a distinction between abstract and executed thought—contemplation versus speech. Here the distinction is a disturbing one because of the transvaluation of traditional values being carried out. Furthermore, this voice disturbs—considered as philosophy—exactly because it appears without transmortal apprehensions. Finally, considered as poetry, as *this* poetical event, it also disturbs by exposing the frailty of the transcendental mind, whose greatest aspirations now begin to appear far more simple and (in every sense) more touching: quotidian apprehensions that, passing through 'single vision', get reified to fear.

Lying (not far) behind this splendid poem is Locke's *Essay*, with its massive reconsideration of the relation of mind and body, matter and thinking.[2] The most ambitious work Gray ever attempted, the *De Principiis Cogitandi*, is explicitly an effort to do for Locke what Lucretius in the *De rerum natura* had attempted for Epicurus. That Gray—again like Lucretius—failed to complete the poem is perhaps unfortunate. What we have is enough to show the general shape of Gray's thinking. Following Locke, he neither affirms nor denies the biblical/historical account of things. Though empirically based, the approach is formally structural: the work means to explicate the fundamental laws of thought, its elements and systematic order (all these meanings being engaged through the Lucretian term 'principium', under whose sign Gray's poem operates). Consequently, when the argument proper begins (lines 32 ff.) Gray imagines a simultaneous emergence of mental and physical elements.

> Principio, ut magnum foedus Natura creatrix
> Fermavit, tardis jussitque inolescere membris
> Sublimes animas; tenebroso in carcere partem
> Noluit aetheream longo torpere veterno:
> Nec per se proprium passa exercere vigorem est,
> Nec sociae molis conjunctos sperneret artus,
> Ponderis oblita, et coelestis conscia flammae.
>   (I.32–8)

---

[2] For a good discussion of Gray's relation to Locke (as well as some shrewd readings of Gray's poetry), see S. H. Clark's two-part essay, ' "Pendet Homo Incertus": Gray's Response to Locke', in *Eighteenth-Century Studies* 24/3, 4 (spring–summer 1991), 273–91, 484–503.

(In the beginning, when Nature, the law-giver of creation, established the great covenant and bade lofty souls grow in sluggish bodies, she did not wish the ethereal part to grow torpid through long inaction in a dark prison; neither did she permit it to exercise its special vigour unchecked, lest it spurn the linked joints of the united mass, forgetful of weight and conscious of celestial fire.)[3]

The general Lockean approach is clear enough. But I want to point out two interesting features of this text. First, the account is quite un-biblical (and far more Lucretian) when it imagines this primordial event in the plural rather than the singular.[4] Second, the system being sketched does more than balance the relation of spiritual and material elements; it functions to stabilize the volatile elements ('the aethereal part'), which, Gray suggests, could easily come disengaged at either the higher or the lower registers of the organism ('Ponderis oblita, et coelestis conscia flammae'). The thought expressed in the phrase 'magnum foedus' is drawn straight from Lucretius (e.g., I.586): this is not 'law' in the modern scientific sense, but (as the translation 'covenant' suggests) a contractual arrangement binding two parties. Here, the contract is between 'membris' and 'animas'.

The presentation thereby establishes a 'material' authority and power at the most primordial level. Gray emphasizes this fact when he opens his discourse of the particulars:

> Primas tactus agit partes, primusque minutiae
> Laxat iter caecum turbae, reciptitque ruentem.
> Non idem huic modus est, qui fratribus . . .
>
> (I.64–6)

(The sense of touch plays the leading role; it goes first, widening the dark path for the lesser crowd, and restrains its headlong rush. This sense is not subject to the same restrictions that its brothers are. . . .)

Gray then elaborates the extensive domain of this primary sense. He follows with a standard movement 'up' the scale of the

---

[3] Text and trans. from *The Complete Poems of Thomas Gray*, ed. H. W. Starr and J. R. Hendrickson (Oxford: Clarendon Press, 1966).

[4] One important consequence, peripheral to my present concerns, becomes quite clear in the context of Gray's full opening treatment (lines 31–63): by speaking of the primordial 'membris' and 'animas', Gray's account of the elemental individual organism opens itself to the kind of cosmological treatment that Blake would later make famous.

organism's structure, from 'lower' to 'higher' senses and thence to the temple of the mind. As in Pope, however, the emphasis falls not on the scale and hierarchy of relationships, but on their intricate balance and structure. Furthermore, the primacy of 'tactus', and its extensive domain, is striking. Gray thereby establishes the 'foedus' of things as 'magnum' by balancing the scale of relationships at the (traditional) scalar extremes. 'Membris' and 'animas' are not just organically structured, 'tactus' is the primary and encompassing state of 'membris'.

I have laboured this rather technical matter, first, because it informs all of Gray's work; and second, because it will help us to understand the crucial importance that the sense of touch plays in the literature of sensibility and sentiment. If one contrasts, for example, the erotics of sensibility with the erotics of the *stil novisti* and their Petrarchan and metaphysical inheritors, a distinct shift is unmistakable. The latter imagine love in its determining (divine) form by associating it with the 'highest' of the senses, with vision and the eyes. In the literature of sensibility, however, the determining sensual place is 'tactus'. Drawn to their most sublimed emblematic *figurae*, the two traditions represent themselves very differently: on one hand we have lovers staring rapt into each other's eyes (or the individual fixed in solitary ecstatic vision); on the other, a pair of embracing lovers (or a mother enfolding a child). Gray's *De Principiis Cogitandi* sets the model for the literature of sensibility when it imagines the primary scenes of human existence as tactile events:

> Necdum etiam matris puer eluctatus ab alvo
> Multiplices salvit tunicas, et vincula rupit;
> Sopitus molli somno, tepidoque liquore
> Circumfusus adhuc; tactus tamen aura lacessit
> Jamdudum levior sensus, animamque reclusit.
> Idque magis simul ac salitum blandumque calorem
> Frigore mutavit coeli, quod verberat acri
> Impete inassuetos artus: tum saevior adstat,
> Humanaeque comes vitae Dolor excipit; ille
> Cunctantem frustra, et tremulo multa ore querentem
> Corripit invadens, ferreisque amplectitur ulnis.
>
> (I.70–80)

(Indeed, even the child that has not yet struggled forth from its mother's womb dissolves the many layers of covering and bursts the chains; although it is as yet wrapped in soft slumber and bathed in warm fluid, nevertheless a very slight breeze has already been stimulating the sense of touch and opening the way for the breath of life. This activity is intensified the moment the child has exchanged the soothing warmth to which it has grown accustomed for the chill of the outer air, which assails its untried limbs with savage fury. Then the more excruciating sense of touch begins to function, and Pain, the constant companion of human life, takes possession. Striking home inexorably, Pain seizes the infant, despite his vain attempts to delay and the many wails of complaint from his quivering lips, and folds him in an iron embrace.)

This is the context for reading Gray's *Elegy* as well as his poems based on the Northern Antiquities. Gray's 'rude Forefathers' (line 16) stand in relation to 'ye Proud' (37) as the pagan world of the Sagas stand to succeeding, Christian Europe; and in each case the relation is, apparitionally, what convention defines as a lesser to a greater order of things. But the *Elegy*, like Death, is a levelling engine. Both return our awareness to primaries.

> Can storied urn or animated bust
> Back to its mansion call the fleeting breath?
> Can honour's voice provoke the silent dust,
> Or Flatt'ry sooth the dull cold ear of Death?
>
> (41–4)

The full force of these rhetorical questions comes through their doubleness. On one hand they cut across the *vanitas* of 'ye Proud', who 'heap the shrine of Luxury and Pride' (71) in a futile gesture of power; on the other they attach themselves sympathetically to those who 'kept the noiseless tenor of their way' (76). 'The silent dust' is a figure of their humble lives; and if 'Honour's voice' will never 'provoke' their vitalities, the poem can imagine a more appropriate vehicle for 'the genial current of the soul', even in its death. The further it proceeds, the deeper the text plunges into the discourse of sensibility.

> Yet ev'n these bones from insult to protect
> Some frail memorial still erected nigh,
> With uncouth rhimes and shapeless sculpture deck'd,
> Implores the passing tribute of a sigh.
>
> (77–80)

Surveying the country churchyard's gravestones with their 'unletter'd' inscriptions (81 ff.), Gray's poem becomes their 'kindred Spirit' (96). His poem reads the inscriptions as the voice of the living dead:

> For who to dumb Forgetfullness a prey,
> This pleasing anxious being e'er resign'd,
> Left the warm precincts of the chearful day,
> Nor cast one longing ling'ring look behind?
>
> On some fond breast the parting soul relies,
> Some pious drops the closing eye requires;
> Ev'n from the tomb the voice of Nature cries,
> Ev'n in our ashes live their wonted fires.
> (85–92)

The passage speaks equally to and of those who both pass away and are left behind. The gravestones' inscriptions are, literally, 'the silent dust' here provoked to communication. The force of human sympathy is so great and foundational that Gray, in a stanza that parodies one of the churchyard inscriptions, imagines it as showing and telling this: 'Ev'n in our Ashes live their wonted fires'. Gray moves to brute matter, the lowest order of things, to engage the highest: energy, vital response, and sympathetic exchange. One thinks of Blake: 'Energy is the only life, and is from the body'. Even more, one thinks of Wordsworth, who turned the 'Immortality Ode' to its redemptive phase by making a reprise of this passage from the *Elegy*:

> Oh Joy! that in our embers
> Is something that doth live,
> That nature yet remembers
> What was so fugitive!
> ('Intimations Ode', 132–5)

Ashes, embers, dust: Gray's poetical flight is earthward, to brute matter in its most extinguished conditions. 'The Descent of Odin. An Ode' is a parable of his philosophic passage to the world of the living dead.

> Right against the eastern gate,
> By the moss-grown pile he sate;
> Where long of yore to sleep was laid
> The dust of the prophetic Maid.
> (17–26)

Odin descends into the earth, the (female) realm of matter, for the knowledge that might secure his power and future dominion. What he gains, to his chagrin, are ominous stories of his rise and eventual fall. When Gray replicates this descent for the eighteenth-century reader, however, the final words of the Prophetess carry even more far-reaching intimations of mortality:

> PR. Hie thee hence, and boast at home,
> That never shall Enquirer come
> To break my iron-sleep again;
> Till *Lok* has burst his tenfold chain.
> Never, till substantial Night
> Has reassumed her ancient right;
> Till rapt in flames, in ruin hurl'd,
> Sinks the fabric of the world.
>
> (87–94)

The prophecy suggests that this brutal figure foreknows more than a pagan imagination ought to foreknow—as if, for example, the Christian final Judgement were some latter-day interpretation of a more primal event. Furthermore, matter itelf—the coarse earth—is here imagined as possessing great, even fundamental power and knowledge. In this context the gendered terms of the poem are quite significant. (Male) worlds rise and fall in violence and flame, encompassed by 'substantial Night' and the prophetess who is the voice of her order. Despite the surface similarities, this imagination of 'substantial Night' is about as far from Pope's misogynist figure of 'Universal Darkness' as one can get. Gray enters his earthy realm in a full act of sympathy.

He does so because 'Hela's drear abode' (line 4) and the 'rosy bosom'd' land of 'Fair Venus' ('Ode on the Sping', 1–2) are equivalents and, for Gray, all that's best of dark and bright. As we have seen, his myth of 'tactus' structures a relation between encompassing sensual experience ('where ignorance is bliss') and a dark, painful knowledge that is its dialectical twin ('Wisdom in sable garb array'd', 'Hymn to Adversity', 25). 'Poesy' replicates this dialectic, as the splendid 'Thoughts, that breathe, and words, that burn' ('The Progress of Poesy', 110) implicitly argues via its subtle reworking of the biblical text 'The letter killeth, but the spirit giveth life'. Gray's pair of figures mirror each other by associating (spiritual) ideas with bodily action and (dead) letters with extreme energetic power.

In each case embodiment measures the order of things, whence the mind may discover its true function and virtue: not as controlling power, but as the source of sympathy:

> What sorrow was, thou bad'st her know,
> And from her own she learn'd to melt at others' woe.
> ('Hymn to Adversity', 15–16)

Gray's ultimate prayer to the 'benign . . . Goddess' (41) is cast in his familiar material terms: 'The gen'rous spark extinct revive' (45). He is sketching a sentimental myth of Eternal Return. If adverse 'Thought . . . destroy[s the] Paradise' of the Eton Ode (98), it is not to establish an empire of the mind, but to perpetuate the circulation of energy, mental as well as physical: 'To breathe a second spring' (20).

4

Ossian as a Poetry of Knowledge

When James Macpherson published his *Fragments of Ancient Poetry* in June 1760, Gray was '*extasie* with their infinite beauty' (Gray, 1925: letter of 20 June 1760). His early reaction forecast the extraordinary career of Macpherson's 'Ossian' over the next fifty years and more. Despite—perhaps even because of—the controversy that raged over the question of the authenticity of the Ossianic materials, this work's influence on the literary scene of the late eighteenth-century eclipsed all others. More particularly, Ossian set the literature of sentiment and sensibility on a whole new footing.

Macpherson introduced a novel and extremely important argument about the moral status of primitive culture—at any rate, of *British* primitive culture. The enlightenment opposition between heroic societies and modern civilizations tried to distinguish the strengths and weaknesses of each: classically, passion and spontaneity versus self-conscious refinement and balance. In so far as a distinction was maintained between sensibility and sentimentality, sensibility was the more primitive of the two. An affect of instinct and 'animal spirits', its signs appear as the body's most primitive registrations: blushes, tears, sighs and faintings, blind and involuntary responses. Sentimentality, by contrast, was a sophisticated acquirement, a sympathetic understanding gained through complex acts of conscious attention and reflection. Achilles' wrath is naïve, Rousseau's reveries, sentimental.

In making that simple and elegant distinction problematic, Macpherson's work helped to develop the resources of the literatures of sensibility and sentiment alike. The fierce argument about the authenticity of Macpherson's Ossian reflects what was at stake. Those who worked to expose Ossian as a fraud argued that Macpherson's supposedly primitive texts everywhere displayed the signs of their modernity. To Macpherson,

however, these philological arguments were based upon errone-
ous ideas exposed by the works of Ossian themselves: that
heroic cultures were founded in codes of violence. On the contrary, Macpherson's texts argued that primitive societies exhi-
bited important variations, and that the early societies of Ireland
and Scotland were models of civilized heroism. Their wars en-
sue, according to the Ossianic texts, from their efforts to establish and maintain a stable and sympathetic social order in face of
a whole array of forces bent upon destroying that order.

In making this argument Macpherson is implicitly suggesting
that sentimental values—self-consciousness, refined aesthetic
taste, sympathy for others—are a second-order extrapolation
of primary human qualities. Sentimentality is taken as an effort
to regain the lost paradise of sensibility. The state of nature is
not fallen and needs no redemption, according to this view
of the matter, though its existence is always perilous. The ethos
(as well as the ethics) of Fingal, of Ossian, of Oscur is impec-
cable. This fact gets underlined in Hugh Blair's introduction to
the *Fragments* when he emphasizes (pp. iv–v) the pre-
Christian integrity of a 'tradition . . . supported by the spirit and
strain of . . . poems . . . which abound with those ideas,
and . . . manners, that belong to the most early state of society'
(p. iii).

The threats to this society come from chance misfortune, from
external threats by those bent upon destroying the good society,
and from internal deviance and betrayal. This last is associated
with the pursuit of selfish ends, and in particular with the desire
for personal wealth (here the emblematic tale is fragment IX, in
which the treachery of 'Euran, the servant of gold' causes the
warrior-brothers Connan and Ronnan to kill each other). The
external threats come from the Vikings of the north, who provide a regular structural focus in the poems. Finally, evil chance
recurrently wounds this world's body, as 'Carthon', one of
the most popular and influential of the Ossianic texts, clearly
demonstrates.

According to Macpherson's (philological) myth, the ruination
of an original state of (civilized) nature is something to be
recovered rather than redeemed. The distinction, a crucial one
for understanding the literature of sentiment and sensibility,
centres in a highly active and moral view of memory. John

Dwyer's explication of the Ossianic epithet 'the joy of grief' goes
to the core of the matter. The phrase defines a self-conscious
cultivation of the past and its sympathetic values: 'The capacity
for "remembrance" was different from mere recollection, for it
involved both an effort of the will and judgment' (1991: 182).
This capacity, according to Macpherson's texts, is not brought
to a primitive order by a saving act of civilization (the 'second
nature' of culture and poetry), it is already a fundamental feature of the original human condition. Indeed, every act of
remembrance suffers a slight retrogression (loss and fragmentation of memory), and the 'progress of society' devolves slowly
but surely from that state of cultivation when memorial acts,
like the acts of the girl in 'We Are Seven', obliterate all distinction between past and present. In Macpherson, Fingal is every
bit as distinguished a poet as his son Ossian, and Fingal himself
is merely *primus inter pares* in a society that maintains itself as
much by deeds of song as deeds of war. In fact, the deeds of war
serve primarily as metaphors in Macpherson, the outward and
visible signs of the Blakean 'mental fight' by which this blessed
society raised itself up.

That way of thinking justifies Dwyer's view that 'The bonds
between [Macpherson's] Caledonians are sentimental ones, that
is, they are mental rather than physical' (1991: 190). This is a
shrewd and important insight, but it obscures, I think, the
tendency of Macpherson's writing to collapse the distinction
between the mental and the physical. This tendency—which
characterizes eighteenth-century Scots writing in general, as
Christopher Lawrence has shown—develops from one of Scottish philosophy's key ideas, that passion and feeling are the basis
of human action. Macpherson clearly shares that form of
thought, and he just as clearly attributes it to the heroic society
created by his writing.

His view of materialized mentality informs the typical
Ossianic landscape, where the inanimate world of earth, wind,
and water comes traversed by the simultaneous presence of all
the noble living and the noble dead. Death does not interrupt
their intimate social intercourse; on the contrary, the reader
regularly confronts vital and articulate human presences
throughout Macpherson's otherwise inanimate, desolate, and
purely geophysical places. The first two of the 1860 *Fragments*

sketch the tale of the warrior Shilric and his beloved Vinvela. Anticipating his death while he has gone to war with his chief Fingal, Vinvela dies of grief. When Shilric returns alive, he haunts the waste places and invokes her ghost. Since in Macpherson all language functions as an instrument of natural magic, his words unveil her deathless presence:

> But is it she that there appears, like a beam of light on the heath? bright as the moon in autumn, as the sun in summer-storm?—She speaks: but how weak her voice! like the breeze in the reeds of the pool. (1966: 14)

The index of her voice's weakness appears exactly in and as this text's resort to simile, a rhetorical form that replicates the desolation of Shilric himself, who appears as yet unequal to his own desire.

The similes turn quickly to unmediated presence when Vinvela responds to Shilric in her own voice and the lovers have a brief conversation. Vinvela then 'fleets, she sails away as grey mist before the wind!' (p. 14) Her departure in simile is crucial, a sign that, in this land of the heart's desire, the invisible dominion of death functions symmetrically with the apparent substantial world. Consequently, Shilric's posture of sorrow at the end of the poem is very different from what it was at the beginning:

> By the mossy fountain I will sit; on the top of the hill of winds. When mid-day is silent around, converse, O my love, with me! come on the wings of the gale! on the blast of the mountain, come! Let me hear thy voice, as thou passest, when mid-day is silent around. (p. 15)

Here simile, a nominal structure, shifts into the mood of verbal imperative. Forms and figures acquire in and through this text a sensitivity conscious of their own power to act and interact.

At the outset of Book II of *Fingal* Macpherson supplies an interesting gloss on this typical Ossianic event. The hero Connal, lying on the earth 'by the sound of the mountain stream', hears 'the voice of the night'. The latter phrase is a magical epithet that unlocks the cryptic messages drifting randomly around Connal. 'The voice of the night' begins to materialize as the ghost of the warrior Crugal, slain by Swaran who is invading Ireland. Crugal tells Connal to advise his chief, Cuthullin, to make peace with Swaran, for if he does not, Cuthullin will be killed in battle by the Viking invader.

When Connal delivers this message to the king he describes the visitation of the ghost in the following terms: 'the ghost of Crugal came from his cave. The stars dim-twinkled through his form' (p. 51). Cuthullin understands that Connal uses this last statement as proof that his ghostly encounter was substantial, and not a mere sound illusion. Macpherson then glosses the text as follows:

The poet teaches us the opinions that prevailed in his time concerning the state of separate souls. From Connal's expression, 'that the stars dim-twinkled through the form of Crugal,' and Cuthullin's reply, we may gather that they both thought the soul was material: something like the *eidolon* of the ancient Greeks. (52n)

The note is establishing a continuity between ancient Greek thought, primitive (*circa* third century AD) Caledonian ideas, and eighteenth-century enlightenment philosophy. All three, according to Macpherson, share similar ways of thinking about the relation of spiritual and material phenomena.

Macpherson's poetry erodes the sharp divisions of matter and spirit, body and soul, at every textual level. Given the translational character of his project, he devotes particular attention to primitive linguistic structures: phoneme, morpheme, individual word. In the opening pair of the *Fragments*, for example, the word 'rushes' locates a distinct field of shifting associational relations. Phrases like 'the rushes are nodding in the wind' (p. 9) get repeated and call out to other repeating phrases, like 'One tree is rustling above me' (13). The word slips into different grammatical forms, nominal, adjectival, verbal ('their memory rushes on my mind', 25). Furthermore, the 's' sounds proliferate and metamorphose, establishing relations between otherwise disparate phenomena: Shilric 'pursues the deer', 'his bow-string sounds' (9). Primary rhymes establish secondary ones, and the developing structure grows in unexpected directions: Shilric's 'bow-string', an instrument of hunt and war, gets a refigured life whenever we read of the harp songs of the poets, or encounter other rhyming phenomena in phrases like 'bright as the bow of heaven' (10), which is here an explicit simile for Shilric.

A similar set of relations builds itself through an even more important constellation of words: son, sun, song. Macpherson opens Fragment XII under a bright sky ruled, however, by a

flying 'inconstant sun' (p. 55). This sharply visibilized order is
then transacted by strong sonic forces, and in particular by 'the
voice of Alpin the son of song, mourning for the dead' (55).
These wordplays, which govern the general organization of the
fragment, get reinforced at the end (where the related pun on
'mourning' is explicitly exposed): 'When shall it be morn in the
grave, to bid the slumberer awake? . . . but the field shall see
thee no more; nor the dark wood be lightened, with the splendour of thy steel. Thou hast left no son. But the song shall
preserve thy name' (58). Such linguistic events populate the
world of Ossian and establish odd relationships that are all the
more compelling and suggestive for their slight disjunctions. In
Fragment XI Arindel dies from an arrow shot from Armor's
bow: 'It sung; it sunk in thy heart, O Arindel my son!' (52–3).
Various fragments connect the sunlight with the glistening of
polished swords.

The environment exploits the sensational and aesthetic features of words. Macpherson treats language as a dynamic and
volatile order, more performative than referential. Indeed, the
world of Ossian appears to subsist as a complex affective system
rather than a machine for transmitting information. Its language
builds knowledge by developing sympathetic relations, not by
labelling, storing, sending, and receiving data. In such a system
the gap between *res* and *verbum*, assumed in an informational
model of language, begins to close, and may collapse altogether,
as happens when Macpherson generates a phrase like 'son of
song'. The words do not name something, they illustrate themselves, they incarnate an idea.

That level of Ossianic language operates most clearly through
its proper names. The person and his or her verbal sign appear
indistinguishable, as if people were words made flesh. When 'the
sighs of Fiona arise' (p. 44) in Book I of *Fingal* to lament the
death of the heroes, Macpherson glosses the semantic meaning
of her name: 'a fair maid'. When we then read, immediately
afterward:

Weep on the rocks of roaring winds, O maid of Inistore. Bend thy fair
head over the waves . . .

the figure of Fiona has become utterly figurative, a presence in
and of this sympathetic language. This kind of effect is solicited

repeatedly in the Ossianic texts. Later in Book I Macpherson introduces another woman, Brassolis, with a note: 'Brassolis signifies *a woman with a white breast*.' Shortly the poetical text represents her

mourn[ing] him in the field of blood; but still she hoped for his return. Her white bosom is seen from her robe, as the moon from the clouds of night, when its edge heaves white on the view. . . . (48)

Or in Book II: 'But who is she that, like a sun-beam, flies before the ranks of the foe. It is Degrena, lovely fair, the spouse of fallen Crugal' (55). When Macpherson's note states that 'Deogrena signifies *a sun-beam*', the point is to establish the *literal* truth of this field of representations.

The whole poem *Carthon*, one of the central and most impressive works in the corpus, pivots around the significance of the hero's name, and its resonance in (and finally as) the poem over which it is set. Macpherson's Argument to *Carthon* tells us that his name means '*the murmur of waves*'. That identification gets explicitly recalled later, after Carthon's death, when Fingal's grief for the hero leads him to command

his bards to mark the day, when shadowy autumn returned: And often did they mark the day and sing the hero's praise. 'Who comes so dark from ocean's roar, like autumn's shadowy cloud?' (p. 183)

The story of Carthon is the story of him and his father, Clessammor, and their fateful passages across the sea. It is equally the story of the bards who tell and retell the story of Carthon, as they are made to do in Macpherson's poem. Carthon the hero and Carthon the tale carry the murmur of waves of rising and falling heroes, of which Macpherson's poem is yet another murmuring repetition. Because Carthon's 'waves' are literal, not referential, they can live (and die) deathlessly in any form of language that chooses to summon them. So Carthon comes and goes through the text that names him. When Fingal himself sings his *Poem of the Hymns*, a poetical injunction to the 'bards' to perpetuate the world of song, Carthon makes arbitrary and recurrent appearances ('The fox looked out from the windows, the rank grass of the wall waved round its head'; 175): Carthon's presence hovers in the air of that sentence because one of its principal verbs is one of Carthon's notable epithets. And in Ossian's final, celebrated address to the sun, it is Carthon the tragic *son* of Clessammor who 'rollest above' and who 'sinks into the western wave' (184). Carthon becomes incarnate in and as poetry, in and as *this* poem.

PART II

'Sensate Hearts': The Poetry of Sensibility

There were some dark and heavy men there then. There were some who were not so heavy and some who were not so dark. Helen Furr and Georgine Skeene sat regularly with them. They sat regularly with the ones who were dark and heavy. They sat regularly with the ones who were not so dark. They sat regularly with the ones that were not so heavy. . . .

They were regular then, they were gay then, they were where they wanted to be then where it was gay to be then, they were regularly gay then.

Gertrude Stein, 'Miss Furr and Miss Skeene'

5

Learning by Doing: The Example of 'The Amourous Lady'

Sensibility is the language of spontaneous overflow. From the perspective of feeling and emotion and all affective philosophy, it is unteachable. That belief is ancient, but in the eighteenth century it began to be scrupulously re-explored. A passion for enlightenment drove the quest for the reasons of the heart. The project is therefore riven with paradox from the outset.

A basic paradox involves the apparent inadequacy of language to sustain the pursuit. In the most elementary (and traditional) sense, language is a formal structure comprising a certain vocabulary (lexis) and a specific set of operating rules (grammar). But every writer who engages the question of the language of feeling recognizes that the heart speaks (and needs) a different kind of language.

Throughout this pursuit the idea recurs that learning and a 'knowledge of letters' are obstacles to be overcome rather than aids to reflection. Wordsworth's thoughts on the matter follow this line.

> Enough of Science and of Art;
>   Close up those barren leaves;
> Come forth, and bring with you a heart
>   That watches and receives.
>   ('The Tables Turned', lines 29–32)

The important books are not in libraries. Like Blake, Wordsworth has gone to a new school that teaches a new and paradoxical discipline: to 'act from impulse, not from rules':

> One impulse from a vernal wood
>   May teach you more of man,
> Of moral evil and of good,
>   Than all the sages can.
>   (21–4)

The general attitude pervades eighteenth-century writing. Wordsworth's geophysical perspective on a 'natural language' is a late-eighteenth century acquirement. Earlier writers tend to put the matter in tropes drawn from social relations (in particular, erotic relations). The anonymous author of 'On being Charged with Writing Incorrectly' (1734) fashions her poetic manifesto from the problem.[1]

> I'm incorrect: the learned say
> That I write well, but not their way.
>
> (1–2)

In two lines we see who will judge the judges: those who have learned by doing. The lovely antitheses generated through these lines might be analysed through technical terms like enjambment and caesurae; they come to the reader, however, as playful surprises, with each of the four phrasal units leaping ahead to say something in excess of what, moment by phrasal moment, one might have expected. So this poem begins with a subtle and significant revision of Pope's brilliant couplet style.

> Shall bright Apollo drudge at school,
> And whimper till he grows a fool?
> Apollo, to the learned coy,
> In nouns and verbs finds little joy.
> The tuneful Sisters still he leads
> To silver streams, and flowery meads.
> He glories in an artless breast,
> And loves the goddess Nature best.
>
> (17–24)

Because a woman is conducting this poetic argument, its delicate eroticism is both startling and very effective. The poet, like all her 'Sisters'—including those original 'tuneful Sisters', the nine Muses—appears to have always had a special relation with Apollo. Schoolmasters know nothing of these lovely academical groves.

> I from my very heart despise
> These mighty dull, these mighty wise,

---

[1] My texts here are from Roger Lonsdale's splendid *Eighteenth-Century Women Poets: An Oxford Anthology* (Oxford: Oxford University Press, 1989).

Who were the slaves of Busby's nod,
And learned their lessons from his rod.

(13–16)

This is bold, even 'incorrect' in an important way. But it is written very well, and in that fact justifies itself and its argument against writing to any rule but the rule of pleasure.

If I a pleasure can impart,
Or to my own, or thy dear heart,
If I thy gentle passions move,
'Tis all I ask of fame or love.

(39–42)

The problem is, how to realize those desired possibilities. And it *is* a problem because language—or the language we learn in the schools—appears a conceptual rather than an affective instrument. The ideal of a learned language is the clear expression of thought. To the degree that language's affective possibilities are addressed, as they are by the rhetoricians, the approach remains scholastic, intellectual, systematic.

In this situation, if one aspires to an effective emotional expression, 'Writing Incorrectly' becomes a poetic *sine qua non*, as the lady argues. The splendid wordplay in the title—the double meaning of the phrase 'Charged with'—defines her general approach. The 'problem of language' (the obstacles thrown up by its scholastic character) becomes the starting point for a more full and vital expressiveness. To free language from its embrained corruption, the poet wants no fugitive or cloistered virtues. She becomes charged with the charges she is charged with, flourishing in her adversaries and her adversities:

Let Dennis haunt me with his spite;
Let me read Dennis every night,
Or any punishment sustain,
To 'scape the labour of the brain.

(25–8)

One thinks forward to Byron, who declares a similar allegiance when he observes: 'The great object of life is sensation—to feel that we exist, even though in pain.'[2] No affective resort is too

---

[2] Or to Keats's less strenuous version of this attitude: 'O for a life of Sensations rather than of Thoughts' (letter to Benjamin Bailey, 22 Nov. 1817: *Letters*

extreme 'To 'scape the labour of the brain', including nightly doses of the most notoriously petty and spiteful critic of the age.

The discourse of sensibility typically develops through an ethics of loss and suffering, and that moral urgency can easily obscure the specifically aesthetic character of the poetries of sensibility. This poet's work is critically useful just because it has set aside those customary moral considerations. As a result, the verse gives us a good look at the logic of the discourse of sensibility. Grounded in dialectic, it builds itself as a network of elaborate and surprising transformations.

Two other poems by the same poet underscore her method, if such it can be called. In 'A Letter to my Love.—All alone, past 12, in the Dumps', eight-syllable couplets run the poem through a series of quickly veering changes of topic, tone, and mood. The poem evolves by feeding on its own circumstances. Desire finds a voice in frustration, and all three of these elements culminate the poem:

> This hour, when pallid ghosts appear,
> Oh! could it bring thy shadow here,
> I every substance would resign
> To clasp thy aereal breast to mine;
> Or if, my love, that could not be,
> I would turn air to mix with thee.
>
> (54–9)

The poem works by playing with its own emptiness—ultimately, by calling attention to its stylistic tricks and purely verbal moves. As much as we might be inclined to admire the poet's wit, as we should, her language succeeds primarily because the poem measures itself through failure. The method here is just like what we saw in the other poem's Dennis passage. There she solicits 'any punishment' in order to 'sustain' her affective needs. Here the desire for actual physical contact is so imperative—the need for the 'substance' of her lover—that she physicalizes her own dissolution in order to imagine an erotic encounter.

Cast in the form of 'A Letter', the poem turns its figurative moves into assertions—as if her desire had made her capable of

---

I.185). See Byron's letter to his future wife, 6 Sept. 1813 (*Letters and Journals* III.109).

anything. The power of that final image, in which she wills
the dispersal of her own identity, is uncanny. She not only
defines herself by passion, her demands reveal passion as a kind
of primary substance. According to the logic of the text,
that substance is her true identity, her substantial self. The
thought is extreme because the problem being addressed is
experienced as a crisis. Of course the extremity is, in another
perspective, all very commonplace: the separation of lovers is an
old story, and so is the inadequacy of language to express what
one feels. Furthermore, the one tropes the other and poets—
like this poet—have exploited the analogy from time immem-
orial. That kind of logic generates and sustains this poetry as
well. What is new here is the way issues of style get
foregrounded when the writing is self-consciously gendered. The
constellation 'men/conceptual mastery/language of ideas/mind'
is ranged against 'women/practical expression/affective lan-
guage/heart', and the latter comes to overthrow the former. The
project is clearly rendered in another of this lady's lyrics of
direct address.

The situation of 'To my Love' is dramatically imagined. The
lovers' tryst is ending, they will shortly separate and return to
their respective spouses. For her the event comes as a catastrophe of language and feeling:

> Fain would my lips have sighed 'Adieu! Adieu!',
>   But rising sorrow would not give them leave;
> My words, like traitors, they forsook me too;
>   My sighs themselves had scarcely power to heave;
> My arms alone with grasping could impart
> The agony that filled my breaking heart.
>
> (7–12)

As in her other poems, the linguistic wit here is remarkable: for
instance, the image of 'My arms alone with grasping', or the
figure (in lines 7–8) of a speechless speaking that is evoked
through the meta-figure of an unheard internal dialogue of the
lady's mind with itself. The stanza, in general, projects the
intensity of her feelings as a struggle of language, a trial and
exposure of the poverty of ordinary discourse.

We glimpse that discourse in the posture of the lady's lover,
who seems (by contrast) quite unshaken. His body registers

none of those outward and visible signs of the language of the
'heart' (the refrain word of each of the poem's five stanzas):

> In vain my weeping eyes thy features traced
>   (And features speak the passions of the mind):
> Still wert thou unconcerned; nor didst impart
>   One sigh of thine to those that swell'st my heart.
>
> (16–19)

The contrast is underscored when the lady imbeds his actual
words, his dead prudential language, within her poem.

> Whilst I was grieved to such a kind excess,
>   Oh! how untimely must thy prudence be,
> To bid me *meet, with artful tenderness,*
>   *The arms that were no friends to love or thee.*
> Beware how you instruct me in that part,
> Lest I give him the true, and thee the faithless heart.
>
> (19–24)

'Beware' brings a threat that signals the extremity of her passion. Illicit love justifies itself, as it were, by faith alone. Her
lover's 'prudence' imperils the entire project, so she warns him
back with a clear demonstration of her own absolute love-
commitment. Coolly delivered, the lady's threat hardly conceals
its extreme measures. Between 'reconcilements' and 'aversions',
between love and marriage, between pure faith and prudential
works: in such circumstances there are no half measures, only
abandonments.

> Bid the rude North be gentle to the spring,
>   Or kiss the new-born flowers with tender care;
> To reconcilements all aversions bring;
>   But oh! to me thy dull advice forebear;
> No faithless maxims to my breast impart,
> To change the nature of my breaking heart.
>
> (25–30)

The continued wit (e.g., 'faithless maxims') should not disguise
the threatened energy being figured here. The menace of the
previous stanza carries over, not least in the erotic violence so
deftly figured in lines 25–6. A liaison with this lady's love must
be dangerous.

  For my purposes, what is most important to see here is the

contrast of styles, the one controlled and calculating, the other beside and beyond itself—so committed to its love purposes that it would choose destruction rather than compromise its desire. The climactic fourth stanza (lines 19–24) therefore moves to oppose two types of cool expression: hers (tense and intense) against his (bland and assured). The difference separates a performative language from an instructional one, 'kind excess' opposed to 'faithless maxims'. Once again the man appears as master, scholar, teacher, but in these circumstances his master's knowledge is an enemy that threatens to destroy his own happiness, as the lady's 'kind excess'—*her* threat—warns him. So the poem *executes* a different form of knowledge, a knowledge in 'excess' of its own mind precisely because it is a performative and not a constative language. One thinks, reading this text, of the contemporary anti-scholastic witticism: those who can, do; those who can't, teach.

6

Frances Greville's 'A Prayer for Indifference'

'The most celebrated poem by a woman of the period', the title promises (through both of its principal terms) a far more subdued performative work than we see in The Amourous Lady's writing. Greville's prayer is a reflective rather than a dramatistic action. None the less, the poem operates through the same logic of sensibility, and its passion, if less demonstrative, may appear all the more affecting for that reason. (Do we rank the passions of Anne Elliot and Catherine Earnshaw? Bring out number weight and measure in a year of dearth.)

Nothing is more characteristic of the poetry of sensibility than its dialectical relation to 'Indifference'. In Ann Yearsley's *Poems on Various Subjects* (1787), for example, the opening text 'Addressed to Sensibility' calls out to (and gets recalled by) the lines 'To Indifference', which appear a bit later in the book. The relation between the two, in the discourse of sensibility, functions as a reciprocity and not an antithesis. That fact is abundantly clear in Hannah More's *Sensibility: An Epistle to the Honourable Mrs. Boscawen* (1782), an unequivocal act of celebration.[1] More specifically addresses Greville's famous poem:

> You, whose touch'd hearts with real sorrows swell
> Or feel, when genius paints these sorrows well,
> Would you renounce such energies as these
> For vulgar pleasures or for selfish ease?
> Would you to 'scape the pain the joy forgo,
> And miss the transport to avoid the wo?
> Would you the sense of actual pity lose,
> Or cease to share the mournings of the Muse?

[1] I quote from *The Complete Works of Hannah More*, 2 vols. (New York: J. C. Derby, 1854); 'Sensibility' appears at I.32–6.

No, Greville, no!—thy song, tho' steep'd in tears,
Though all thy soul in all thy strain appears;
Yet would'st thou all thy well sung anguish choose,
And all the inglorious peace thou begg'st refuse.

(179–90)

More understands that Greville's prayer for indifference expresses exactly the opposite of what it appears to call for. It
prays for indifference the way Jesus prays to his father on the
cross, and for the same reasons. Both are (literally) prayers of
passion. They reveal that the demands of an absolute love
commitment are extreme, and that they are felt in the blood, and
felt along the heart.

According to the poem's induction, Greville's prayer comes as
a sort of timely utterance. All earlier prayers having proved
unavailing, she decides to address not 'the gods' but 'Oberon,
the fairy' (4). The move serves two functions. First, the implicit
Shakespeare reference virtually allegorizes the poem as a prayer
not to God or the gods, but to the powers of poetry. Second,
Greville introduces her prayer on a playful note, suggesting that
nothing serious is at stake.[2]

That suggestion gets dispelled even as it develops itself
through the first four stanzas. Greville's playfulness, we come to
realize, is part of her act of prayer, an apparent insouciance
gesturing at 'indifference'. By the fifth stanza of Greville's 'A
Prayer for Indifference', the mask has utterly fallen away.

I ask no kind return in love,
    No tempting charm to please,
Far from the heart such gifts remove,
    That sighs for peace and ease.

Nor ease, nor peace that heart can know,
    That, like the needle true,
Turns, at the touch of joy or woe,
    But, turning, trembles too.

Far as distress the soul can wound,
    'Tis pain in each degree;

---

[2] When Helen Maria Williams interprets Greville's work, in her poem 'To Sensibility' (*Poems*, 1786), this is the meaning she assigns to Greville's use of fairy
materials.

>   Bliss goes but to a certain bound,
>   Beyond is agony.
>   (17–28)

If More's verse commentary seems quite pedestrian beside this, it does supply a useful gloss. According to More, those driven through sensibility discover the paradoxical logic of the heart:

>   That, while we clasp the phantom, we destroy;
>   That perils multiply as blessings flow,
>   That sorrows grafted on enjoyments grow;
>   That clouds impending dim our brightest views,
>   That who have most to love have most to lose.
>   (206–10)

Unlike More, however, Greville writes to enact rather than to analyse, to pray and not to preach. Greville's opening mask of playfulness emphasizes her felt need to 'speak' beyond the limits of a semantic or purely rational discourse. And when the mask falls away, Greville's true voice of feeling appears in its naked simplicity. Furthermore, and as More's gloss emphasizes, it is poetry—'well sung woes'—that most approximates the difficult (yet elementary) language of the heart.

But a new kind of poetry, according to its votaries and exegetes. Once again More's commentary is useful. She organizes her epistle as an exploration of true and false forms of sensibility, and in particular true and false poets of sensibility. Affect is haunted by the demon of affectation, virtue by virtuosity, the language of the heart by the tricks of art:

>   Sweet Sensibility! Thou secret pow'r
>   Who shed'st thy gifts upon the natal hour,
>   Like fairy favours; Art can never sieze
>   Nor Affectation catch thy power to please . . .
>   (231–4)

Like souls issuing from the hands of a loving God, poets of sensibility are born and not made. More delivers this axiom because the power of art is so great that false souls can use it to construct artificial signs of true feeling. So More runs through a catalogue of eighteenth-century 'counterfeit' forms:

She does not feel thy power who boasts thy flame,
And rounds her every period with thy name;
Nor she who vents her disproportion'd sighs
With pining *Lesbia* when her sparrow dies . . .

(249–52)

And so forth. More is well aware that sensibility and sentiment are growth industries of the age. She applies an interesting test to distinguish the real from the factitious:

There are whose well sung plaints each breast inflame,
And break all hearts—but his from whom they came.

(273–4)

In poetical terms, this rule impicitly names 'failure'—a loss unredeemed by one's own skill or effort—the grace beyond the reach of art.

More is acute to take Greville's poem as a model of this writing ideal. Every gesture the poem makes to unwind its 'agony' of intense feeling simultaneously confirms the logic of insuperable need. Through all this effort and expectation and desire, there is always a something evermore about to be: the eternal present of the need as well as its perpetual future, both of which appear in the effort to unimagine them. Greville writes:

The tears, which pity taught to flow,
My eyes shall then disown;
The heart, that throbb'd at others' woe,
Shall then scarce feel its own.

(41–4)

Shaped as the agon of a future simple rather than a future perfect, the poem defines the perpetual presence of all its reciprocal desires and sufferings ('The wounds, which now each moment bleed,/ Each moment then shall close', 45–6). To imagine, to pray for, 'nights of sweet repose' (48) simply refires the enginery of her needs and desires.

So the poem ends in a dying fall—in a quatrain that More quite rightly reads 'against the grain'.

And what of life remains to me
I'll pass in sober ease,

> Half-pleas'd, contented will I be,
> Contented, half to please.
>
> (61-4)

The lines belie themselves, as More clearly saw. Recalling the poem as a whole, these final half measures become figures of the perpetually suffering heart. They suffer, literally, in their silence.

Greville's poem serves up an appearance of beginnings, middles, and ends, of pasts, presents, futures. It frames these traditional orders in an appropriate form: a prayer comprising a clear induction, body, conclusion. But the final quatrain's anticlimax realizes (or enacts) a logic of impossibility. The prayer issues her heart's call—for what? Its own destruction?

> Take then this treacherous sense of mine,
> Which dooms me still to smart;
> Which pleasure can to pain refine,
> To pain new pangs impart.
>
> (29-32)

This kind of conscious suffering will take many to their deaths, most memorably Clarissa and Werther. Greville turns aside from such absolute gestures. When she imagines a state of half-pleasure, however, it comes to the poem as a kind of death-in-life, yet another treacherous figure of Greville's treacherous sensibilities. The poem aspires to 'new-string' her 'shatter'd nerves' (33-4), which is exactly what it does. If we imagine it succeeds, then it will have rebuilt the infrastructure of its suffering; and if we imagine it as failing, Greville simply goes on as before, 'shatter'd' by her feelings. At every turn it can only expect to tremble again.

7

Ann Yearsley's 'Remonstrance in the Platonic Shade, Flourishing on an Height'

Among eighteenth-century poets, Yearsley carried out the most extensive exploration of the discourse of sensibility. She was doubly prepared for her task by being doubly deprived: a woman, and without privilege or formal education. Yearsley *thinks* about sensibility repeatedly, as if an effort of self-education—an experience she well understands—could reveal its full meaning. In her work sensibility appears as an endless struggle of suffering thought. As a result (and somewhat paradoxically) her writing is strongest when it appears most contorted. Yearsley's style then becomes an elaborate index for the torturous intensities of her mental affect.

The most immediate (aesthetic) sign of her suffering mind appears as the biographical drama of her poetry. Her writing tells the story of how Hannah More and Elizabeth Montagu 'discovered' her poetical gifts and promoted her work. Her expensively produced books, with their elaborate dedications and long lists of well-to-do subscribers, establish an apt material framework for the story of WORTHY TALENT lifted from obscurity by CONSCIOUS BENEVOLENCE. Yearsley's poems replicate the theme often.

> O, Montagu! forgive me, if I sing
> Thy wisdom temper'd with the milder ray
> Of soft humanity, and kindness bland:
> So wide its influence, that the bright beams
> Reach the low vale where mists of ignorance lodge,
> Strike on the innate spark which lay immers'd,
> Thick clogg'd, and almost quench'd in total night—
> On me it fell, and cheer'd my joyless heart.
>
>   ('On Mrs. Montagu', 30–7)

Light meets light, genial sunlight evaporating the rural mists to reveal Yearsley's hidden 'innate spark'. Montagu joins 'STELLA' (i.e., Hannah More) and 'the pair/ Conspire to clear my dull, imprison'd sense' (48–9).

More and Montagu bring to Yearsley two gifts: benevolent sympathy and cultivated thought. The first affirms and confirms Yearsley's 'innate' powers, the second promises to set them free. Yearsley translates their relations in the following terms:

> Oft as I trod my native wilds alone,
> Strong gusts of thought wou'd rise, but rise to die;
> The portals of the swelling soul, ne'er op'd
> By liberal converse, rude ideas strove
> Awhile for vent, but found it not, and died.
> Thus rust the mind's best powers. Yon starry orbs,
> Majestic ocean, flowery vales, gay groves,
> Eye-wasting lawns, and Heaven-attempting hills,
> Which bound th' horizon, and which curb the view;
> All those, with beauteous imagery, awak'd
> My ravish'd soul to extasy untaught,
> To all the transport the rapt sense can bear;
> But all expir'd, for want of power to speak;
> All perish'd in the mind as soon as born,
> Eras'd more quick than cyphers on the shore,
> O'er which the cruel waves, unheedful, roll.
> ('On Mrs. Montagu', 51–66)

The passage begins to develop a fruitful contradiction prevalent in subaltern writing from Chatterton through Keats and Clare. Between the 'fanatic' and the 'poet', according to Keats's later version of this myth, stands a 'fine spell of words' that 'alone can save/ Imagination from the sable charm/ And dumb enchantment' ('The Fall of Hyperion', I.9–11). Yearsley's text appears to execute a proof of this thought: erased 'cyphers' give way before an achieved poetic expression.

At the same time, however, the success of the passage is clearly represented as a 'bound' and 'curb'—poetic figures that replicate Yearsley's 'native wilds', where her 'innate spark' was originally 'awak'd . . . to extasy untaught'. As a consequence, Yearsley's poetic success here turns to a string of second-order figures, 'cyphers' pointing elsewhere 'To all the transport the rapt sense can bear'. Poetry comes not as an expressive achievement but in forms of passion and desire.

These forms shape themselves through the drama of her 'clogg'd' and frequently turgid poetic style. Never simple or harmonious, her writing struggles with an elaborate, largely Miltonic rhetoric that has been filtered through her study of Young. Like the induction to Wordsworth's *Prelude*, the opening (lines 1–48) of Yearsley's impressive 'Remonstrance in the Platonic Shade' builds a self-conscious drama of a failed poetic effort. Both texts preserve these lines as essential figures of the mind's struggling activity. The second part of Yearsley's poem (48–91) proceeds to gloss the opening section.

> These feeble sounds
> Give not my soul's rich meaning; or my thought
> Rises too boldly o'er the human line
> Of alphabets (misused). Why should I wish
> For words to form a picture for the world
> Too rare? O world! what hast thou in thy sounds
> So dear as silent memory when she leads
> The shade of the departed? Ask despair
> What renovation is, when friendship bends
> To kiss her tears away;—but ask her eyes;
> The pleasing anguish dwells not on her tongue.
> Will Friendship stay, when love and virtue fly?
> Sooner Leviathan shall pierce the skies,
> Roll 'mid the burning thunder of the sun,
> And hate the chrystal caverns of the deep!
>   (48–62)

Coiled within these splendidly convoluted lines are the commonplace ideas of an art of sensibility. They get lifted through their thought by their style, which repeatedly thwarts a conceptual transaction of the poetic field.

Equally important, the passage parades its deliberateness and deliberation—as it were a creature with a purpose, and its eyes were bright with it. Though turned by her benefactors to the very emblem of a 'naïve' poet, Yearsley accepts as an aesthetic given all those stylistic devices that Wordsworth would repudiate as mannered, false, and artistically dead. So her verse lacks altogether the cultivated simplicities fashioned in the sophisticated minds of writers like Schiller and Wordsworth. Yearsley's poems are anything but simple for she does not wear her elaborate style with ease. Rather, it seems a kind of shirt of Nessus, an angel to be wrestled with.

> 'Folly' could ne'er o'ertake me. Oft I verge
> When warm'd by fancy, to the farthest bound
> My sense of words can bear; but at the extreme
> Contemn the sense that chastity throws off.—
>
> (64–7)

What kind of logic makes these lines follow the passage just quoted? It is very difficult to say or—in the immediacy of one's reading experience—to know what they are about. As the poem continues we see that Yearsley is drawing a complex relation between her writing, her commitment to Ideal forms, and the preservation of her sexual virtue. The relation is maintained, however, only by an 'extreme' expressive effort—in verse that occupies 'the farthest bound/ My sense of words can bear'. Line 67 culminates the effort with a tortured poetical inversion that must be carefully worked out to be comprehended and that continually slips away regardless.

A close explication of the lines is illuminating. Their syntax, unravelled, yields the following: 'oft I verge to the farthest bound, but when I reach the absolute extreme of my effort, I contemn the sense that throws off chastity'. Many features of the sentence contribute to its obdurate convolution. The subordinate clause ('When warm'd by fancy') subtly erodes the temporal argument of the main clause, as it also interrupts its literal movement. The phrase 'my sense of words' is quite difficult in a context that insists so strongly on the physicality of this experience—as if the mind were a body struggling with its intellectual purpose. Finally, that subject—which is the principal topic of the verse—gets radically distorted by the governing image signalled by the obscure (and technical) term ' "Folly" '. As becomes clear only much later in the poem, Yearsley summons this term to operate as a virtual allegorical sign for lost female virtue. Even so, it does not function in a straightforward way. It is in fact a second-order sign. The syntactic inversion of line 67 thus has to contend with a figural set which is itself quite obscure and difficult. As readers we have to struggle on through the verse to discover that the phrase 'the sense that chastity throws off' only bears *at the literal level* the meaning 'an extreme passion that leads a woman to abandon her virtue'. Yearsley works the image into a figure for a certain kind of poetical conscience, a particular ('Platonic') way of using language when brought (as Keats will later say of imagination in 'To J. H. Reynolds Esq.') 'beyond its proper bound, yet still confined,/ Lost in a sort of purgatory blind'.

In short, Yearsley's 'clogg'd' verse perfectly represents her difficult mental environment, including her own (mental) self as it struggles to negotiate its obscurities, which replicate those of its world:

> 'Folly!' Good heaven! have I not climb'd an height
> So frightful, e'en from comfort so remote,
> That had my judgement reel'd, my foot forgot
> Its strenuous print, my inexperienced eye
> The wondrous point of view; or my firm soul,
> Made early stubborn, her exalted pride;
> Though of external poor, the stagnant lake
> Of vice beneath, than Cocytus more foul,
> Had oped its wave to swallow me. . . .
>
> (68–76)[1]

This kind of verse enacts its own message: that success comes only to 'rough laborious spirits' (82) whose understanding has been schooled by lived experience. Writing poetry is Yearsley's spiritual agon, which her readers must re-experience to understand.

A remarkable feature of Yearsley's writing is the way it *literally* identifies her spiritual difficulties with cultivated 'poetical' forms. Her thought (though not her poetic practice) replicates a writer like Wordsworth. So she concludes her poem 'Addressed to Sensibility' with the familiar distinction between natural and educated feelings:

> My rough soul,
> O Sensibility! defenceless hails,
> Thy feelings most acute . . .

---

[1] The stylistic difficulties persist, most apparently in a phrase like 'Though of external poor', which clearly pushes to the very limit 'the sense of words can bear'.

> Does Education give the transport keen . . . ?
> No, Nature feels
> Most poignant, undefended . . .

But if 'Education' is not the source of sensibility, it is, for Yearsley, its (paradoxically) clarifying medium. Yearsley does not make a myth of fleeing the cultivated world, like Rousseau and Wordsworth, she makes a myth of entering fully into its demonic illusions. Her clotted style figures a wilderness of false visions that her 'rough soul', entering into, exposes and finally even transforms.

According to Yearsley, sensibility is an essential means for carrying out those transformational actions. It operates a logic of (Platonic, not worldly) refinement:

> 'tis thine
> To give the finest anguish, to dissolve
> The dross of spirit, till all essence, she
> Refines on real woe; from thence extracts
> Sad unexisting phantoms, never seen.
> ('Addressed to Sensibility', 37–41)

Though in ultimate Truth 'unexisting', these 'phantoms' are none the less powerful forces, all the more so because their unexisting natures are 'never seen' except through sensibility's refining processes.

> Then, with viewless pencil, form his sigh,
> His deepest groan, his sorrow-tinged thought,
> Wish immature, impatience, cold despair,
> With all the tort'ring images that play,
> In sable hue, within his wasted mind.
> ('Addressed to Sensibility', 44–8)

In making these revelations, sensibility generates a sympathetic energy field within the 'afflicted heart' (59). This state corresponds precisely to that 'farthest bound' verged by Yearsley's 'sense of words' in her 'Remonstrance in the Platonic Shade'. It is a boundary not to be crossed—she calls it 'the line for ever plac'd/ 'Mid the platonic system' ('Remonstrance', 125–6). It marks the limit of the powers of Sensibility herself:

> yet—yet beware,
> Nor stoop to seize from Passion's warmer clime

> A pois'nous sweet.—Bright cherub, safely rove
> Through all the deep recesses of the soul!
> Float on her raptures, deeper tinge her woes,
> Strengthen emotion, higher waft her sigh,
> Sit in the tearful orb, and ardent gaze
> On joy or sorrow. But thy empire ends
> Within the line of SPIRIT.
>   ('Addressed to Sensibility', 59–67)

But if the angels of Sensibility may 'safely rove . . . the deep recesses of the soul', these are perilous regions for the human 'SPIRIT'. Yearsley writes her poem 'To Indifference' as a further move toward the intellectual clarity she is pursuing. Sensibility is a creature of extremes, 'what is not bliss/ Is woe':

> No placid medium's ever held
> Beneath her torrid line, when straining high
> The fibres of the soul. Of Pain, or Joy,
> She gives too large a share . . .
>   ('To Indifference', 30–4)

'Indifference' comes then 'for one short hour' (39) as a respite from the struggle. Yearsley's climactic figure for this moment of relief is a telling one:

> Soft Indiff'rence, come!
> In this low cottage thou shalt be my guest,
> Till Death shuts out the hour: here down I'l sink
> With thee upon my couch of homely rush,
> Which fading forms of Friendship, Love, or Hope,
> Must ne'er approach. Ah!—quickly hide, thou pow'r,
> Those dear intruding images . . .
>   ('To Indifference', 46–52)

Because Yearsley's spiritual agon is so physically imagined, relief takes a corresponding form. Furthermore, those 'fading' Platonic shapes are the shadows of her former patronesses, who sought to cultivate her powers of sensibility and separate her from her rude origins. 'Indiff'rence' is (as it were) a sleep and a forgetting, whose mists were once penetrated by the refined benevolence of More and Montagu. Yearsley's cottage appears now to measure and judge the limits of 'Those dear intruding images' and the light they brought.

The poem concludes with a final, stunning pair of lines:

> IDEA, smother'd leaves my mind a waste,
> Where SENSIBILITY must lose her way. (55–6)

'Indiff'rence' returns Yearsley to a primal state, a pristine wilderness. It is a condition where the difference between platonic IDEA and virtuous SENSIBILITY gets clarified.[2] Yearsley frames this condition in dark and paradoxical terms: at once a maze to thwart the dangerous projects of sensibility, and a dark night of the soul where pure light, being wholly extinguished, revives as an impersonal form of a personal desire. As a later poet would say, 'In a dark time the mind begins to see'.

That is precisely the argument of 'Remonstrance in the Platonic Shade'.

> THOU purest spirit bestow'd by bounteous Heav'n,
> To bless the world and dignify the man,
> Think not I leave the cool Platonic shade,
> Haunt of the God invisible . . .
>
> (1–4)

Such a thought might come because Yearsley has started to write, has moved into the 'selva oscura' of this very poem. But she rings various changes on the word 'shade' to suggest that this writing, this poetic act, is itself a form of Intellectual Beauty:

> In this sacred shade,
> Whilst cruel duty fetter'd every sense,
> I saw my morning sun ascend with tears,
> And sink at eve with heaviness; the night
> Came burthen'd with despair; yet unsubdued,
> I frown'd indignant on my chains, and tun'd
> My rural lay to universal love.
>
> (6–12)

The platonic shade is her writing as well as the rude life it represents. And it is her mind as she incarnates the grace of primal Mind:

> Such grandeur works his mighty scenes thro' shades
> Where sober contemplation plumes her wings,

---

[2] Yearsley's poem explicitly associates sensibility with the cultivation of virtue ('*her* loud boast/ Is VIRTUE' (12–13)). But in Yearsley's view, all such virtue rests in a state of subsistent grace, which Yearsley associates with platonic IDEA.

And calls her Plato from behind the stars.
Love breathes corrected sentiment, inspires
. . . truth serene, which makes our bliss below,
By luring virtuous spirits to repose.

(40–6)

The intellectual structure of Yearsley's thought is remarkable and remarkably coherent. This 'repose' corresponds to the restorative sleep of 'To Indifference'. It is a rest, a condition of primitive darkness, most needed by 'virtuous souls' who struggle in the obscurities of their own commitments to virtue, most understood by poets committed to Ideal Forms of thought.

In the 'Remonstrance', Petrarch functions as Virgil to Yearsley's Dante. From his grave, paradoxically, he is flourishing on the height toward which Yearsley's desire is carrying her. After narrating, in the central section of her poem, how she 'attained/ With wretchedness this summit' (82–3), and how this attainment gave her an exalted view of the world-historical nature of human wretchedness (83–92), Yearsley halts the progress of her verse:

O forbear,
My muse! turn from the vision, lest thou wake
Emotion, and compare that heart with thine—
There gentle Petrarch sleeps; mild victim long
To that serene despair, which once imbib'd
The soul grows fond of, and withdraws, to give
Her tints of sympathy, ideal grace,
Languishing sentiment, and faithful tear,
To the wild woodland.

(92–100)

This move turns Petrarch's 'heart' to the platonic *cor cordium* of sensibility. And she is able to 'compare' his heart with her own because she perceives an ideal analogy between their circumstances *at this very moment in time*. Like Shelley later, Yearsley is thinking toward the Euganean Hills, to the small village of Arqua.[3] Petrarch's tomb is in the churchyard, nearby the modest house where he died. House and grave together exalt the 'wild

---

[3] Petrarch's symbolic place in the culture of sentiment and sensibility, and later in romanticism, is a central one. The influence of *The Florence Miscellany*—see below, Part II Chapter 5—can be seen in its promotion of Petrarch as a key poetic point of departure.

woodland', and reaffirm the spiritual significance of Yearsley's own 'Rural Lyre' (the title of the volume in which her poem appears).

The 'Remonstrance' thus ends by turning into itself, conflating literal with ideal forms, and representing the process as the act of writing a poem, *this* poem. In the event, Idea becomes Act, thought the bride of thinking (rather than a conceptual form). Yearsley's platonic ideal therefore does not emerge into the light, it merges with its own evolving Petrarchan darkness (where her 'soul . . . explores/ The utmost limit of her gloomy sphere', 119). Petrarch leads her home, back to the obscurity and 'shade' of a world 'far from the noise' (101) of the larger world. Exactly in keeping with her studied Miltonic (re)vision, it appears a darkness visible. Like her cottage in 'To Indifference', 'Remonstrance' becomes the fulfilment of her primal 'retreat' (121), a lowly place 'Flourishing on an Height'. In that state her life becomes a sleep and a forgetting, the platonic anamnesis of her soul perpetually rising up through its own inarticulate darkness: as Petrarch, as 'Plato from behind the stars', as (not least aptly or memorably)

> Sweet Philomel sings to the warrior[']s shade—
> Far o'er the plain, beneath the midnight moon.
>
> (110–11)

It is a nice, final touch. The poem ends with the song of the nightingale, the bird of Sappho: her emblem and, according to ancient tradition, her very self.

8

Motherhood and the Self Unknown

Yearsley, Greville, and The Amourous Lady pursue love through a context of deprivation, and the literature of sensibility does largely function in a world assumed to be 'fallen'. Yearsley's Platonic remonstrance, however, suggests the possibility of a wholly uncorrupted realm, a glimpsed world of pure forms. Indeed, among the sub-genres of sensibility one does stand apart, trailing clouds of the glory of a condition of absolute purity. This is the literature of the child: 'Infant Joy', 'The Lamb', 'The Idiot Boy'.

Such verse assumes a particularly telling form when a mother appears the medium of the child's inarticulate life. More's Mrs Boscawen is turned to an emblem of perfect sensibility not because she is a poet but because her feelings are incorrupt, and her purity is imagined as a direct function of her motherhood ('And you . . . fondly melt,/ In raptures none but mothers ever felt', lines 199–200). These 'raptures' develop to include a broad range of sympathies. They empower Boscawen to

> view, prophetic, in your race,
> All Levison's sweetness, and all Beaufort's grace;
> Yet dread what dangers each lov'd child may share,
> The youth, if valiant, and the maid, if fair.
>
> (201–4)

Writers tell the stories of endangered valour and beauty, the tales of sensibility. But these tales are immediate apprehensions to a mother like Mrs Boscawen—'felt in the blood, and felt along the heart'. The future opens itself to view through an intensity of present affect.

According to Blake's grand (romantic) representations, an elemental and unfallen condition is a state of being where 'eternal Life sprung' (*The [First] Book of Urizen*, plate 3). This is the state (not revived but played out) in a poem like 'The

Lamb', which is an engine of pure reciprocities, perpetual motion figured as perfect sympathy. The course of romanticism shows that the state of primal blessedness gets figured in mythic terms when it lapses into a fallen condition, or agrees that the authority of fallenness cannot be neglected. But writers may indeed refuse to acknowledge the dominion of that authority. Blake's *Songs of Innocence*, in general, do so, as does (in general) the tradition of 'children's literature' that those songs exemplify.

In later Blakean terms, the formula 'to become what one beholds' defines a lapse of imagination. It is a romantic figure of visionary catastrophe. But in a poem like 'The Lamb', the formula signifies perpetual blessing, as it does in Joanna Baillie's 'A Mother to her Waking Infant' or Anna Laetitia Barbauld's 'To a Little Invisible Being . . .' (see Lonsdale's *Eighteenth-Century Women Poets*). A conscious reflection on that blessedness, whether as lost or found, is a characteristic feature of this kind of poetry. As a result, the writing begins to turn from a poetry of sensibility into a poetry of sentiment.

Insignificant by any reasonable measure, Baillie's child yet exerts commanding force: not to call out obeisance, as might a monarch, but to make eternal life spring:

> Each passing clown bestows his blessing,
> Thy mouth is worn with old wives' kissing:
> E'en lighter looks the gloomy eye
> Of surly sense, when thou art by . . .
>
> (33–6)

In Barbauld's poem, the mere promise of such a creature transforms the world:

> And see, the genial season's warmth to share,
> Fresh younglings shoot, and opening roses glow!
> Swarms of new life exulting fill the air—
> Haste, infant bud of being, haste to blow!
>
> (9–12)

As in William Carlos Williams's *Spring and All*, which this kind of poem anticipates, the act of writing instantiates its subject. In one sense this nature and these roses are little invisible beings called to an ideal life by the literal imperative of the text.

Because the writing is pregnant with the reality it celebrates, however, the words themselves appear to come not as through Barbauld's personal act of artistry. This is an art of self-efface-ment, an art that realizes it*self* when it comes as a determinate part of a pure and primal process. Barbauld's perceived inability to control this process of energies becomes a poetic figure of a new kind of artist (one who 'watches and receives').

Barbauld's is therefore partly a poem about poetry. This new art does not create *ex nihilo*, however: it brings forth and reveals. It is exactly the same kind of art discussed by Mary Shelley in her famous introduction to (the 1831 reprint of) *Frankenstein*:

Every thing must have a beginning, to speak in Sanchean phrase, and that beginning must be linked to something that went before. The Hindoos give the world an elephant to support it, but they make the elephant stand upon a tortoise.

In Shelley, when a modern Faust seeks to command this elemen-tal process, the consequence is disaster. Barbauld's poem, by contrast, like the child of promise it celebrates, emerges as another creature of the process itself.

It is the simplest of processes, known to all, endlessly re-peated, yet ceaselessly mysterious and wonderful. Its key feature is that while it must be undergone, it can never be compre-hended.

> What powers lie folded in thy curious frame—
> Senses from objects locked, and mind from thought!
> How little canst thou guess thy lofty claim
> To grasp at all the worlds the Almighty wrought!
>
> (5–8)

Lines 7–8 deftly conceal the figure of a little invisible being with little invisible hands. Barbauld does not have to 'create' a poetic image of a child with outstretched arms and grasping fingers; the figure is known to all and need simply be recalled. This con-cealed figure therefore appears a second-order sign for Barbauld's new poetical practice. A foetus is here poetically born as an image of an artistic ideal. This is not the child as father of a man, it is non-gendered being, the free object of maternal devotion.

The line 'Senses from objects locked, and mind from thought' is particularly telling. It casts the child as an existential absolute—a kind of living soul laid asleep equally in body and in mind. This is the soul of vital phenomenal life, a radical recasting of traditional humanist vision. The aspiration is not to 'Know Thyself' but rather, as it were, to *un*Know Thyself:

> She longs to fold to her maternal breast
> Part of herself, yet to herself unknown;
> To see and to salute the stranger guest,
> Fed with her life through many a tedious moon.
>
> (21–4)

Maternal embrace becomes a self-enfolding and thereby a self-unfolding. Barbauld's identity emerges, paradoxically, with the birth of the child, as both grow (w)rapt in a secularized (mortalized) Cloud of Unknowing. Freedom comes according to the Blakean proverb 'The most sublime act is to set another before you' (*The Marriage of Heaven and Hell*, plate 7), with its splendid wordplay on the preposition.

> Haste, little captive, burst thy prison doors!
> Launch on the living world, and spring to light!
> Nature for thee displays her various stores,
> Opens her thousand inlets of delight.
>
> (29–32)

Endless and reciprocal, the action depends at all points upon minute but determinate (and ultimately human) particulars. As in lines 7–8 earlier, here lines 31–2 elaborate a general philosophical statement by sketching the figure of an infant: 'Nature' appears and opens not abstractly or in general, but at every child's birth, in every infant's form.

Though much less philosophically self-conscious, Baillie's 'A Mother' is more apt with its particulars. This happens because hers is not a promised but a present child. The birth figure that focuses Barbauld's poem becomes a figure of awakening in Baillie's. So the infant's concrete features and specific acts can be catalogued ('Thy curled nose and lip awry,/ Thy up-hoist arms and nodding head', 2–3; etc.). These beauties of inflection do not come in an orderly way, however, but as it were randomly, as it were imitating the mother's thirteen ways of looking at her infant. The randomness signals the child's special virtue: that its vitality is an absolute, beyond good and evil. Baillie writes:

> When sudden wakes the bitter shriek,
> And redder swells thy little cheek;
> When rattled keys thy woes beguile,
> And through the wet eye gleams the smile,
> Still for thy weakly self is spent
>   Thy little silly plaint.
>
> But when thy friends are in distress,
> Thou'lt laugh and chuckle ne'er the less;
> Nor even with sympathy be smitten,
> Though all are sad but thee and kitten . . .
>   (13–22)

Trivial, fortuitous, and silly things not only define the child's universe, they found (and ultimately judge) every higher moral order, as the word 'sympathy' comes to show. The infant is literally careless in its laughter and its tears alike.

At the poem's climax, the imaginary mother imagines a useful future for her child, a time when the infant might tender a sympathetic return of its mother's love:

> Perhaps when time shall add a few
> Short years to thee, thou'lt love me too.
> Then wilt thou through life's weary way
> Become my sure and cheering stay . . .
>   (39–42)

This imagining, however, is Baillie's rhetorical artifice fashioned to dismantle a shallow and ultimately utilitarian conception of love:

> Wilt care for me, and be my hold,
>   When I am weak and old.
> Thou'lt listen to my lengthened tale,
> And pity me when I am frail—
> But see, the sweepy spinning fly
> Upon the window takes thine eye.
> Go to thy little senseless play—
>   Thou dost not need my lay.
>   (43–50)

The portmanteau phrase 'senseless play' signals a mortal grace beyond the reach of every art. It is the sign of Grace Abounding, an absolute imagination of a way of life that throws into relief the inadequacy of even the most exalted moral conceptions, the best of 'good works'. Here the woman considers her child as Jesus considered the lilies of the field when he went up to the mountain to preach to the multitudes (Matthew chapters 5–7, especially 6:28). The child appears a kind of mortal divinity, not a free but a freed spirit: as it were, free flesh. This vision of the child is begotten of its mother, whose power comes—like her child's—from her humanity. Like her poem, she does not create, she brings forth and then 'sets another before her'.

As a consequence, the mother also appears new born (or here, new wakened) through her maternity. Barbauld's poem helps to elucidate the action:

> She longs to fold to her maternal breast
> Part of herself, yet to herself unknown . . .
>
> (21–2)

In 'freeing' her child 'living from thy living tomb' (20), the mother also gains her new life, that part of herself previously 'unknown' and 'invisible'. Unlike Barbauld, however, Baillie represents this self-consciousness as a pervasive rhetorical feature of her poem, which is (self-consciously) constructed as a dramatic monologue. The unknown self thus appears to Baillie, to the reader, as the woman in the poem, who promises a new life. This new life separates the woman from her previous social roles, most especially her role as wife or lover. In motherhood, Barbauld and Baillie imagine their emergence as non-dependent and free agents.

Let it be remembered, however, that this imagination reflects certain historical and social conditions. 'Motherhood' is not a transcendental moral category. Indeed, an antithetical reading of these poems, against the grain I have been following here, could and should be imagined. Under the horizon of an age of sensibility, however, the category 'mother' had gained such ideological power that it supplied poets, especially women poets, with remarkable new aesthetic possibilities. A generation later, in the work of Felicia Hemans, the situation has already changed dramatically.

Hemans focuses nearly all her work on an exploration of the figural constellation of motherhood. The emotional consequence is not Barbauld's and Baillie's sense of wonder, however, but the running drain of her melancholic imagination. What appears to Hemans as most unstable, most threatened, is what she most values: the child and its immediate world, the family unit (centred in the mother). Hemans' central myth represents a home where the father is (for various reasons) absent. This loss turns the home to a precarious scene dominated by the mother. As in Wordsworth, one of Hemans' important precursors, the mother's protective and conserving imagination presides over a scene of loss (see 'The Homes of England', for instance, or 'The Graves of a Household'). But whereas Wordsworth's (male) myth of (feminine) nature licenses what he called a 'strength in what remains behind', Hemans' is an imagination of disaster because (unlike Wordsworth's nature) Hemans' mothers are so conscious of their fragile quotidian state.

The disaster is clearly displayed in poems like 'The Image in Lava' and 'Casabianca'. Theatrical by modernist conventions, these lyrics deploy Byronic extravagance as a vehicle for measuring social catastrophe and domestic loss. 'The Image in Lava', a dark rewriting of Barbauld's 'To a Little Invisible Being', studies the epic destruction of Pompeii in a bizarre silhouette of a mother cradling her child. The artist of the end of the world is here imagined not on a grand scale—as a Blakean 'history painter'—but rather as a miniaturist. For Hemans, catastrophe is finally what Byron famously called 'home desolation', and world-historical events are important only because they help to recall that fact.

> Babe! wert thou brightly slumbering
>   Upon thy mother's breast,
> When suddenly the fiery tomb
>   Shut round each gentle guest?
>   (13–16)

Hemans' poem is imagining a new burning babe and a new sacred heart. The events at Pompeii comprise a mere figure for the 'impassioned grasp' that bonds child to mother. Burning in the fire of their relationship—setting their fires against 'the cities of reknown/ Wherein the mighty trust' (39–40)—mother and child transcend the Pompeiian world. As Blake might have said, they 'go to Eternal Death' (*Jerusalem* 39.16), which now reveals itself in and as the poem Hemans is writing, what she calls a 'print upon the dust' (38).

In 'Casabianca', another poem of fiery immolation, Hemans emphasizes the psycho-political basis of destruction in 'the cities of reknown'. Explicitly set in a modern context (the Battle of the Nile, August 1798), the poem anatomizes the ideology of glory in the death of the thirteen-year-old 'son of the admiral of the Orient', Commodore Casabianca. Standing to his duty in a secular fiery furnace, the boy is the central figure of a complex iconograph of the violence society exacts of itself as payment for its pursuit of power and glory. The sentimentalism of the scene is a feminizing textual move. The boy pleads for a word from his 'unconscious' father that would release him from 'the burning deck', but the language of the fathers is defined as a fearful symmetry of heroic silence and awful noise. The upshot is a poem of violent death brooded over by a beautiful but ineffectual angel of (maternal) love.

It is crucial to understand that Hemans' feminine imagination does not solve the problems it exposes. Her sentimentalism is revelatory.[1] Readers cannot forget that her poem recollects one of Nelson's mythic victories over the French, and a turning point in the Napoleonic wars. But Hemans' poem deliberately forgets to remember that saint of English imperialism. Nelson and England's sea power supply the poem with its obscure and problematic scene. Standing with the young Casabianca on the burning French flagship, Hemans puts the war and its champions in a better perspective.

The poem's unusual ideological move exposes as well the special (historic) function that Hemans' poetry has gained for itself. According to Hemans' poem, in worlds where power measures value, imaginative truth discovers itself through its apparent powerlessness. That idea presides over the entire poetic tradition of sensibility and sentiment. The young

---

[1] Indeed, it is crucial to recall that poems like 'Casabianca' are, in another perspective, jingoist tracts. Hemans was a conservative poet and her works were appropriated for the most conservative ideological causes. Their force *as poetry* comes exactly from the extent of their own reactionary commitments, and the contradictions that emerge therefrom.

Casabianca's moral and emotional position, what the poem calls his 'still, yet brave despair' (24), defines the equivocalness of what he represents. Like Byron's Prometheus, Hemans' boy 'make[s] of death a victory'. Unlike Byron, however, Hemans does not end her poem with a romantic gesture of eternal defiance. She concludes by imagining the death of the heart she values:

> But the noblest thing that perish'd there,
> Was that young faithful heart.
>
> (39–40)

No words of comfort or uplift follow that imagination, though they could easily have been added. Their absence speaks to the character of the poem, and not to any possible doubt in Hemans about the 'nobility' of the boy's death. The poem ends by doubting itself and its own powers to rise above its subject. It discards the last infirmity of those minds who make poems to celebrate the mastery of art.

To think of poetry in that way distinctly anticipates the full-blown critique developed one hundred years later by Laura Riding. Hemans' melancholia turns to Riding's pitiless philosophical reflections on the lying and joking words of the poets and their poems.

9

The Literal World of the English Della Cruscans

A REBOURS

Not many remember that the eighteenth century had a literary *fin de siècle*. It was called the Della Cruscan movement. Of course no one now takes this body of work seriously, and its readers are rare. The received judgement—that it's trash—comes to us as naturally as the leaves to the tree. Nor do many now recall the immense notoriety the Della Cruscans quickly gained after their initial appearance in the 1780s. William Gifford, the movement's first public enemy, launched his (once celebrated) attack in 1791 because Della Cruscan writing was so successful, becoming what Gifford called an 'epidemic malady...spreading from fool to fool' ('introduction' to *The Baviad*, xii).[1] The disease ran out of control when Robert Merry (alias 'Della Crusca') returned home to England from Italy

and immediately announced himself by a sonnet to Love. Anna Matilda [Mrs Hannah Cowley] wrote an incomparable piece of non-sense in praise of it; and the two 'great luminaries of the age', as Mr. Bell calls them, fell desperately in love with each other. From that period not a day passed without an amatory epistle...and a thousand other nameless names caught the infection; and from one end of the kingdom to the other, all was nonsense and Della Crusca. (xii–xiii)

Gifford's terms of abuse are interesting: for example, 'high flown', 'prurient', 'obscene', 'unintelligible'. Three good couplets in an impossibly turgid satire summarize his views:

[1] My texts from Gifford are taken from *The Baviad and Maeviad*, 6th edn. (London, 1800).

Lo, DELLA CRUSCA! In his closet pent,
He toils to give the crude conception vent.
Abortive thoughts that right and wrong confound,
Truth sacrificed to letters, sense to sound,
False glare, incongruous images, combine;
And noise, and nonsense, clatter through the line.
(*The Baviad* 39–44)

Leaving aside the indiscriminate abuse—can it really be the case
that *all* this writing comes out as shit?—we will find, I think,
that Gifford here betrays a good general comprehension of what
this ('unintelligible') writing is about. His understanding is just
marked with a negative inflection. The 'incongruous images' are
everywhere, elaborate sound patterns build primary stylistic
devices, and knowledge (moral or otherwise) generally lies
closer to a surface of textual 'letters' than to a sub-surface of
deeper 'Truth'.

If we want to reacquire an understanding of Della Cruscan
poetry, Gifford's fustian points us in the right direction, but it
won't take us very far. We need a more serious antagonist for
that. Fortunately we find what we want exactly at the end of the
decadent and Della Cruscan nineties—in the poetry written by
Wordsworth and sponsored in his 'Preface' to the 1800 *Lyrical
Ballads*. This great prose text is a conscious critique of the Della
Cruscans and the kind of writing inspired by their work. When
Wordsworth speaks of his subject as 'incidents of common life',
when he says he wants to trace 'the primary laws of our nature'
in a rural language of 'simple and unelaborated expressions',
and when he attacks 'arbitrary and capricious habits of expression [that] furnish food for fickle tastes and fickle appetites
of their own creation', he is setting his project apart from the
manner of the Della Cruscans. The famous paragraph on 'the
general importance of the subject', where Wordsworth attacks
literary London's 'degrading thirst after outrageous stimu-
lation', is levelled squarely at the Della Cruscans, whose influence on the theatre of the decade had earlier (1795) drawn
Gifford to his second attack, in *The Maeviad*.[2]

Wordsworth's response proved effectual for a simple but

---

[2] See *Lyrical Ballads: Wordsworth and Coleridge*, eds. R. L. Brett and A. R. Jones
(London: Methuen, 1965; new and rev. imp.), 244–6, 248–50.

profound reason: unlike Gifford, he could write good verses, so he put into play a practical alternative to what was, after all, not a set of ideas (confused or otherwise) but a style and programme for writing. Of course such conflicts of style always reflect broad social and cultural issues. The ideological stake for Wordsworth involves the relation of language to 'feeling', both natural (so-called) and poetic. Feeling is the central issue because the Della Cruscans had launched their own writing fifteen years earlier under the same sign. From Wordsworth's perspective, however, nothing could be more strained or artificial than the feelings pursued by writers like Robert Merry and Mrs Cowley. And (so the imagination goes) when feelings are stimulated rather than spontaneous, when poetic language cultivates artifice rather than sincerity, Wordsworth's mind turns catastrophic, fantasizing a world reduced 'to a state of almost savage torpor'.

All such totems and taboos aside, clear lines are being drawn here that will have marked effects upon the course of writing and culture. (I note in passing, for example, that Shelley's and Byron's hostilities with Wordsworth, like Blake's earlier, come from their greater sympathy with a Della Cruscan approach to language.) The differences come sharply into focus if we compare the way Wordsworth renders external nature with a typical Della Cruscan text. The first passage is the well-known quatrain from Wordsworth's 'Lines written in early spring', the second is from Robert Merry's 'Monody Addressed to Mr. Tickell'.

> To her fair works did nature link
>   The human soul that through me ran;
> And much it grieved my heart to think
>   What man has made of man.
>
> Through primrose tufts, in that sweet bower,
>   The periwinkle trail'd its wreathes;
> And 'tis my faith that every flower
>   Enjoys the air it breathes.
>
> The birds around me hopp'd and play'd:
>   Their thoughts I cannot measure,
> But the least motion which they made,
>   It seem'd a thrill of pleasure.
>   (5–16)

Yes, *she was mild and lovely as the star*
That in the Western hemisphere afar,
Lifts its pure lamp above the mountain's head,
To light *meek Evening to her dewy bed.*
And as the waning moon displays,
With mirror clear, Morn's rising rays,
She, in decay, show'd VIRTUE'S ORB refin'd,
Reflected *fairer* from her angel mind;
Till at the last too fierce a blaze was given,
And then she sunk from sight, and FADED *into* HEAVEN.

(I.72)[3]

Both of these passages involve what a later criticism, unhappy with romantic conventions of writing in general, would call 'affective fallacy'—the ascription of sensibility to the inanimate or vegetable world. The two texts represent, however, very different approaches to the natural world, human feelings, and the language of poetry.

Wordsworth's lines, a *locus classicus* of 'romantic nature', call for little comment at this late hour. As everyone knows, the text illustrates how one might 'see into the life of things' in the broad (religious and philosophical) sense Coleridge invoked when he spoke of 'the one Life within us and abroad'. Merry's natural scene at first appears shot with a similar kind of spiritual presence and activity. In fact, Merry is far from perceiving, much less arguing, that some kind of objective 'soul' or transcendent Spirit 'runs through' the natural world.

O TICKELL! in the murm'ring gale
Oft have I found thy plaintive voice prevail;
When the wet fingers of the morn
Shook the cold pearl-drops from the bending thorn;
Or when, at close of day,
To the lone vale I took my way,
The *sad vibration* of *faint* ECHO'S *breath,*
Brought to my heart the dirge of Death.

(I.70–1)

---

[3] From *The British Album.* In Two Volumes. (London: John Bell, 1790). The notoriety of Della Cruscan verse was largely a consequence of these volumes, where the amatory exchanges of Della Crusca and Anna Matilda, reprinted from Bell's periodical *The World,* were first anthologized. Citations hereafter are given in the text by volume and page number.

Here the lively features of the natural world come forward as signs of a power Blake called 'the Human Imagination'. In this respect Merry's poem is unconcerned with nature as such—for example, whether or not it is invested with spirit. What interests him is art's capacity to deal with fatal circumstance. In trying to console Tickell, Merry celebrates what he elsewhere calls the 'Eternal beauties in [the] mind' (I.12).

The natural figures conjured in Merry's poem are thus, paradoxically, signs of their opposite, signs of an anti-nature. Merry's poem doesn't simply construct an artificial order of nature, it puts its own act of construction on display, makes that act one of its primary concerns. The infamous extremities of Della Cruscan poetry are self-consciously theatrical and spectacular, like the self-conscious wit cultivated in (for example) metaphysical poetry. Here is Anna Matilda describing dawn in a landscape she imagines Della Crusca is travelling through.

> And when her tints of various dye
> Burst from the pallid sickly sky,
> *There* rush in violet, *there* in green,
> *Here* in soft red imbue the scene,
> Then lose themselves by growing bright,
> 'Till swallowed up in one vast flood of light—
>   (I.103–4)

This is the metaphysical verse of a period that has put itself to school to sensationalist rather than faculty psychologies. Everything is as it is perceived. So while 'nature' is constantly invoked in Della Cruscan verse—while the entire movement took the meridian graciousness of Italy as its point of departure—the Della Cruscans definitely operate under the Blakean proverb: 'Where Man is not Nature is barren'.[4] The primary forms of nature dwell in 'the feeling mind' (II.26):

> Why does thy stream of sweetest song,
> In many a wild maze wind along;
> Foam on the Mountain's murm'ring side;
> Or through the vocal coverts glide . . . ?
>   (I.78)

---

[4] Several of William Parsons' contributions to *The Florence Miscellany* (Florence, privately printed, 1785), the movement's first important publication, explicitly address this topic of nature as imaginative reconstruction. See 'On the Pleasures of Poetry', pp. 134–6, esp. stanzas 8 and 13–14.

Della Crusca's artful questions to Anna Matilda are asked in the 'vocal coverts' of this text, which is constructed as a linguistic landscape—indeed, which is (implicitly) arguing that the primary forms of nature are inward, imaginative: human.

So when Della Crusca answers his own questions by saying these things happen 'because thy HEART can feel', we register the difference between this order of feeling and (say) Wordsworth's. The 'one Life' perceived and celebrated by Wordsworth and Coleridge is a religious vision, an imagination of the

> workings of one mind, the features
> Of the same face, blossoms upon one tree;
> Characters of the great Apocalypse,
> The types and symbols of Eternity
> Of first, and last, and midst, and without end.
>   (*Prelude* VI.636–40)

While such a vision, like Della Crusca's, is ultimately grounded in eighteenth-century sensibility, it also reaches for the sublime, an effect (or what we now call an 'aura') that is explicitly refused in the tradition followed by Merry, Cowley, and their immediate precursor, Sterne.

REFINING DECAY

Wordsworth and Coleridge have embarked on a quest for permanence, for a 'primal sympathy/ Which having been must ever be'. By contrast the Della Cruscans, for all their celebrated extremities, operate at a distinctly mortal level. Wordsworth's transcendental functions appear in Della Crusca as imaginative ornament and decorative wit. What we observe are not the workings of one transcendent mind, but the artificial constructions of a particular poet—'one' mind in a distinctly lower case. So whereas Wordsworth's poetry typically aspires to the spontaneous and sublime, Della Cruscan poetry seems self-conscious and erotic. These differences signal different approaches to poetic style and a desired mode of address towards the reader. Della Cruscan verse is conversational where Wordsworth's is meditative, theatrical rather than overheard. The Della Cruscans court passion and intensity, but in doing so they leave no doubt that these are all splendid and wonderful *im*permanences. The Della Cruscans thereby erect what Blake will call 'the buildings of Los[s]'—extreme artifices of an eternity in love with the productions of time, and hence in a permanent condition of impermanence.

We see this approach very clearly in Merry's 'Monody' for Tickell. Tickell's wife Maria has passed away like the moon before the dawning sun; 'FADED *into* HEAVEN' is a pure grace of art, an imagining as fragile as it is lovely, and a splendid figure of the permanence of impermanence. As the rest of the poem makes quite clear, Merry writes—*sympathizes*—out of an understanding that '*all of Nature, as of Art, must end*' (I.72). The superb (and distinctly proto-Shelleyan) figure of Maria Tickell fading into heaven is not a transcendental but a quotidian sign. Working from the same Enlightenment traditions out of which Merry came, Shelley will name it a sign of 'Intellectual Beauty'.[5]

The point is that while both Wordsworth and Merry wish to celebrate 'the mind of man', that mind is for Wordsworth the type of a higher Mind, whereas for Merry it is always a particular mind. Wordsworth's 'types and symbols of Eternity' are Merry's 'Eternal beauties *in thy* mind' (my italics): 'thy' signifying that the addressee, in this case Anna Matilda, comprehends such eternities; and 'in' specifying the locus of what we might otherwise take for an appeal to a transcendental norm. Furthermore, Della Cruscan beauties are 'Eternal' in a distinctly Lucretian or Heraclitian (rather than a Platonic or neo-Platonic) sense. In this respect the writing draws explicitly upon the materialist tradition of sensibility defined by Sterne, the immediate (and acknowledged) precursor of the Della Cruscan movement.[6]

To the Della Cruscan imagination, one enters nature only to reconstruct its orders in a finer tone. The transformation doesn't occur, however, as an act of creation—a unique Fiat—but as *re-creation*, a multiplying of particular repetitions. Eros therefore defines this second-order creation, which emerges—in current

---

[5] So will Coleridge, in 'The Eolian Harp', line 47. Coleridge was strongly influenced by the Della Cruscans in the early nineties. His ambivalence is evident in 'The Eolian Harp' (composed in 1795). His later, famous critiques of sensationalist philosophies, as we know, are as much recantations as anything else.

[6] See e.g. Arley's 'Elegy on the Death of Mr. Sterne' (*British Album* II.88–90); but Sterne is echoed and glanced at throughout Della Cruscan verse.

terms—by fusion rather than fission energy. In this context, we can appreciate why the typical form of Della Cruscan writing came to be the *tenso*, and its defining event the poetic interchange of 1788–9 between Della Crusca (Robert Merry) and Anna Matilda (Mrs Hannah Cowley).

A word or two about the general form of these interchanges might be useful at this point. Consciously following the example of the troubadours and the *stil novisti*, the English Della Cruscans refined the *tenso* into a specifically heterosexual erotic exchange. The *tensi* of their European precursors were more typically between male poets, whether friends or rivals or both. In English Della Cruscan verse, by contrast, what were once poetic subjects for male poets—their blessed damozels—assume positive textual roles, become themselves agents in the poetic exchanges. Furthermore, the focusing interchange (in this defining case between Della Crusca and Anna Matilda) generates further textual relations with third or fourth parties. For example, the first *tensi* of Della Crusca and Anna Matilda are complicated when two other figures ('Reuben' and 'Laura') enter the central poetic conversation.

These kinds of development and complication are inevitable, however, given the erotic and dialectical character of the writing. Indeed, the Della Cruscan movement came into such rapid cultural dominance during the 1790s, I think, because the writing explicitly encouraged further writing, whether response or elaboration. Its erotic formalities appealed as much to women's as to men's imaginations. Such a catholic (hetero)sexuality elsewhere provoked the hostile reactions best known through Gifford's *Baviad* and *Maeviad* and the other attacks of the period, like Polwhele's *The Unsex'd Females*. Conventional literary history now likes to imagine that those attacks undid the English Della Cruscan movement, but the truth is that it pursued a vigorous life well into the 1830s. Byron and Keats are both deeply marked by Della Cruscan forms, and the resources of the style are not fully exploited until it is undertaken by Moore and Shelley.

None the less, its basic poetic structure is clearly visible from the start. We may trace its unwindings, for instance, in the central passage of Della Crusca's early lines 'To Anna Matilda' (from *The British Album*, I.86–8).

Let but thy lyre impatient seize,
Departing Twilight's filmy breeze,
That winds th' enchanting chords among,
In ling'ring labyrinth of song:
Anon, the amorous *Bird of Woe*,
Shall steal the tones that quivering flow,
And with them soothe the sighing woods,
And with them charm the slumb'ring floods;
Till, all exhausted by the lay,
He hang in silence on the spray,
Drop to his idol flow'r beneath,
And, 'midst her blushes, cease to breathe.

(I.87)

Anna Matilda's poetry is being imagined here as a kind of eolian harp whose chords 'seize' an otherwise inarticulate natural world and compel it to a form of complex, world-creating music. The verse thus produces a landscape of intoxicating sound out of which appear music-generated super-natural forms: in this case, a watered woodland covert where the eternal loves of the rose and the nightingale are replayed.[7] The verse is profoundly synaesthetic and transformational. It is a 'labyrinth of song' where lyre and breeze wind into each other, where *flow*ers alternately *flow* like water or turn to sculpture (idle idols), and where the nightingale's erotic suspension quivers like (or into) a drop of dew that is falling into (its) love and in that ecstatic moment of morning, dying.

Della Crusca ascribes such events to the power of Anna Matilda's poetry, but of course this magical world appears only in the here and now of Della Crusca's poem. None the less, the relation of rose and nightingale, of lyre and breeze, and of the various other interchanges evoked by the verse are all *figurae* of the defining interchange, the poetic *tenso* between Della Crusca and Anna Matilda. The basic structure of the verse is exactly erotic because it proceeds by acts of intercourse that are at once perfectly immediate and purely imaginative.

'Sex in the head' then; but after all—so the Della Cruscans,

---

[7] Della Crusca's footnote to the passage is explicit: 'This alludes to the idea of the Nightingale being enamoured of the Rose, so frequently expressed in Persian poetry.'

like Blake, will ask—where else *should* it be? In our vegetable
nature? An injunction to cultivate a sensate mind involves here
the imaginative reconstruction of Blake's vast polypus of death,
our (erstwhile and otherwise) brute flesh. As Blake was fashioning that reconstruction in cosmic and world-historical terms, the
Della Cruscans—like Oscar Wilde one hundred years later—
rediscovered it in the pulsation of very ordinary arteries.

The miniatures of Della Crusca, the movement's apparently
precious trifles and triflings, mark a self-conscious effort at a
comic recovery of energy. Gifford and others were appalled that
the Della Cruscans' fame should have emerged through
low-brow periodical organs like the *Oracle* and the *World*. But
the movement gloried in its scorn for 'those the VULGAR call
the GREAT' who 'strive a consequence to find/ By seeming more
than Human kind' (I.79). 'Consequence' follows rather when
'The lustre of poetic ray/ [Shall] wake an artificial day' (I.11):
'artificial' here standing as the sign of an imagination that
aspires to be at once supremely self-conscious and wholly
voluptuous.

The eighteenth-century term for that ideal was Intellectual
Beauty. Though commonly understood to involve mental as
opposed to sensuous phenomena, intellectual beauty defines a
project to undermine the body/soul distinction altogether. When
Merry opens his exchange with Mrs Cowley by publishing his
intention to quit poetry, she writes to dissuade him:

> O! seize again thy golden quill,
> And with its point my bosom thrill;
>
> (I.3)

The self-consciousness of such eroticism—it is nothing less than
the metaphysical verse of sensibility—is exactly the 'point'.
Cowley calls for a 'blended fire' of poetry and sexuality:

> The *one*, poetic language give,
> The *other* bid thy passion live;

Later romantic writers become preoccupied with Paolo and
Francesca, Launcelot and Guenevere, Tristan and Isolde, in
order to explore what D. G. Rossetti would call 'the difficult
deeps of love'. The kiss is the earliest figure of those deeps, and
it focuses a great deal of Della Cruscan writing.

We have to pause a bit—it isn't difficult—over this matter of kissing, for it locates an important feature of the Della Cruscan experience. Recalling the troubadours and the *stil novisti* is here once again useful. Unlike their medieval precursors, as we have seen, the *tensi* of the English Della Cruscans involved women as much as men. We mark a related difference in the importance the Della Cruscans attach to the so-called lower senses. Troubadour poetry is dominated by vision, the 'highest' of the senses, the one (it was thought) closest to the mind's intellectual powers. In the sense of touch, on the other hand, we are truly imbruted, our debasement fully manifest.

A brief digression—interesting, I hope, and relevant to the question of the Della Cruscans. Though kissing in one perspective—Dante's, for example, in *Inferno* Canto V—has been made a *figura* for a (lower) sensual corruption of the highest good (Love), an even more ancient Christian tradition was able to see the kiss otherwise. Among primitive Christians what we now call the French kiss, or soul kiss, was called the kiss of peace, and was widely practised among the faithful. Through the kiss of peace Christians engaged a spiritual intercourse—the exchange of breath being meaningful not simply as a cultic sign but, more significantly, as a sacramental (i.e., outward and material) event.[8]

Della Cruscan kissing makes a secular return to that kind of imagination. The inheritance of Locke, especially as it passes through Sterne, opened doors of perception that had been shut or hidden for centuries. Eyes closed, kissing lovers enter the voluptuous rooms of a long-forgotten palace, the tactile body, at once electric and material.

Blake's work is preoccupied with this move to redeem the erotic corpus. It is a literal subject in *The Book of Thel*, the *Songs*, and *The Visions of the Daughters of Albion*, but it appears in more cosmological forms everywhere. 'The lust of the goat is the bounty of God', for (according to Blake) a certain 'Metaphysics' has turned the body to a cavern, a 'palace of eternity' to 'the jaws of the hungry grave' (*Visions* 6:1). When Blake drives the angel before him in plates 17–19 of *The Mar-*

---

[8] See Nicholas James Perella, *The Kiss Sacred and Profane* (Berkeley and Los Angeles: University of California Press, 1969), 20–8.

riage of Heaven and Hell the event transforms a dungeon to a pastoral paradise. The underground hell of the Bible becomes a Venusberg.

Similar experiences preoccupy all romantic poets. Keats's work is especially important. When 'Kisses four' take Keats's knight-at-arms into *his* Venusberg, he wakens not to a Blakean heaven but 'the cold hillside'. A nightmare imagination intervenes 'To turn a palace to a tomb' ('The Giaour', 281). The nightmare is ancient, Platonic, ultimately misogynist: the body, which is woman, promises heavens of pleasure, but these heavens, real enough in themselves, are also impermanent. Erotic love, grounded in the body, cannot escape the body's limitations.

Like Blake, however, the Della Cruscans escape Keats's nightmare by starting from a different imagination of the relation of pleasure and pain. The hell of Keats's Paolo and Francesca is flawblown by a 'melancholy storm', and the darkness proceeds from the same imagination announced by Urizen when he destroyed the world:

> I have sought for a joy without pain,
> For a solid without fluctuation.
> Why will you die, O Eternals?
> Why live in unquenchable burnings?
> (*The [First] Book of Urizen* 2:3)

Hidden in those troubled questions are their ecstatic answers: one dies in order to love, and one enters the fiery furnace because to do so is exactly to display the triumph of eternal life.

Della Cruscan poetry dwells on these subjects repeatedly, 'to a fault' in several senses. In the exchanges of Anna Matilda and Della Crusca, the lady recurrently draws herself toward 'INDIFFERENCE' because the pleasures of 'SENSIBILITY', coming and going, inflame and tear her nerves. To inhabit such a world is precisely to 'live in unquenchable burnings',

> where the Sun, with downward torrid ray
> *Kills*, with the barb'rous glories of the day.
> ('Ode to Indifference', I.76)

The elision in 'barb'rous' is telling, and a typical feature of Della Cruscan wit. Gifford deplored it as a trick of mere 'letters', which is of course true enough, so far as that idea of the matter goes. Anna Matilda takes it farther, picking up various motifs in the couplet (in particular 'barb'rous', 'torrid', and the killing Sun) and playing transformations on them:

> Oh! she has torn the slumbers from my lids:
> Oft rous'd my torpid sense to living woe,
> And bid chill anguish to my bosom grow.

While the conceptual subject is pain, and the referential experience suffering, the immediate *poetic* event signals the triumph of art over—say rather, *within* and through—its embracing limitations.

What is absolutely crucial to understand about this kind of writing is its extreme formality. Its world is figured, consciously artificial. To read it one would do well to recall one of Pound's famous 'don'ts' in 'A Retrospect':

When Shakespeare talks of the 'Dawn in russet mantle clad' he presents something which the painter does not present. There is in this line of his nothing that one can call description; he presents.[9]

There is in Anna Matilda's lines, in Della Cruscan writing generally, nothing that one can call description. All is present-ed through and as letters. Anna Matilda's world is her text—immediate, material, self-conscious, limited to language. Her art reflects (upon) a reality imagined in a similar design.

Immersed in that textual condition, however, Anna Matilda cannot comprehend its truth. In this respect she utters words, like Blake's Urizen, whose entire meaning she cannot herself realize. So her 'Ode to Indifference' is answered—really, is read and interpreted—by Della Crusca.

> O CEASE MATILDA! cease thy strain,
> That wooes INDIFFERENCE to thy arms;
> For what are all her boasted charms?
> *But only to be free from Pain!*
> (I.78)

Della Crusca begins to develop Anna Matilda's poetic thought—her 'feeling mind', her 'sensate heart'—by invoking the multiple meanings carried in the word 'strain' (familial,

---

[9] Printed in Pound's *Pavannes and Divisions* (New York: Alfred A. Knopf, 1918).

musical, poetic, biological). Pleasure is fraught with its reciprocal pain, and Anna Matilda's expressed desire for untormented love, being itself a form of desire, generates 'the LUXURY OF WOE'. This is Della Crusca's phrase, however, not Anna Matilda's; that is, Della Crusca gives a local habitation and, most importantly, a name to Anna Matilda's style. He reveals part of its *luxurious* meaning. In doing so, he begins to establish the signs of the limits of his own imaginings. His admonition 'CEASE', for example, is in an important sense the precise opposite of what he wants of her, of the truth of his true desire.

The *tenso* format is the key device for gradually unfolding more of the literal truth to the conversing writers. (Of course the *full* truth can never be disclosed, only *fore*closed—by ceasing to enter and regenerate the world of letters.) Anna Matilda first responds to, then resists, the 'Poetic ardors' (II.160) aroused by Della Crusca. For his part, Della Crusca is 'recalled to love' by his own impulse of renunciation, and the recall is literalized in Anna Matilda's first lyrical response. But that response builds up its own structure of internal resistances, so that a complex pattern of nested tensions gradually unfolds itself. The whole exchange comprises a dialectic of ambiguous resistances and stimulations: 'flights' alternating figures of fear and of ecstasy, binding 'strains' of music and tortured nerves.

A LIVING THEATRE

To Wordsworth (to return to Wordsworth), these literalists of imagination were deplorable not for having failed in their art, but for having proposed such an artistic procedure in the first place. It was, in a word, insincere: a game of words rather than a true expression of true feeling. The language of poetry is not to be measured by a norm of artifice but by what Wordsworth calls the 'real language of men'. Poetry succeeds, for Wordsworth, to the degree that it approximates such a language, for only that 'real' language can hope to express what is 'permanent' and 'universal' in our nature and our feelings.[10]

[10] For a good contextual treatment of sincerity see Leon Guillamet, *The Sincere Ideal. Studies in Sincerity in Eighteenth-Century English Literature* (Montreal and London: McGill-Queens University Press, 1974).

Of course Wordsworth skirts the problems of his position—for example, that his 'real language of men' is an artificial construction of his own (certainly in his own poetry), and that it by no means comprehends the full range of the 'English' language, even the English spread abroad the kingdom in 1800. Furthermore—and speaking only of poetry—'sincerity' is, after all, strictly a poetic style, a rhetorical stance. Wordsworth's project, however, was to argue the need of translating that style into a moral norm for artists. (Byron, recognizing this, laid down his parody-decalogue in *Don Juan* to expose the over-weening presumptuousness of Wordsworth's position.) The second of the essays 'Upon Epitaphs' supplies an excellent gloss on the (often recondite) argument of the *Lyrical Ballads'* Preface:

when a man is treating an interesting subject, or one which he ought not to treat at all unless he be interested, no faults have such a killing power as those which prove that he is not in earnest, that he is acting a part. . . . This is one of the most odious of faults; because it shocks the moral sense.[11]

This comment explains why Wordsworth found Della Cruscan verse so abhorrent. Love and sympathy, the relation of thought and feeling, or art and life: these are the large and 'interesting' subjects addressed by the Della Cruscans. Their work is 'odious' because of its theatricality, because it is 'not in earnest' as Wordsworth imagines it should be.

Coleridge's views on these matters in *Biographia Literaria* are relevant and instructive.[12] Taking up the 'second defect' in Wordsworth's poetry, Coleridge expands his earlier remark about the momentary 'willing suspension of disbelief . . . that constitutes poetic faith' (II.6). The root of the defect Coleridge locates in Wordsworth's idea that poetry 'proposes *truth* for its immediate object, instead of *pleasure*' (II.130). Wordsworth's project tries 'to make [poetry] what it ought to be', that is, a form of expression where no gaps open between *res* and *verba*.

---

[11] See *William Wordsworth: The Literary Criticism*, ed. Paul M. Zall (Lincoln: University of Nebraska Press, 1966), 107.

[12] I quote from the two-volume edition (eds. James Engell and W. Jackson Bate) in *The Collected Works of Samuel Taylor Coleridge*, Bollingen Series LXXV (Princeton: Princeton University Press, 1983). Citations are in the text.

But this is to place a demand upon poetry that could only be realized when

the blessed time shall come, when truth itself shall be pleasure, and both shall be so united, as to be distinguishable in words only, not in feeling. (II.130)

Coleridge is saying that poetry creates virtual worlds. This being so, the poet will only destroy the rhetorical effect of his fictions if he asks the reader to judge them by measures of truth or reality. For Coleridge, poetry works by a delicate kind of '*negative* faith': viz., the 'willing suspension of *dis*belief' (my italics) in what a critical intelligence, if permitted to operate, would judge unreal, things of mere words, 'letters' (as Gifford called the *unbelievable* language of the Della Cruscans).

Much closer to the Della Cruscans than Wordsworth, Coleridge came under their influence for a brief time in the early nineties[13] (Wordsworth was never influenced, except by antithesis). He differs from them in one crucial respect: for Coleridge, the verbal structures erected by the poet will ideally comprise symbols of the transcendental order that Wordsworth wants to imagine. The logical form of this symbolical relation eventually gets expressed in the theory of the primary and the secondary imaginations. The latter constructs a figural totality analogous to the primal (Judaeo-Christian) act of creation—a finished and unified form wherein various opposite and discordant qualities are balanced and reconciled.

This context of more traditional romantic thought throws the differential of the Della Cruscans into bold relief. As we have already seen, the dialectics of the Della Cruscan *tenso* do not permit the symbolist approach to writing favoured by Coleridge. Furthermore, as Coleridge seeks communion with 'the one Life within us and abroad', the Della Cruscans pursue change, variety, and a succession of diverse experiences. That feature of the work comes out early, in *The Florence Miscellany* (Florence, privately printed, 1785), the volume that brought the movement into public attention. The title is itself an index of a writing committed to change and variety. The book mixes

---

[13] See especially the poems of 1792–4 (e.g. 'Kisses', 'The Sigh', and 'The Kiss', among others). These are explicitly Della Cruscan works.

Italian and English poets and poetry, men and (at this point only) one woman (Mrs Piozzi). The Miltonic model of l'allegro/ il penseroso is explicitly invoked in numerous poetic pairings, the most important being Merry's 'Il Viaggio' and 'La Dimora'. In the ambitious poem 'Valombrosa', a culminant text in the book, Merry sets 'the ardent love of change' and a 'Lavish . . . maze' of experience against an 'unvaried round' of existence bound by 'chains of habit' (186–7): in typical Della Cruscan style, 'change' versus 'chains'. The point is not to bring order to variety but to stimulate and provoke. Artificial reconstructions of nature everywhere spread and multiply into further textualities.

The mechanism generating these generations is the theatricality of the verse, its conscious pursuit of illusion and surface effects. Where Coleridge understands poetry to function through a suspension of critical disbelief, the Della Cruscans argue that it comes exactly from the self-conscious display of disbelieved forms and fanciful gestures. In poetry, being earnest becomes important only when you're not.

The Della Cruscan who explores this paradox most thoroughly is William Parsons. His 'The Story of Francesca, from the fifth Canto of DANTE'S INFERNO' (in *The British Album*) uses the method of what Parsons calls 'Free Translation' to weave his Della Cruscan interpretation into the reworked Dantescan original. The clear differences between Dante's text and what Parsons makes of it can be seen in Francesca's famous climactic comment upon the sinful event:

> Galeotto fu il libro e chi lo scrisse:
> Quel giorno piu non vi leggemmo avante.

> Thus did that cursed book, with pois'nous art,
> To us perform it's Galeotto's part;
> That day no more the luscious page we priz'd,
> For all it feign'd in us was realized.

> (p. 122)

Throughout the episode Dante's text wants us to see that the lovers have been bad readers. Had they gone on reading 'that day' (to the end of the story), had they even paid attention to the text they did read (rather than to each other), their sin might have been averted. Francesca here acknowledges her culpability, but Parsons—like Dante—wants us to see that she does not understand what she knows. She speaks like that figure of contemporary legend, the reader of *Werther*, who finishes the book by committing suicide.

Parsons thus extends Dante's thought most tellingly in his climactic line, which has no linguistic equivalent in the original. The line is impossible to overpraise, at least if one values economy of rich expression. It works by the simplest of devices—locating the prepositional phrase simultaneously in two syntaxes. Parsons thus adds an unexpected gloss on Dante, a comment amounting to a brief theory of poetic mimesis: the 'luscious page' loses its artistic value when its artificial status is compromised. According to Parsons' reading, text works to build a 'feign'd' world 'in' the lovers, a significant experience they might imaginatively engage. In this case, however, the lovers don't engage an erotic text, they choose to enter its 'realiz'd' equivalent.

Parsons implicitly argues that disaster looms for readers who suspend the self-consciousness ('disbelief') promoted by textual experiences, in particular poetic experiences (for example, in spontaneously overflowing texts, or 'sincere' verse).

> One day we read how Lancelot's throbbing heart
> Felt the soft torments of love's piercing dart.
> Alone we were, in innocence secure,
> For till that moment all our thoughts were pure;
> But then too oft as our uplifted eyes
> Each other met, the conscious blushes rise.

Like a fever, those blushes signify that her body knows more about Francesca's danger than her mind. The text marks her mind's ignorance by her (yet maintained) idea about their mutual innocence and mental purity. 'The fatal crisis' plays out Francesca's culpable lack of awareness, and the text, which might have been a Virgil to Francesca, becomes instead a Galeotto:

> When as we read how first the kiss of flame,
> On fair Ginevra's smiling mouth impress'd,
> Rais'd love's wild tumults in her yielding breast;
> The youth beside me sought an equal bliss,
> With trembling lips I met his burning kiss.

But texts are not to be thus abandoned and misused. These lovers have forgotten their book, have forgotten how to read. The desire to establish a real equation between textual and personal erotics means, in this text, disaster.

Parsons translates Dante as a warning against forms of reading (or writing) that seek a real equivalence between expression and feeling, between the poetic and the personal. Parsons has turned Francesca to a monitory emblem of the poetry of sincerity. His 'free translation' involves an argument about the moral function of textual fictions, whose obligations to reflection and self-consciousness (style and art) stand prior to all (rhetorical) demands for expression and sincerity. One is not surprised, consequently, that Parsons typically addresses the problem of poetry through explicit or implicit analogies between poetry's virtual worlds and the illusions of the stage.

The 'Song' to his coy mistress Melissa, for example (*Miscellany*, p. 142), functions as a kind of allegory of art. As 'Melissa's voice' 'outvies' the loveliest natural sounds, it becomes a figure for, and a challenge to, the 'Song' itself. But Parsons moves to meet the challenge:

> Yet can I meet devoid of fear
>   The matchless splendor of her charms;
> And when she sings unmov'd can hear,
>   Nor dread the tyrant Love's alarms.
>   (5–8)

Reimagined, Melissa has met more than her match in Parsons' verse, as we see in that splendid—and typically Parsonian— wordplay on 'unmov'd'. For the 'studied airs' (16) of Melissa's singing, he goes on to say, have taught Parsons to make a theatre of her art.

At the outset of his song Parsons allows that Melissa's voice 'outvies' the 'wood-lark's melting lays'. At the end, however, he compares himself to a 'free bird high-pois'd in air', 'sing[ing] secure' from the 'downward lure' (21–4) of Melissa's dangerous art. Like any craftsperson (see the 'crafty fowlers', 22), Melissa has gained her skill through 'studied' work. When she sings she is therefore 'unmov'd', and in the eyes of an imaginatively aware listener may be judged 'by affectation sway'd' (13). Labelled as such, as in Brechtian theatre, that affectation gives up its unexpected virtue. It appears (now) the gift of art. Parsons takes the gift and sings Melissa a responsive song, wherein her 'unmov'd' song turns through its 'unmov'd' hearer to a kind of meta-song about the freedom that art offers.

We want to see that Parsons does not romanticize either Melissa or the art she teaches and practices. The labels 'affectation' and 'studied' and 'fantastic' all carry their negative overtones through the text. By the same token, Parsons doesn't want to diminish her achievement, as his own song plainly indicates. If there is a grace beyond the reach of art—something this song suggests in its critique of Melissa—we can *know* its absent presence only through the measure of art: that is one of the key ideas promoted in work of this kind.

The 'romantic' poems of the Della Cruscans—I have in mind significant works like Merry's 'Madness' and 'Sir Roland. A Fragment'—always come labelled as such. In this respect they are literally 'theatrical' works; they call attention to themselves as artistic constructs. They make one remember Charles Lamb's acute displeasure when Coleridge changed the title of the 1798 'Rime of the Ancyent Marinere' to the 1800 'Ancient Mariner: A Poet's Reverie':

it is as bad as Bottom the Weaver's declaration that he is not a lion, but only the scenical representation of a lion. What new idea is gained by this title but one subversive of all credit—which the tale should force upon us—of its truth.[14]

Coleridge's change is a move in the direction of Della Cruscan self-consciousness. The 'new idea . . . gained' by the revision is precisely an *idea* rather than an affect. It introduces an intellectual element into the work. Nor is this to suggest—*pace* Lamb— that the affective order of Coleridge's verse does not undergo a similarly decisive change. Bottom's declaration of his role-playing is not 'bad', it is a gesture bringing pleasures of awareness to the audience's experience. Not many would prefer Lamb's version of *A Midsummer Night's Dream* to Shakespeare's. Not many wouldn't think the original a far richer work, both intellectually and affectively.

---

[14] See Lamb's letter to Wordsworth of Jan. 1801, quoted in Brett and Jones, *Lyrical Ballads*, 277.

10

Mary Robinson and the Myth of Sappho

Describing the scope of her study of the *Fictions of Sappho 1546–1937*, Joan DeJean points out that the reception history of the Greek poet 'is almost exclusively a French preserve' until the eighteenth century, at which point 'the English and the Germans really began to play a role'. These facts explain why DeJean focuses on French traditions. But she then adds:

Once other traditions become active, I refer to all the major contributions to the composite portrait of Sappho that originate outside of France. I dwell especially on those foreign traditions when they create original fictions that subsequently serve as models for French authors.[1]

But the truth is that the single most important English contribution to the Sapphic tradition is never mentioned in DeJean's study.[2] This is Mary Robinson's *Sappho and Phaon* (1796).

Far more is at issue here than filling an omission in an important scholarly study. Robinson's work in fact had little influence on subsequent treatments of Sappho in *any* language, so we can understand why DeJean overlooked her book. To say that *Sappho and Phaon* is a central document in the poetry of sensibility—which it is—already hints at the problem. The literature of sensibility has been, as we say these days, securely marginalized. And the *poetry* of sensibility has long been virtually invisible. Of course the impact of the great original writings

---

[1] *Fictions of Sappho 1546–1937* (Chicago: University of Chicago Press, 1989), 4.

[2] One other signal contribution, Swinburne's, is treated rather perfunctorily, as if it were simply a footnote to Baudelaire (see 272). But Swinburne's is a highly original contribution to the tradition (see Jerome McGann, *Swinburne: An Experiment in Criticism* (Chicago: University of Chicago Press, 1972), esp. 112–17).

of sensibility, both prose and verse, has scarcely been negligible. Touchstone writers in the tradition—say, Rousseau and Sterne, Goethe and Richardson, or the 'major romantic poets'—are canonical figures. But tradition and the profession of letters has not preserved their work *because of its sentimentality*. Their cultural value is judged by other measures, with their sentiment-alism being viewed in neutralized 'historical' terms. That pro-cedure, at any rate, has governed critical practice to this point in time.

As a result, the literatures of sensibility tend to be read through categories that bracket out the question of the (aes-thetic) value of sensibility as a mode of expression. Of course the styles and the culture of sensibility maintain a vigorous life in western society to the present day. But this life typically func-tions in low cultural and social registers: in popular music, pulp fiction, the movies. More fastidious souls—often splendid enough, in their own way—look with judgmental eyes on figures like Marianne Dashwood and Mary Robinson. Sometimes these looks are censorious, sometimes condescending, occasion-ally sympathetic. They are nearly always conscious of their superiority.

Robinson's *Sappho and Phaon* is not itself low-brow; on the contrary, it is a learned production fully aware of the major works serving the tradition it interprets. Two of the key docu-ments, Ovid's culminant epistle in the *Heroides* and Barthelemy's *Voyage du jeune Anarcharsis en Grèce* (1788), are given special prominence by Robinson, and her handling of both tells us much about the distinctive features of her work, as we shall see. Indeed, what most disturbs contemporary readers of *Sappho and Phaon* are its serious and radical philosophical pretensions. Most reactionary critics in the 1790s lacked the intellectual tools to combat these pretensions when they took imaginative forms—for example, in Della Cruscan poetry—so the attacks came as invective, travesty, ridicule. The prominent antagonists were Gifford, Polwhele, Mathias, and the *Anti-Jacobin* writers, though only the latter achieved true poetic distinction. A major figure of reaction would soon emerge in the person of 'the later Coleridge', himself a lapsed Della Cruscan poet.

One needs to recall this history in order to revise it radically.

The complete excision of Della Cruscan poetry from the history
of English writing has been a cultural disaster. This consequence
has followed not because the work of the original English Della
Cruscans was in itself a major poetic achievement, though they
certainly have their impressive moments. One wants to understand Della Cruscan poetry because:

1. it provides an invaluable corpus for studying the conventions
   of the poetry of sensibility;
2. understanding those conventions gives greater access to the
   work of the major poets who worked in the first phase of the
   tradition, that is, in the years 1760–1840;
3. understanding the poetry of sensibility in that period opens
   new avenues for (re)reading the poetry that succeeded it.

To this point in time we possess virtually no studies of the
formal and rhetorical conventions of the kind of verse that Mary
Robinson cultivated. How then can we read with any confidence
the poetry of Robert Merry, Charlotte Smith, or Ann Batten
Cristall, much less the work of Felicia Hemans or Laetitia
Elizabeth Landon? Or how evaluate what we may read? Much
of this writing is currently under historical recovery through the
efforts of cultural historians, feminist and otherwise. But such
readers tend to have little interest in the *art* of this writing,
which is interrogated for its social, or moral, or ideological
significance.[3]

We can scarcely manage distinctions between sentimental
poetry, poetry of sensibility, and romantic verse. As for the
latter, which we pretend to understand, its conventions are
widely misunderstood or ignored. Indeed, the fact that romantic
poetry operates with *conventions* of sincerity—that the famous
'true voice of feeling' is an artful construction—remains widely
unappreciated. Poe and Wilde, it is true, have provided brilliant
guides for studying such work, but neither are taken seriously as
poets, so that their criticism of poetry remains to this day badly

---

[3] In his good study *Radical Sensibility: Literature and Ideas in the 1790s* (New
York: Routledge, 1993), Chris Jones says that 'I have used the two terms inter-
changeably, as much from a conviction of their continuity as from the inconvenient
absence of an adjectival form for "sensibility" ' (5). His move is common and seems
to me symptomatic of a wholly inadequate critical procedure—and all the more
inadequate if, as Jones believes, there is a 'continuity' between the terms. (For
'continuity' I would myself put 'close relation'.)

misunderstood. (We have yet to plumb the depth of Poe's serious joking in 'The Raven' and 'The Philosophy of Composition', or of the profound inconsequence of Wilde's various elucidations and critiques of romanticism and sincerity—for example, in *The Importance of Being Earnest*.)

While the ultimate issues here are aesthetic ones—and socio-political to the extent that we can appreciate the socio-political dimensions of aesthetic action—the immediate problems are critical. We want to elucidate the rhetorics of sentimentalism, sensibility, and sincerity in a way that might correspond to the early twentieth century's critical exploration of the metaphysicals and their Augustan inheritors. To do this demands a return to formal analysis and close reading. But in the present case the acts will have to be self-consciously (re)historicized, so that the classicist histories (and evaluations) established through the discourse of modernism can be fundamentally relativized. If you demand of 'poetry' what can be followed through Pound, or Eliot, or Yeats, or Stevens, you will have great difficulty understanding, much less appreciating, most of the poetry written between 1760 and 1900; and you will work hard to exorcize a poet like Stein, who is the chief modernist inheritor of those traditions. You will also select from the poetry of 1760–1900 those writers who can be shown to have broken with—in fact 'romanticized'—the original spirits of sentimentalism and sensibility.

This is the context in which one wants to reread Robinson's *Sappho and Phaon*. The book was written as a comprehensive manifesto for poetry (that is to say, for poetry of a certain kind—for a poetry of sensibility). It is in this respect a polemic for 'modern' poetry (that is to say, for verse that was understood at the time to be new and innovative, or—in the rhetoric of its hostile critics—dangerous and newfangled). The manifesto comes at once as a theory and a practice, with the two moves formally marked in the work's prose and verse sections. Indeed, one key (dialectical) argument of *Sappho and Phaon* is that a proper poetical practice ought to be fully 'theorized' (self-conscious, philosophical, and in Schiller's sense 'sentimental'), just as an adequate theory of poetry would have to establish feeling and emotion as intellectual and philosophical grounds.

ROBINSON'S MYTH OF SAPPHO: GENERAL THEORY

Robinson's manifesto—like the more celebrated ones of Wordsworth, Percy Shelley, and others—directly engages current poetical theory and practice. Most important, *Sappho and Phaon* follows eighteenth-century theory in taking 'sensibility' and 'feeling' as distinguishing marks of poetical writing. From Edward Young's 'Discourse of Lyric Poetry' (1828) through Dugald Stewart's *Elements of the Philosophy of the Human Mind* (1792–1827), poetry is associated with a feminized 'feeling' and 'imagination', and is opposed to the sober and practical 'masculine power[s] of the mind' (Stewart, 1854: I.416). The opposition gets codified as a distinction between reason and imagination. Like later romantic writers, Robinson contests the invidious judgement often implied in the comparison.

Her argument, both as theory and as practice, is specifically gendered female. This comes about not simply because of Robinson's sex, but—more crucially—because the substance of her argument demands it. She takes it for granted—as everyone else at the time did—that sensibility is a feminized 'experience'. She is equally aware, however, that the philosophical *discourse* of sensibility has been dominantly masculine. Robinson's work proceeds to turn this cultural limit to her polemical advantage. If sensibility (in theory) is to have a discursive form, it will have to be an 'experiential' one, that is to say, a poetic (aesthetic) form.

This context of thought explains the purposes of Robinson's book. First, it will elucidate the contradiction that Robinson perceives between the discourse of poetry and the discourse of philosophy. Second, it will argue the philosophical case of poetry *in the discourse of poetry* (and implicitly critique the relevance or effectiveness of any philosophical discourse that eschews the practice of sensibility and what is in this book taken as its chief discursive vehicle, poetry). Her position puts her at odds with the two dominant (and masculinist) theories of poetry articulated in the volatile 1790s, the one reactionary, the other revisionist. As one target of Gifford's anti-Della Cruscan satire *The Baviad* (1791), Robinson means to disestablish a 'dead but sceptred' view of poetry that clung to its authority in face of the many bold new writing ventures of the later eighteenth century.

On the other hand, her book of sonnets constructs its own positive interpretation (or 'myth') of this new poetical scene. In this respect her argument anticipates Wordsworth's defence of poetry against the emerging cultural claims of science and philosophy. As a specifically Della Cruscan myth, however, Robinson's approach would be undermined in Wordsworth's revisionist 'Preface' to *Lyrical Ballads* (1800), which seeks to restore poetry—including the poetry of feeling and imagination—to its 'manly' heritage.

Sappho and Phaon perfectly illustrates Schiller's theoretical dialectic of naïve versus sentimental poetry. Robinson's work is fully sentimental exactly because it (imaginatively) constructs a naïve body of sapphic writing. The construction draws a running parallel between a model of ancient cultural 'enlightenment' and the contemporary world (both Europe in general, but England in particular).[4] The prose shape of the argument is set forth in Robinson's 'Preface', her address 'To the Reader', and her 'Account of Sappho', all of which introduce the sonnet sequence.

Robinson's Sappho is first of all a model of the passionate 'naïve' poet. Her poems are 'the genuine effusions of a supremely enlightened soul' (p. 25). 'Distinguished by the title of the tenth Muse' (21), Sappho's 'Fame . . . spread even to the remotest parts of the earth' (22). Again and again Robinson associates Sappho with cultural enlightenment:

for it is known, that poetry was, at the period in which she lived, held in the most sacred veneration; and that those who were gifted with that divine inspiration, were ranked as the first class of human beings. (18)

In the consciousness of the golden age of Greek civilization, Sappho and her work embodied the highest values available to a civilized culture, and 'the most competent judges' of later ages 'esteemed' her work 'as the standard for the pathetic, the glowing, and the amatory' (24).

In associating cultural enlightenment with poetry, and in (implicitly) proposing a poetry of sensibility as a touchstone of

---

[4] Robinson stresses the term 'enlightened', its various cognates, and related words (like 'lustre'). For eighteeenth-century thinkers, the term was an all-purpose figure for advanced and liberal thought. As early as 1732 Berkeley (*Alciphron* 1.9) refers to 'the select spirits of this enlightened age'.

poetical work, Robinson is doing two important things at once. First, she is feminizing the Schillerian dialectic by replacing Homer with Sappho as the paradigm naïve writer of ancient Greece. In contemporary terms, Robinson is accepting eighteenth-century sentimentality and sensibility as (the) distinctive features of poetical expression. That acceptance, however, does not lead Robinson to neglect the more broadly social functions and responsibilities of the poet. On the contrary, in fact. The move to Sappho is part of a general argument on behalf of the enlightenment powers of 'pathetic . . . glowing [and] amatory' verse. A 'lustre of intellectual light' (10) inheres in this poetry and diffuses throughout every enlightened society. Robinson explicitly associates it with the entire movement of progressive cultural views that men like Polwhele and Gifford in the 1790s so deplored.

It is the interest of the ignorant and powerful to suppress the effusions of enlightened minds: when only monks could write, and nobles read, authority rose triumphant over right; and the slave, spell-bound in ignorance, hugged his fetters without repining. It was then that the best powers of reason lay buried like the gem in the dark mine; by a slow and tedious progress they have been drawn forth, and must, ere long, diffuse an universal lustre; for that era is rapidly advancing, when talents will tower like an unperishable column, while the globe will be strewed with the wrecks of superstition. (14–15)

But 'that era' of full enlightenment is not yet come, even (!) in 1796, and Robinson's Sappho also functions in this argument as the exponent of an unripened historical evolution.

In this last respect Robinson's Sappho is at once the index of a current (inadequate) condition and the prophet of a future day. Though herself 'supremely enlightened', Sappho's very sensibility—her greatest virtue—became through circumstance a kind of defect or error:

That Sappho was not herself insensible to the feelings she so well described is evident in her writings; but it was scarcely possible, that a mind so exquisitely tender, so sublimely gifted, should escape those fascinations. (24)

In Robinson's myth, Sappho's love for Phaon appears a madness because he proves completely unworthy of her devotion. This explanation comes in the sonnets proper rather than in the prefatory prose documents, although in the latter it is sketched in the theme of Sappho's detractors. Following Rousseau and Goethe, Robinson turns Sappho's apparent madness to a psychological sign of a general social disfunction, of which Phaon is the emblem. Her love for him therefore functions as prophecy, the forecast of a time when a Phaon might come who would be worthy of such love. In the meantime Sappho exhibits a soul tortured by the failures of time and circumstance.

This is to express Robinson's myth in interpersonal terms, and perhaps to recall the less happy events of her personal life-experience. As such it is to court a view that was probably quite far removed from Robinson's specific intentions, which are clearly much more social and even—in their own way—Wollstonecraftian, as we shall see. The more broadly cultural purposes of Robinson's myth of Sappho are clear in the following key passages:

Addison was of the opinion, that the writings of Sappho were replete with such fascinating beauties, and adorned with such a vivid glow of sensibility, that, probably, had they been preserved entire, it would have been dangerous to have perused them. They possessed none of the artificial decorations of a feigned passion; they were the genuine effusions of a supremely enlightened soul, labouring to subdue a fatal enchantment; and vainly opposing the conscious pride of illustrious fame, against the warm susceptibility of a generous bosom. (24–5)

If her writings were, in some instances, too glowing for the fastidious refinement of modern times; let it be her excuse, and the honour of her country, that the liberal education of the Greeks was such, as inspired them with an unprejudiced enthusiasm for the works of genius; and that when they paid adoration to Sappho, they idolized the MUSE, and not the WOMAN. (27)

In her critical presentation of Sappho Robinson is not prepared to say that her poetry is ever censurable as such. Sappho's writings constitute the essence ('the MUSE') of poetry. That they might appear terrible, excessive, even frightening can be admitted and should be said, but those qualities are a function of unripened conditions. Addison's admiration for Sappho is limited and 'fastidious', a sign that his soul is not as enlightened as it might be. In this respect Addison is a figural avatar of Phaon. His position in Robinson's argument is important because he shows how 'enlightenment' is never uniformly distributed, either across history or within a particular epoch. Robinson's critical myth of Sappho, finally addressed to her 'enlightened' contemporaries, shows that the differences between ancient Greek civilization and the more 'fastidious' society of late eighteenth-century England can be regressive ones.

When Robinson stresses Sappho's prophetic importance she is thinking in these historical terms. 'Sappho . . . knew that she was writing for future ages' (26), Robinson says, and the remark applies as well to Robinson herself in writing *Sappho and Phaon*. For the epoch forecast by Sappho's work is not yet come ('that era is rapidly advancing'), as Robinson knows because of the persistent 'neglect . . . of literary merit' (16) in the present— a neglect shadowed, Robinson repeatedly argues, in Sappho's own neglect by her later detractors who envied her fame. *Sappho and Phaon* comes therefore to history as a song before the sunrise of that new day whose advent is clearly marked in the prophetic signs of the present:

I cannot conclude these opinions without paying tribute to the talents of my illustrious countrywomen; who, unpatronized by courts, and unprotected by the powerful, persevere in the paths of literature, and ennoble themselves by the unperishable lustre of MENTAL PRE-EMINENCE! (16)

Here Robinson's basic argument is being summarized and repeated at the level of a strong rhetorical address. At the end of her 'Preface' Robinson comes out as 'a woman speaking to women' about feminized sources of poetical power. With Sappho as their progenitor, Robinson's 'illustrious countrywomen' have entirely restructured the philosophy of literature in terms of the feelings and the passions. Here sensibility is being represented as a pre-eminent intellectual force, and the emblem of whatever social and philosophical advancement the present age can claim for itself. Well might Wordsworth, in face of such a consciously feminized prophecy, step slightly back and try to re-establish poetry as the discourse of 'a man speaking to men'.

THE MYTH AS POETICAL TECHNIQUE

The sonnets of *Sappho and Phaon* re-read, and re-write, their sources, and in particular Ovid's famous epistle 'Sappho to Phaon'. Historicizing her materials in her prefatory prose texts,

Robinson develops a general interpretive rationale in order to undermine the commonplace and narrower focus. In the latter Sappho is the emblem of a mind deranged by excessive love; she serves future generations as a monitory sign of the danger of ungoverned passion. In Robinson's work Sappho becomes a kind of Promethean figure who will inaugurate a new age of enlightenment and higher 'Reason'.

To understand Robinson's poetical method we have to stay a while with her prose preface; in particular, with the opening section where Robinson conducts a technical discussion of poetry. The text forces us to reflect upon the poetical form of Robinson's recreative verse. Robinson's Sappho speaks (in 1796) in the most finished of verse forms, the 'legitimate sonnet'. The choice of form sharply distinguishes Robinson's Sappho from the way she is represented in Ovid (and Pope). In the latter the epistolary form emblematizes the extinction of Sappho's poetic gift, as Sappho herself famously declares in Ovid's text;

> Flendus amor meus est, elegeia flebile carmen;
> Non facit ad lacrimas barbitos ulla meas.
>
> (7–8)

This is in fact the epigraph Robinson places at the head of her sonnet sequence, along with Pope's transliteration:

> Love taught my tears in sadder notes to flow,
> And tun'd my heart to elegies of woe.

The startling form adopted by Robinson for her retelling of Sappho's story suggests the exact opposite of what Ovid wants to intimate when he has Sappho discuss her abandonment of the sapphic for the elegiac measure, 'cum lyricis sim magis apta modis' ('since I am more apt with lyric measures', line 6). In Robinson, the Italian sonnet—a sign of the presence of a firmly self-conscious artistic intelligence—argues that Sappho's poetical genius must be seen to persist even during the period of her silence and apparent derangement. Ovid's elegiacs misrepresent Sappho and her love for Phaon.

This subject is worth further attention, not least because Robinson herself spends a substantial part of her preface discussing her chosen verse form, the Italian (or Petrarchan, or 'legitimate') sonnet. Her remarks explicitly draw a relation be-

tween this form and Sappho via Milton's sonnet to the nightingale, which Robinson reads as an address to Sappho.[5]
Robinson stresses the technical skill required to work in the
form in order to reinforce the Sapphic connection. Ovid's elegiacs are an index of Sappho's poetic desuetude:

> Nec mihi, dispositis quae iungam carmina nervis,
> Proveniunt, vacuae carmina mentis opus.
>
> (13–14)

(Songs no longer come for me to compose on harmonizing strings,
songs that are the works of an untroubled mind.)

In Robinson, however, Sappho's emotional condition does not
affect her art of poetry.

The 'legitimate sonnet'—which is Robinson's shrewdly
chosen term for the form—explicitly represents not merely a
sure artistic control but 'A chaste and elegant model' (p. 3 n.) of
poetic style. These terms all reflect back upon the image of
Sappho that Robinson is building. When Robinson reflects upon
the current craze for sonnet writing, she observes a *mélange* of
bastard forms, 'the non-descript ephemera from the heated
brains of self-important poetasters' (10). The 'legitimate sonnet'
thus comes to stand for the possibility of a poetry of strong
passion and emotion that yet preserves its artistic power and
integrity.

The entire discussion of the sonnet, which opens Robinson's
preface, grounds the argument of her general manifesto for
poetry. Being 'an enthusiastic votary of the Muse', Robinson is
writing to prevent the

chaos of dissipated pursuits which has too long been growing like an
overwhelming shadow, and menacing the lustre of intellectual light,
should, aided by the idleness of some, and the profligacy of others, at
last obscure the finer mental powers, and reduce the dignity of talents
to the lowest degradation. (10)

This is at once brilliant and pointed: brilliant, because
Robinson's wit has stolen the language of the enemies of the
new poetry of sensibility and thrown it back at them; and
pointed, because she simultaneously recurs to her central sub-

---

[5] It scarcely needs pointing out that the most ancient traditions associate Sappho
with the nightingale.

ject, the need to promote the 'intellectual light' of poetry and its relation to 'the finer mental powers' of the soul.

The emergence of the authority of sensibility tended to narrow poetry's authority to the field of personal or interpersonal emotions. While Robinson by no means wants to undermine this culture of sensibility, she is intent upon arguing its largest philosophical and social claims. So she begins by declaring that

the LEGITIMATE SONNET, may be carried on in a series of sketches, composing, in parts, one historical or imaginary subject, and forming in the whole a complete and connected story. (5)

It is not without good reason that Robinson chooses Milton to authorize her resort to the Italian sonnet. Her claim here establishes the importance of 'major form', a poetic vehicle capable of dealing with matters that transcend the merely personal.[6] Robinson concludes her discussion of the sonnet by expanding upon the significance of being able to form 'in the whole a complete and connected story'. Clearly anticipating the later arguments of Wordsworth and Percy Shelley, Robinson asserts the power of 'grand and harmonious compositions' to 'look beyond the surface of events' (11). Such works are prophetic and historically visionary, and she concludes her discussion of the sonnet by aligning *Sappho and Phaon* with the claims made by perhaps the most admired poet of the day, William Cowper:

> So when remote futurity is brought
> Before the keen inquiry of her thought,
> A terrible sagacity informs
> The Poet's heart, he looks to distant storms,
> He hears the thunder e'er the tempest lowers,
> And, arm'd with strength surpassing human pow'rs,
> Seizes events as yet unknown to man,
> And darts his soul into the dawning plan . . .

Once again we are struck by the extremity of Robinson's wit. Cowper's text is being read by an 'enlightened' mind in complex contemporary terms, as the shrewd use of the feminine pronoun in the second quoted line shows. The word literally refers to

---

[6] The legitimate sonnet, according to Robinson, has the power to generate 'a complete and connected story' because of its formal structure. In this it is unlike 'the modern sonnet [which concludes] with two lines, winding up the sentiment of the whole [and confining] the poet's fancy' (5).

'the MUSE' (just mentioned in the previous prose text), but of course in the context of Robinson's work it carries several more pointed references: to Sappho, to Robinson, and (generally) to the 'MENTAL PRE-EMINENCE' of those 'illustrious countrywomen' whom Robinson finally determines to celebrate (16).

Though never explicitly named, the most important of these is Mary Wollstonecraft, not only because of her general celebrity, or her friendship with Robinson, but more especially because *Sappho and Phaon* clearly steps away from certain key Wollstonecraftian positions. How does *Sappho and Phaon* relate, for example, to the following?

Women subjected by ignorance to their sensations, and only taught to look for happiness in love, refine on sensual feelings, and adopt metaphysical notions respecting that passion, which lead them shamefully to neglect the duties of life, and frequently in the midst of these sublime refinements they plump into actual vice.[7]

In certain (obvious) ways, *Sappho and Phaon* might be taken as a perfect illustration of Wollstonecraft's complaint: its central subject is love, it scrutinizes 'sensual feelings', it works up an elaborate philosophical rationale for itself, it tells the story of a suicide. And behind it all stands the notorious figure of 'Perdita' Robinson, whose personal life was a scandal.

Another famous passage from the *Vindication* (p. 130) can help to clarify the issues:

Novels, music, poetry, and gallantry, all tend to make women the creatures of sensation . . . This overstretched sensibility naturally relaxes the other powers of the mind, and prevents intellect from attaining that sovereignty which it ought to attain to render a rational creature useful to others . . . : for the exercise of the understanding, as life advances, is the only method pointed out by nature to calm the passions.

In this context one can see that Robinson wants to argue with Wollstonecraft about the social, philosophical, and intellectual power of 'sensibility'. Robinson does not disagree with Wollstonecraft about the terms or issues at stake; what she contests is Wollstonecraft's recurrent tendency to denigrate the

---

[7] *A Vindication of the Rights of Women*, in *The Works of Mary Wollstonecraft* vol. 5, ed. Janet Todd and Marilyn Butler (London: William Pickering, 1989), 255.

importance of 'passion', 'love', and the philosophy of sensibility that underpins those ideas and experiences.

Of course Wollstonecraft's personal life regularly set her public positions at defiance, as her many detractors liked to point out. The contradiction is important for Robinson, since it draws certain telling parallels between Robinson and Wollstonecraft and—most salient—Sappho. Like Sappho (and Robinson), Wollstonecraft is a prophetic soul, and her contradictions are an index of her historical position and significance. Furthermore— and this is the most crucial point of all—Wollstonecraft's philosophical work (as opposed to her personal history) replicates the contradictions of her life. The theorist who regularly argues down the passions is not in fact unaware of their power and importance: 'They . . . who complain of the delusions of passion, do not recollect that they are exclaiming against a strong proof of the immortality of the soul' (*Vindication*, 143). Wollstonecraft is not an atheist, so that her remark here introduces an important qualification to the paragraph of arguments against the pursuit of love and happiness which this sentence finishes. And the next short paragraph elaborates the point:

But leaving superior minds to correct themselves, and pay dearly for their experience, it is necessary to observe, that it is not against strong, persevering passions; but romantic wavering feelings that I wish to guard the female heart by exercising the understanding: for these paradisiacal reveries are oftener the effect of idleness than of a lively fancy. (143)

Here is exactly where *Sappho and Phaon* enters Wollstonecraft's argument. Like Wollstonecraft, Sappho is one of those 'superior minds' who—to borrow and adapt Percy Shelley's splendid later description of Byron as the emblematic poet—'learn in suffering what they teach in song'. *Sappho and Phaon* is Robinson's explication of the 'strong, persevering passion' that Wollstonecraft must finally defend.

THE MYTH IN POETICAL PRACTICE

The central object of the sonnets will be to provide a new answer to the traditional question re-posed by Robinson at the outset of the narrative:[8]

[8] The fourth sonnet of the sequence begins the narrative proper of the events in Sappho's story. Sonnets I–III are not 'spoken' by Sappho at all; Sonnet I is 'Introduc-

> Why, when I gaze on Phaon's beauteous eyes,
>   Why does each thought in wild disorder stray?
>   Why does each fainting faculty decay,
> And my chill'd breast in throbbing tumults rise?
> Mute, on the ground my Lyre neglected lies,
>   The Muse forgot, and lost the melting lay;

As Robinson's retold story develops, we realize that the answer to these initial questions comes through a more broadly based, less 'prejudiced' study of the situation and materials. This is what the whole work *Sappho and Phaon* does. When Ovid's 'Sappho *to* Phaon' becomes Robinson's *Sappho and Phaon* the changed middle term signals an important change of attention. Sappho is placed in a larger context of understanding, as Robinson's prose materials emphasize, and this widening includes a closer investigation of Phaon.

Robinson's work underscores the relevance of the investigation, for Sappho's beloved is a highly problematic figure. Most important is that he has proved himself faithless to their love devotions. He exhibits the very opposite of Wollstonecraft's (and Sappho's) 'strong, persevering passion'. At the level of narrative, Robinson represents his corruption in two principal ways. First, she associates him with an inclination to pursue dark pleasures, love that is hidden away or practised at night (see for example sonnet IX). Second, in his (traditional) departure from Greece to Sicily he is represented as forsaking Sappho for lesser lovers. In each instance his debasement is associated as a retreat from 'enlightenment', the meaning of his Sicilian adventures appearing through a contrast of mortal and immortal fires, Aetna and the maidens of Sicily versus Apollo and Sappho.

> Ah! think, that while on Aetna's shores you stray,
> A fire, more fierce than Aetna's, fills my breast . . .
>   (XXII)

That fire is explicitly poetical and Apollonian. When it pores and focuses upon Phaon ('Oft o'er that form, enamour'd have I hung': X.5), it brings him to a new and higher (poetical) life:

---

tory' while sonnets II and III set the allegorical terms within which the Sapphic events will be explained.

> So, on the modest lily's leaves of snow
> The proud Sun revels in resplendent rays!
> Warm as his beams this sensate heart shall glow,
> Till life's last hour, with Phaon's self decays.

The figure here startles because of its gender reversals (Sappho as the sun, Phaon as the lily), and the explicit equation of Sappho's love and poetry with the sun/Apollo's natural heat and ideal inspiration. 'Sensate heart' is a particularly fine epithet, echoing as it does the diction of Della Cruscan verse and its feeding source, the poetry of sensibility. Its function here is metaphysical: to argue (in poetic figuration) that a certain movement in modern writing (sensibility) most fully represents the tradition and 'original genius' of poetry.

Sappho and Phaon will therefore repeatedly explore the ambiguous significance of passion and reason, chastity and pleasure, feeling and thought. Robinson introduces Sappho's dramatic monologue of sonnets with an allegorical pair (sonnets II and III) that set the terms of what will follow. One describes the Temple of 'Chastity divine' (I.3), the other a 'vale beneath' (II.1), 'The bow'r of Pleasure' (II.4). The Temple, though 'rear'd by immortal pow'rs' (I.2), appears cold and inhuman—its promise of 'celestial joys' (I.8) marred by the forms in which those promises are carried:

> On the frozen floor
> Studded with tear-drops, petrified by scorn
> Pale vestals kneel the Goddess to adore . . .
>   (11–13)

The contrast with the 'bow'r of Pleasure' is clear and explicit: 'There witching beauty greets the ravish'd sight', and 'birds breathe bliss! light zephyrs kiss the ground' (III.6, 9). None the less, the bower's limitations are also clearly marked, not least in the figural fact that its 'tangled shade/ Excludes the blazing torch of noon-day light' (1–2). In a work where the sun/Apollo represents an 'enlightened' norm, both Temple and Bower suffer from its diminished presence. The text maintains Chastity and Pleasure as ideal forms, but equally as forms that are operating under constraint and limitation.

As a prophetic instrument, Robinson's Sappho is the voice through which the topics raised by the text get expressed. Like

the mythic creatures in Blake's prophetic books, she is transacted by everything her texts reveal. The derangement of her
mind and heart enacts an incompetent social and philosophical
situation, which is itself figured in Robinson's work as the
unbalanced relations of thought and passion, pleasure and chastity. As a consequence, spiritual absolutes like 'Love' and 'Reason' become, along with Sappho, disordered, and (literally) lose
their identities—as we see with special clarity in sonnet V, for
example:

> O! How can Love exulting Reason quell!
>   How fades each nobler passion from his gaze!
>   E'en Fame, that cherishes the Poet's lays,
> That Fame, ill-fated Sappho lov'd so well.
> Lost is the wretch, who is his fatal spell
>   Wastes the short Summer of delicious days,
>   And from the tranquil path of wisdom strays,
> In passion's thorny wild, forlorn to dwell.
>
> (1–8)

The initial ambiguous syntax operates through the entire poem,
which represents with fine poetic exactitude a confusion of heart
and mind in a soul committed to a full realization of the virtues
of both. Hence Sappho addresses 'Reason' in despair, for in her
quotidian experience 'Reason'—Sappho's commitment to full
and conscious awareness of herself and the meaning of her
desires—comes only in demonic form:

> Around thy throne destructive tumults rise,
> And hell-fraught jealousies . . .
>
> (XI.11–12)

hence too her despair when her ideal quest is experienced as the
commitment to Love: 'Ah! why is rapture so allied to pain?'
(XVIII.14) Perfection is clearly defined in the sonnets as 'endless
rapture' (XXXVII.12), but in the immediate event this rapture
grows debased by circumstance. Both heart and mind, Love
and Reason get confused and overthrown: a 'potent mischief
riots in the brain' and 'in the heart [a] Tyrant lives enshrin'd'
(XVII.6, 8).

Robinson's Sappho is not by any means arguing for an ordinary balance of head and heart, or reason and feeling. In the

traditional (masculine) version of an ideal of balance, order is established at a literally undesirable level. The apothegm 'Moderation in all things' governs the terms by which thought and feeling get measured.[9] On the contrary, this new Sappho is imagined as finally realizing the exalted demands upon heart and head that the Greek poetess originally, if ineffectually, sought. What is required is a balance of raptures, according to the analogous Blakean proverb of hell: 'The road of excess leads to the palace of wisdom' (*The Marriage of Heaven and Hell*, plate 7).

In this frame of reference, Sappho's love for Phaon is not only explicable but emblematically appropriate. Phaon is for Sappho an ideal form of both mind and heart exactly because he is masculine. Cultural tradition has to this point in time regularly cast that ideal form in masculine terms; indeed, even idealized female figures, like Richardson's Clarissa or the Venus de Milo, are masculine forms of expression, 'emanations'—to borrow Blake's neoplatonic term—of the 'human imagination' (i.e., the *male* imagination). Robinson's work moves upon this context in order to transpose its terms, though not its (ultimate) values of an enlightened heart and head.

A Sapphic perspective perceives Phaon not as a figure of heterosexual promise but as a traditional sign of the exalted power of thought and liberated pleasure. Phaon-as-ideal is to be transformed through the passion and desire of Sappho, whose love is determined to strip him of his corruptions. Sappho's love is committed to *this* Phaon, whose ideal form (literally) is at once glimpsed in and betrayed by the 'historical' Phaon pursued by Sappho. Phaon's own sexual wanderings therefore become yet another figural representation of Sappho's own desire and pursuit of the whole—even more particularly, her desire and pursuit of the whole in the ideal immediacy of a mortal and historical existence. The ideal demands made by Robinson's work are thus revolutionary ones in a social and political sense. At the time they would be (and were) seen as jacobinical.[10]

[9] To the degree that Wollstonecraft adheres to such a view, to that extent Robinson is critiquing her work. Wollstonecraft draws her adherence to a philosophy of moderation from Dissenting traditions, whereas aristocratic contexts dominate Robinson's life and imagination.

[10] When Richard Polwhele deplores the 'Philosophism' of Robinson's writings, he is in effect labelling the work 'jacobin' (see *The Unsex'd Females*, 93 n.). In the same

Robinson's way with Phaon is brilliantly illustrated in sonnet XII, which her index titles 'Previous to her Interview with Phaon'. The heading is important.

> Now, o'er the tessellated pavement strew
> Fresh saffron, steep'd in essence of the rose
> While down yon agate column gently flows
> A glitt'ring streamlet of ambrosial dew!
> My Phaon smiles! the rich carnation's hue,
> On his flush'd cheek in conscious lustre glows,
> While o'er his breast enamour'd Venus throws
> Her starry mantle of celestial blue!
> Breathe soft, ye dulcet flutes, among the trees
> Where clust'ring bows with golden citron twine;
> While slow vibrations, dying on the breeze,
> Shall soothe his soul with harmony divine!
> Then let my form his yielding fancy seize,
> And all his fondest wishes blend with mine.

The sonnet invokes an absent and imagined Phaon, an ideal figure with idealized desires that match Sappho's own. Their ecstatic union is an imagined 'harmony divine' achieved within the orbit of the planet of (Sappho's) love. It is crucial to see that this union is sexual, even as it is being literally cast in ideal erotic terms. The ideal thus summons its full achievement by arousing an as yet unfulfilled reality, which is itself figured as the absent Phaon. The splendid double-meaning worked into the syntax of the final two lines emphasizes the character of Sappho's desire, which imagines a perfect equality between lovers.

The desired conjunction (and hence the actual *dis*junction) of real and ideal orders gets nicely replicated at various subordinate textual levels—for example, in the first appearance of the imagined Phaon in the sonnet:

> My Phaon smiles! the rich carnation's hue,
> On his flush'd cheek in conscious lustre glows,
>
> (5–6)

---

critique he appears to be thinking specifically of *Sappho and Phaon* when he urges Robinson 'to dismiss the gloomy phantom of annihilation; to think seriously of a future retribution; and to communicate to the world, a recantation of errors that orginated in levity, and have been nurs'd by pleasure'.

This extremely complex figuration ultimately stands for the whole 'meaning' of Phaon. The imaginary flush rises through the erotic conjuring of lines 1–4, to which Phaon responds—indeed, within which he is literally brought to life, like a male Galatea ('*My* Phaon'). The flush's 'conscious lustre' locates one of the sonnet's most brilliant metaphysical moments. Here we see a traditional figure of involuntary desire being imagined at a higher level, as it were—as a figure of supreme consciousness, the very image of Sappho's highest desire (of a fully conscious eroticism, a complete integration of the highest desires of the head and of the heart).[11]

That the sonnet situates all these events at the level of Sappho's fantasy and desire provides the (modern) reader with a perspective that fully answers to the 'conscious lustre' imaged on Phaon's face. Phaon registers his desire at the most primitive level, as a blush; Sappho registers hers in the prophetic figuration she gives to this blush, the text's 'conscious lustre'; finally, Robinson frames both of these events in a contemporary context that explicates their prophetic truth. The blush is a recurrent and central figure in the writing of sensibility, where it signifies the body's instinctive knowledge of good and evil, and where that knowledge is no longer judged by dark biblical norms; on the contrary. In Robinson's text, Sappho refigures Phaon's blush in enlightened terms. The phrase 'conscious lustre' raises up the body's knowledge from its low estate by asserting its powers of intelligence. As a figure for blushing, the phrase is a virtual emblem of enlightened sensibility, a fact underscored by the term 'lustre', which in the sonnet sequence is explicitly associated with poetry and Apollo, the 'Lord of Lustre' (IX.7). The phrase is therefore at once Sappho's prophecy on the body of Phaon, and Robinson's hymn to the intellectual beauty of her enlightened ideal of the fully liberated body and mind, and their harmonious union.

The sequence's fundamental argument gets nicely articulated in the opening sonnet, in the sestet especially:

[11] For good discussions of the crucial term 'conscious' see Jean H. Hagstrum, *Eros and Vision* (Evanston: Northwestern University Press, 1989), ch. 1; and A. Sherbo, *English Poetic Diction from Chaucer to Wordsworth* (East Lansing: Michigan State University Press, 1975).

> For thou, blest POESY! with godlike pow'rs
> To calm the misery of man wert given;
>   When passion rends, and hopeless love devours,
> By mem'ry goaded, and by frenzy driv'n,
>   'Tis thine to guide him 'midst Elysian bow'rs,
> And shew his fainting soul,—a glimpse of Heav'n.

The tradition of erotic poetry establishes the sexual import of the figures in the last two lines. Equally, the tradition of masculinist ideology establishes a privileged meaning for the term 'man', so that the blessings and powers of 'POESY' are especially secured for 'men' rather than 'women'. In this text, however, Robinson works a transvaluation of these values by playing that privileged term 'man' off against the pronouns 'him' and 'his' (in lines 12–13). In the context of a work dealing with the loves of Sappho and Phaon, where the latter's frustrations and failures in love are exposed through the poetic sufferings of Sappho, those pronouns acquire a particular reference. The passage is another (at this narrative point, a secret) prophecy that Sappho's poetry will liberate Phaon from his frustrate condition. This meaning hidden in the text takes Phaon as a figure of 'man', and thus prophesies that Sappho's 'POESY' will ultimately redeem 'his' condition.

The meaning of all this is patent. Robinson is the avatar of Sappho, and through her 'POESY' the benighted condition of 'man' will get redeemed. In literal terms, the verse exposes the ideological freight concealed in the term 'man', and proposes a new standard of 'POESY' to be re-imagined through a female, a specifically Sapphic, perspective. So despite its ostensible subject (personal and erotic love) and form (poetic), Robinson's is finally a political and republican work. Indeed, its most cherished positions are probably (*a*) that 'the personal is the political' and (*b*) that 'poets are the unacknowledged legislators of the world'.

Robinson doesn't try to conceal the politics of her work, as we see from her prefatory prose materials, the final section of which comprises an extended quotation from 'the learned and enlightened ABBE BARTHELMI' (p. 27). With this text Robinson fairly labels her work 'republican'. Nevertheless, her treatment of Barthelemy's celebrated *Voyage* is subtle and indirect, and very much in keeping with her poetical commitments. Quoting the

Voyage for a culminant 'vindication and eulogy of the Grecian Poetess' (27) might even be expected, given the well-known views of both Robinson and Barthelemy. More to the point, one of the most startling features of the *Voyage* is its new and specifically political interpretation of Sappho's life. According to Barthelemy, Sappho's move from Lesbos to Sicily is a political act, a flight from a society corrupted (like eighteenth-century Paris) by luxury and licence.[12]

Robinson's long quotation from the *Voyage* is notable, however, precisely because it betrays no reference whatsoever to any of these matters. On the contrary, the quoted texts all focus on the 'sensibility' of Sappho, as well as her great influence in maintaining a culture of 'sensibility':

'Sappho undertook to inspire the Lesbian women with a taste for literature; many of them received instructions from her, and foreign women increased the number of her disciples. She loved them to excess, because it was impossible for her to love otherwise; and she expressed her tenderness in all the violence of passion: your surprize at this will cease, when you are acquainted with the extreme sensibility of the Greeks.' (28)

This is nothing but a (current) politics of sensibility, a feminized equivalent of Sade's politics of pornography. Where Sade is outrageous, however, Robinson is nuanced. In the first place, she invokes political issues with a cool presence-by-absence technique. Beyond that, she elaborates a subtle politicized critique of all those, whether on the right or on the left, who uncouple a social and political consciousness from 'extreme sensibility'. Sappho's detractors have regularly deplored the sensual excess of her loves, but Robinson wants not merely to defend the poet on these counts, she wants to defend the *politics* of the poet. So 'To this hatred' which her life and writings provoked, Sappho 'replied by truths and irony, which completely exasperated her enemies' (28–9).

This last comment exposes the remarkable self-reflexiveness and wit of Robinson's quotation. Not only does she transform

[12] The historical effect of this new intrepretation was notable. As DeJean observes, 'In Barthelemy's wake, Sappho was enshrined as a political exile, a revolutionary who had fought alongside Alceus to overthrow tyranny. This reading won acceptance despite the fact that Sappho's poetry, unlike Alceus's, is resolutely apolitical' (*Fictions of Sappho*, 160).

the political significance of Barthelemy's Sappho, she does this by verbatim quotation of his own commentary. This is to reply 'by truths and irony' indeed—to reply with those 'finer mental powers' (10) that Robinson attributes to the poets. The subtlety of her technique seems especially fine when we register the text's autobiographical motifs. Throughout *Sappho and Phaon* Robinson builds a shrewd retort to the facile slanders regularly directed at herself. Robinson's and Sappho's histories come to reflect each other because (and as) their poetries are made reflective through *Sappho and Phaon*. It is the poetic sensibility that exposes these relations, according to Robinson, and the poetry of sensibility that puts them into most effective (social) action. Not that the more polemical views and approaches of Barthelemy (or Wollstonecraft) are unimportant or ineffective. But for Robinson the poet is especially favoured with the power to wed the longest kind of philosophical view ('the whole', 5) with full, intense, and immediate awareness ('passion').

PART III

The 'Feeling Mind' of Sentimental Poetry

Here is direct expression—pages and pages of it. And if you don't understand it, Ladies and Gentlemen, it is because you are too decadent to receive it.

Samuel Beckett, *Our Exagmination* . . .

II

Sentimental Grounds: Schiller, Wordsworth, Bernardin, Shelley, Keats

'Rosebud'—the characters ignite and shrivel in the last fiery frames of *Citizen Kane*. A child's sled holds a key for understanding the history of a Great Man, and of the King's Treasury he accumulated. The film tells the story of the search for that key, of the failure to find it, and—not least of all—the irony in the final revelation of its loss.

For it might have been found, Kane threw nothing away. But who could have known where to look, or how to look? The film's cavernous warehouse is a Borgesian emblem of the labyrinth of culture—an elaborate system for accumulating, sorting, and finally evaluating what it has come to possess. The movie warns us that 'Rosebud' is unlikely to pass through the fire that refines. Rather, it will be set aflame and 'disappeared', having little apparent importance in a 'larger scheme of things'.

Citizen Kane is a nostalgic film—in terms of Schiller's famous naïve/sentimental formulation, a sentimental film. More than that, its sentimentality is directed at 'the sentimental' itself, as one sees quite clearly in the soft-focus technique and flashback method that frames the recollected world of 'Rosebud'. Kane's unspoiled childhood is represented as a kind of dream memory, a backward-projected fantasy (of the elder Kane and the imaginary world over which he presides). The film's treatment of this psycho-social structure is at once sympathetic and critically reflective. In Schiller's terms, the film desires a 'naïve', an entirely sympathetic absorption in the Rosebud world; but its self-conscious awareness of the fantastic character of that world blocks any simple, naïve engagement.

Welles's lucid, ironic treatment of 'the sentimental' supplies a useful point of departure for reconsidering the early history of sentimental poetry, when its formative stylistic conventions were established. Much of this poetry has vanished from cultural view, and what remains is rarely read in sentimental terms. Having acquired a distinctly negative valence during the past one hundred years or so, the idea of the 'sentimental' resists our critical appropriation. But it is an important concept for two reasons. First, it named a cultural horizon (and hence a set of enabling conventions) under which a great deal of important writing was produced. Second, some of that writing has been handed down to us under false pretenses (as if, like Keats's work, it weren't and must not be considered 'sentimental'); and some of it has not been handed down at all, or only carelessly delivered, as if it weren't worth our thoughtfulness. But an historicist move towards sentimental poetry—an effort to see it on its own terms—is a *sine qua non* for a fully critical recovery of the work.

The term has been a 'keyword' for more than two hundred years, though its negative inflection is much more recent. In its early (modern) history it signalled a range of highly prized values, as one sees in two of the foundational treatments of the subject: Schiller's great and greatly influential essay 'On Naïve and Sentimental Poetry' (1795), and Bernardin de St Pierre's study of the subject in the fourth volume of his *Etudes de la nature* (1783, 1788). The aesthetic focus of Schiller's essay slightly displaces the important moral implications of its subject. For Bernardin, by contrast, moral issues order the horizon of his thought.

Schiller builds his argument around the elementary distinction between 'modern' poetry, which tends to be sentimental (i.e., reflective and self-conscious); and ancient (paradigmatically Homeric) poetry, which tends to be naïve (i.e., simple, direct, 'natural'). Though the terms relate dialectically to each other, it is crucial to understand that the category 'naïve' is a function of the category 'sentimental'. In Schiller's argument, naïve poetry is an expressive form that characterizes an integral psychic and cultural condition. As such it represents an ideal projection of a sentimental attitude, where self-consciousness measures as well the desire for an immediate sense of the organic wholeness of experience. Poets like Burns and the marvellous boy Chatterton acquired special importance—symbolic cultural meaning—exactly because they suggested that a naïve style remained culturally available.

The 'Preface' to the *Lyrical Ballads* replicates Schiller's argument, just as the book's poetry comprises an existential proof that a 'naïve' style remains, like Nature, a permanent resource. For Wordsworth 'lyrical' signifies a personal, subjective, and sentimental style, whereas 'ballads' are an index of impersonal, objective, and naïve writing. For Schiller and Wordsworth (and Coleridge too), a marriage of the two represents a poetical (and moral) ideal, a visioned integration of the inner and the outer world, of the soul and the body.

In this perspective, sensibility tends to function as a 'modern' type of the naïve ideal. The view is quite apparent in Wordsworth's 'Preface', which is a sentimental manifesto in the strictest sense. According to Wordsworth, the debasement of contemporary culture represents a falling away from a natural condition of 'organic' healthfulness. Wordsworth's rural ideal is a Rousseauist trope for an 'original' psychic simplicity. Read in social terms, the trope argues that England can reverse its process of historical corruption. Appeal is made to a population 'originally possessed of much organic sensibility'—as if the bad manners and poetry of the day were evil visitations upon an otherwise innocent social body. By valorizing the term 'organic sensibility' Wordsworth is implicitly arguing that the eighteenth century's traditions of sensibility are in themselves 'healthful'. Wordsworth's critique of culture is directed against what he saw as '*false* refinement and *arbitrary* innovation'. While the traditions of 'sensibility' and poetic experiment fed virtually all the poets of the 1790s, those traditions were not always correctly received or used. Consequently, some of his contemporaries seemed rightful inheritors (Coleridge, Mrs Smith, Bowles), others (the Della Cruscans) were not. If 'all good poetry is the spontaneous overflow of powerful feelings', no good poetry permits linguistic extravagance.

Keats's historical belatedness illustrates a second-order form of the simplicity idealized by Schiller and Wordsworth. Keats begins (as a poet) by sentimentalizing sentimentalism. The move is clearly made in his important early sonnet 'On First Looking into Chapman's Homer'. The poem comes forward, addresses its readers, as a work of discovery, a text for defining the moment when the poet acquired an entire (sentimental) consciousness of his poetic powers and cultural inheritance. The sonnet figures his advance out of a naïve order ('Homer') to a sentimental order ('Chapman's Homer', i.e., Schiller's Homer, Wolf's Homer—Homer enlightened).

> Much have I travell'd in the realms of gold,
> And many goodly states and kingdoms seen;
> Round many western islands have I been
> Which bards in fealty to Apollo hold.
> Oft of one wide expanse had I been told
> That deep-brow'd Homer ruled as his demesne;
> Yet did I never breathe its pure serene
> Till I heard Chapman speak out loud and bold:
> Then felt I like some watcher in the skies
> When a new planet swims into his ken;
> Or like stout Cortez when with eagle eyes
> He star'd at the Pacific—and all his men
> Look'd at each other with a wild surmise—
> Silent, upon a peak in Darien.

In the land of the heart's desire, one can get suddenly quite lost, often without knowing it (perhaps the deepest kind of loss). Here Keats writes a poem he did not know he was writing, a poem about getting lost (though he thought it was a poem of discovery). A naïve text falls out of a sentimental project.

The crux of the poem involves its infamous 'mistake', which is rarely taken as seriously as it ought to be. Among schoolchildren Keats would have been told, correctly, that Balboa, not Cortez, discovered the Pacific Ocean. Among scholars, on the other hand, the error is casually glossed as trivially 'factual', the result of a confused set of literary memories. But the 'wild surmise' of the poem, its *poetic* success, comes exactly from its having gotten lost. We shouldn't ignore or try to explain away its confusions; better far to follow their inviting nonsense and (il)logic, and try to explain them.

Like Hazlitt on going a journey, Keats's prescribed and 'much . . . travell'd' course leads to a wholly undiscovered country. Cortez standing silent on the peak in Darien: the image is at once ludicrous and wonderful, like everything else in the poem. Keats's schoolboy error transforms and redeems the poetical machinery and fine rhetoric he wants to parade. The poem transports us to the most forbidden world of all—the Rosebud world of adolescence, barred out more securely by the adult consciousness (Blake called it 'the Atlantic Deep') than perhaps any other realm has ever been. The poem's absurd error is the sign that it has pledged its allegiance to what would mortally embarrass a grown-up consciousness. (And so scholarship, than which nothing else is more grown up, hastens to explain the error away.)

Where has Keats taken us? To a land beyond what could be fashioned in desire or figured in imagination? But surely such terms are too grandiose for a poem built on such a naïve conception of the sublime. If it weren't so naïve—if it lacked that mistake about Cortez, for example—the sonnet might well strike us as less sublime than trumped up and factitious. But in fact it *has* escaped the serious business of Culture. The poem drops us to a place of actual magic, an embarrassing place that here should not and will not embarrass. That is its magic. It matters that the poem's realms are always second order, even second-hand realms—*Chapman's* Homer (elsewhere, *Elgin's* marbles, that is, 'Culture' at an even further—and a stolen— remove!). And it matters that Keats can represent himself as unselfconscious of the 'objective truth' of his poetical situations. The gold here is all pyrite—which is partly why Keats secures an effect of such unguarded expression. The child of this poem, blindly at strife with its naïve blessedness, thereby becomes father of its man.[1]

Schiller (and Wordsworth) understood that a commitment to the sentimental can easily set the naïve ideal at an impossible remove. As we know, Wordsworth's fear of losing touch with that ideal was so great that he constructed a (sentimental) myth that would redeem the foregone conclusion of its loss. Keats's poem—like the early work of Blake, or the poetry of Burns—is an important text exactly for the way it shows what Schiller explicitly argued, that the naïve remained a perpetual possibil- ity, even in sophisticated cultures. But the poem shows that the possibility cannot be self-consciously achieved, that it must come (to the cultivating mind) as it were by accident.

Unlike the Keats of this sonnet, when Schiller and Coleridge approach the same subject they tend to philosophize the issues,

---

[1] This discussion of Keats stands in heavy debt to Marjorie Levinson's reading of the sonnet, and of her brilliant Keats book in general (*Keats's Life of Allegory: The Origins of a Style* (Oxford: Blackwell, 1988)).

even in their own poetry. Unlike Schiller and Coleridge, when Wordsworth approaches the issues he tends to moralize his subject. In this respect his work follows Bernardin, who explicates his sentimental philosophy in the *Etudes* (1783) and then illustrates his ideas in the immensely influential prose apologue *Paul et Virginie* (1788).[2] The twelfth *Etude* makes a specific study of the sentimental.

There are two primal powers in human beings, one corporeal, the other divine. The first supplies the perduring sentiment of our wretchedness, the other the sentiment of our pre-eminent being. (IV.iii.33–4)

The double meaning of the French term ('sentiment' as both 'conscience' and '*élan*') is here redoubled. Functioning through both of our primal powers, sentiment appears a kind of higher third term that not only operates through both spirit and sense, it establishes the ground of their integrity.

Bernardin's chief concern is to construct a moral programme that can evade or abrogate the authority of the analytic mind. Sentiment is the key to this programme. Pervading both our spirits and our senses, sentiment 'subjugates our reason' and 'itself becomes the noblest and most pleasurable instinct of human life'. It does this by what Wordsworth would later call 'the power/ Of harmony' flowing from pleasure, 'the deep power of joy'. Unlike reason, sentiment puts one (rather literally) 'in touch with' the absolute. This physicalized (pleasure-driven) intimation of immortality and infinitude ensures, on one hand, an immediate and consuming sense of the absolute; and, on the other, an equally consuming awareness of its flights and evanishments.

Bernardin wrote *Paul et Virginie* to illustrate his sentimental ideas, and his tale influenced Wordsworth in the most direct way, far more directly than Rousseau.[3] Wordsworth's sentimen-

---

[2] Until the recent work of Elizabeth Fay, Wordsworth scholars had seriously neglected the importance of Bernardin for the English poet. The entire structure of the Wordsworthian Myth is fully present in *Paul et Virginie*. Indeed, it is clear that Wordsworth studied this work very closely, and made considerable borrowings from it. See Fay's new book on the Wordsworths, *Becoming Wordsworthian: A Performative Aesthetics* (Amherst: University of Massachusetts Press, 1995).

[3] Wordsworth's borrowings from Bernardin are many, the most noticeable being, perhaps, the 'Poems on the Naming of Places', which replicate a key structural feature of Bernardin's tale.

tal style grounds itself in a Bernardinien myth of a vital natural world, a geophysical order that is animated by a spirit of benevolence ('nature never did betray/ The heart that loved her'). Indeed, he does not shrink from declaring:

> And 'tis my faith that every flower
> Enjoys the air it breathes.
>
> ('Lines Written in Early Spring', 11–12)

Later critics misunderstand Wordsworth when they see 'affective fallacy' in such verse. The style is more radical than that. Far from ascribing human attributes to non-human phenomena, Wordsworth turns human experience into a figure for exploring the transhuman. His purpose is to reveal what a human-centred world, economically and socially preoccupied ('getting and spending'), often cannot see: the presence of suprahuman spirit. Giving one's self up to the influence of Nature leads to

> that serene and blessed mood,
> In which the affections gently lead us on,
> Until, the breath of this corporeal frame,
> And even the motion of our human blood
> Almost suspended, we are laid asleep
> In body, and become a living soul:
> While with an eye made quiet by the power
> Of harmony, and the deep power of joy
> We see into the life of things.
>
> ('Tintern Abbey', 42–50)

This is one of the triumphs of sentimental writing. The spiritual condition it celebrates comes through a regimen grounded in the senses. Harmony is (paradoxically?) a function of pleasure, whose increase transports one to a new sensual order—an order where one may at last experience 'the life of things'. We must read this great passage in the simplest and most literal way. 'Things' apparently dead or sub-human are filled with mysterious and harmonic life. The near-cliché of the phrase 'the life of things' is brilliant exactly because it registers the subjective genetive 'of things' so indirectly. The lines thereby partly enact the argument, or rather the experience, they are celebrating.

Wordsworth's sentimentalism typically appears as the climactic moment when a self-conscious mind thinks it has discovered the presence of a higher mind in an order of reality commonly thought to be 'lower'. Affective fallacy (so-called) proves an essential feature of his kind of writing because the device prevents this marriage of true minds from appearing in conceptual forms—those abstract terms that characterize Schiller's self-conscious, sentimental man. So throughout *Lyrical Ballads* Wordsworth's poetical surrogates typically get their understandings corrected ('Repaired and . . . Restored') through disciplines of feeling. The healing of the abstracted mind is the object of this writing, as one sees clearly in poems like 'We Are Seven' or 'Anecdote for Fathers'. The method of healing, however, is through what Blake called 'an improvement of sensual enjoyment'—a restoration of the mind's highest powers by moving it through cleansed doors of perception. The child becomes the father of the man. All this is a strictly sentimental project, however, because this child and those affective doors are—as Schiller's work reminds us—the ideal forms generated by the sentimental subject in the first place.

12

Enlightened Minds: Sir William Jones and Erasmus Darwin

In Wordsworthian sentimentalism, the re-balancing of affect and thought appears under a vast non-subjective horizon, a personal experience of the overwhelming 'diurnal course' of things. In this respect it stands significantly skewed from the sentimentalism of a poem like the following (late Della Cruscan) piece by Charlotte Dacre:

THE KISS

The greatest bliss
Is in a kiss—
A kiss by love refin'd
When springs the soul
Without controul,
And blends the bliss with mind.

(1–6)

Poetry like this explains why Coleridge wrote Della Cruscan verse (something Wordsworth never did), and why he (later) felt relatively easy with the conventions of the Gift Books and Annuals (something Wordsworth never was). 'The Kiss' recalls 'The Eolian Harp' not so much in its eroticism as in the brainy way it handles its erotic subject. Unlike either Lake poet, however, Dacre's poem does not construct a psychic drama of its thought, does not appear to be discovering itself as its lines unfold. The poem's rhetoric assures us that it entirely possesses its own thought from the beginning. The point is to illustrate that thought in a telling way.

And the poem's idea is complex: it lays down a definition of the structure of sentimental experience. Grounded in sensibility, the sentimental also discovers the radical involvement of mind and body. In each case the discovery appears as an enactment of understanding. Dacre's work pivots upon a witty rhetorical move that prevents us from deciding whether it is the kiss or the soul that 'blends the bliss with mind'. The poem thereby generates a *precise* sense of the (con)fusion it wants to define. As a consequence, its key terms—kiss, love, soul, mind, pleasure ('bliss'), and refinement—all neatly constellate in a firm order of relations. The poem is not an organic structure, it is the gravity field of a mind conscious of its own physicalities.

Some of the most consequential work of this kind in the period was written by Erasmus Darwin and Sir William Jones. Jones's poetical expositions of Vedic philosophy reveal the presence of strange, unencountered beings:

> Hail, self-existent, in celestial speech
> > NARAYEN, from thy watry cradle, nam'd;
> > Or VENAMELY may I sing unblam'd,
> > With flow'ry braids that to thy sandals reach,
> > Whose beauties, who can teach?
> > > ('A Hymn to Na'ra'yena', 73–7)[1]

Jones's prose writings on Indian culture and antiquities develop a vast set of contextual commentaries for his poetry and the originals upon which he drew. Orientalist in every sense, the commentaries bring the structure of an imperial (western) intellect to elucidate the original documents. The ultimate point is to establish a (universalist) common ground for the meeting of East and West. Jones's Vedic hymns carry an

> > attestation strong,
> > That, loftier than thy [i.e., poetry's] sphere, th' Eternal
> > Mind,
> > Unmov'd, unrival'd, undefil'd, reigns . . .
> > > ('Hymn to Su'rya', 192–4)

Jones's translations are forcing the Sanskrit texts to deliver up a vision of an originary and transcendent order of things. In point of fact, it is the 'Mind' of a certain kind of rationalist neoplatonism—distinctively English, distinctly Enlightened.

As is clear from the splendid 'Hymn to Na'ra'yena', which constructs a revelatory myth, this mind is distinguished by its creative powers—not its form but its capacity to build forms.

---

[1] The text of the hymn is here taken from *The New Oxford Book of Romantic Period Verse*, ed. Jerome McGann (Oxford and New York: Oxford University Press, 1993), 1–5.

Or high PEITAMBER clad in yellow robes
   Than sunbeams brighter in meridian glow,
   That weave their heav'n-spun light o'er circling globes?
   Unwearied, lotos-eyed, with dreadful bow,
     Dire Evil's constant foe!
Great PEDMANABHER, o'er thy cherish'd world
   The pointed *Checra*, by thy fingers whirl'd,
   Fierce KYTABH shall destroy and MEDHU grim . . .

                        (78–85)

In Vedic thought, a primal source generates a host of subordinate powers and gods, each of whom may undergo further
replications. These transformations exfoliate through an existence that has been perceived as a ceaseless play of energy. When
Jones chooses to 'translate' this world-view into verse, he is
implicitly arguing that, for a western mind, a poetical discourse
approximates Vedic thought more closely than expository
prose. Jones's 'Hymn' aspires to incarnate the Vedic understanding of the world in occidental terms. In this passage, a
series of bizarre creatures make up a selection of such forms, by
no means complete.

From a purely stylistic point of view, the names should—and
they still do—fall strangely under western eyes. These alien
forms partly disclose how the occident neglects its own 'secret
philosophy'. Even more important, coming here as words, as
names, these creatures bear witness to their poetical and imaginative character. Like Macpherson and Blake, Jones exploits
these strange nominations to telling effect. In this case divine
names get decorative elaborations to signify that Jones's poem
replicates the primal energy celebrated in Vedic thought.

The highest of these names is 'Full-gifted BREHMA' (60),
though he too, like all the creatures of this visionary world, is
wholly transformational. But Brehma is 'Full-gifted' because he
represents the unnameable 'Spirit of Spirits' (1) as that Power
assumes the design of self-consciousness.

   Full-gifted BREHMA! Rapt in solemn thought
     He stood, and round his eyes fire-darting threw;
     But, whilst his viewless origin he sought,
     One plain he saw of living waters blue,
       Their spring nor saw nor knew.

                  (60–4)

Like Shelley's Asia, Brehma strives vainly to discover 'What were his pow'rs, by whom, and why conferr'd' (67). In the end,

> With doubts perplex'd, with keen impatience fir'd
>   He rose, and rising heard
>   Th' unknown all-knowing Word,
> 'BREHMA! no more in vain research persist:
> My veil thou canst not move—Go, bid all worlds exist.'
>
> (68–72)

That is to say, the knowledge Brehma desires is a material and creative practice, the enactment of the desires that constitute his very being. Brehma's conceptual efforts must give way to performative acts, and the model of Brehma's existence is supplied in the imperative (performative) command issued in this text. Like Goethe, Jones's 'all-knowing Word', this very poem, declares: 'In the beginning was the deed'.

The clear intellectual character of this kind of desire defines its peculiar senti-mentality. Exactly like Blake's and Shelley's work, Jones's poem reveals the visible world as an index of the exhaustless power of this primal energy. Indeed, the poem unfolds itself as an immediate instance of that energy at work. As such, it illustrates (or executes) what

> the wisest among the Ancients, and some of the most enlightened among the Moderns . . . believe, that the whole Creation [is] rather an *energy* than a *work*. (1)

Jones's hymn climaxes when the sensuous and active mind working through it dismisses all its gorgeous Mayan veils in order to identify completely with its essential being, what Shelley called Intellectual Beauty.

> Smooth meads and lawns, that glow with varying dyes
> Of dew-bespangled leaves and blossoms bright,
>   Hence! vanish from my sight:
> Delusive Pictures! unsubstantial shows!
> My soul absorb'd One only Being knows,
> Of all perceptions One abundant source,
> Whence ev'ry object ev'ry moment flows:
>   Suns hence derive their force,
>   Hence planets learn their course;
> But suns and fading worlds I view no more:
> GOD only I perceive; GOD only I adore.
>
> (116–26)

Mind perfectly enacts its powers in those excellent wordplays on the keyword 'Hence'. The term locates the poem's final set of transformations, as 'the *vulgar notion of material substances*' (1) (Coleridge's '*object*, dead, fixed')[2] collapses into Jones's sentimental performative thought. In this text the material world literally follows the orders of self-conscious Mind—indeed, it appears *as* self-conscious Mind operating through the rhetorical enginery of the hymn.

Jones's poetical reconstructions of the Vedas, along with his elaborate and learned prose introductions, ultimately celebrate the mind's ability to perceive and reconstruct higher-order levels of being—in this case, an ethnographic structure of Indian myth and culture. A very similar work is *The Botanic Garden*, Erasmus Darwin's brilliant poetical explication of Linnaean taxonomy. In Darwin's case, however, we also get useful prose discussions of the function poetry serves for an intellectual subject like Darwin's. These come in the dialogic Interludes that punctuate the four Cantos of *The Loves of the Plants*. The dialogues are conducted by two notional characters, 'Bookseller' and 'Poet' (the latter being Darwin's surrogate).

The first of the Interludes develops out of an inquiry into the difference between prose and poetry. Darwin's thought anticipates Wordsworth's famous 'Preface' in several respects, not least in arguing against any essential difference between prose and poetry. Setting aside (for a later Interlude) the question of 'measure', Poet says that 'The Poet writes principally to the eye, the Prose-writer uses more abstracted terms' (pp. 41–2). The visionary character of poetical discourse produces a condition of wholly self-contained perception ('a compleat reverie', 48).[3] Appropriating a phrase from Lord Kames, Poet calls this state an 'ideal presence'.

Poet's argument finishes by assigning a remarkable *scientific* function to poetical discourse. Incompetent before a world of Ideal Presence, a prose treatment of scientific subjects cannot convey science's most 'sublime' ideas.[4] (Shelley will later argue

---

[2] See ch. 12 of *Biographia Literaria* (II.279).

[3] Coleridge's dicussion of poetic probability and 'the willing suspension of disbelief' manifestly borrows from Darwin's treatment of the same subjects in this Interlude (see *Biographia Literaria*, ch. 14).

[4] Darwin also explicitly associates Ideal Presence with the eighteenth-century 'Sublime'. This is important because it also shows that he refuses the sharp Burkean

much the same thing in his 'Defence', as we see from his famous injunction on behalf of poetry's intellectual obligations: 'we want . . . to imagine that which we know'.)[5] The highest ideas of science are best approached through poetry, which is peculiarly fitted to render 'the ideal presence of the object' (48). In the case of *The Botanic Garden*, that 'presence' is not just the total structure of the Linnaean taxonomy, it is the 'ideal' form (the Intellectual Beauty) supporting that or any other scientific model.

When Poet later takes up the bracketed topic of verse measure (in the third and last Interlude), the sentimentalism of his thought becomes very clear. Working from Berkeleyan ideas, he extrapolates a theory of the synaesthetic sub-structure of all language. According to Poet's view, not only is there 'the strictest analogy between colours and sounds', colours and sounds 'are both but languages, which do not represent their correspondent ideas; but only suggest them to the mind' by association (122). Though complete signifying systems unto themselves, morphemes and phonemes are also the primitive (visible and audible) units of a higher-order language; as such, they correspond with each other at the formal level. The discussion culminates (129–30) when Poet cites a philosophical paper on *Ocular Spectra* by 'Dr Darwin of Shrewsbury' (128), which 'shews' that 'the same laws must govern the sensations of both' vision and hearing. Because this congruence is, in Darwinian terms, an 'ideal presence', Darwin's Poet demands the muse:

it is to be wished that some ingenious musician would further cultivate this curious field of science: for if visible music can be agreeably produced, it would be more easy to add sentiment to it by the representation of groves and Cupids and sleeping nymphs amid the changing colours, than is commonly done by the words of audible music. (130)

Heard melodies are sweet, but those unheard are sweeter still. And the latest orchestration of this music of the spheres is even

---

distinction separating the sublime from the beautiful. As a result, sublimity, Ideal Presence, and the sentimental are constellating terms for Darwin. For a good discussion of the general significance of this way of thinking see Julie Ellison, 'Redoubled Feeling: Politics, Sentiment, and the Sublime in Williams and Wollstonecraft', *Studies in Eighteenth-Century Culture* 20 (1990), 197–215.

[5] *Shelley's Poetry and Prose*, ed. Donald H. Reiman and Sharon B. Powers (New York: W. W. Norton and Co., 1977), 502.

now issuing from the 'ingenious musician' named Dr Darwin. The passage is a witty description of his own poetical project, of which this very work, *The Loves of the Plants*, is a major part.

Darwinian 'sentiment' functions as the conscious eroticism of his poem ('conscience' and '*élan*'). Unlike Wordsworth or Bernardin, however, Darwin does not attack the analytic powers of the mind. On the contrary, throughout his work these powers—which he associates explicitly with prose discourse—respond to the discourse of imagination and poetry (as Interludes, as the book's front and back matter, and as the brilliant set of footnotes to the different poetical set-pieces). On one hand, the prose checks the poetical flight toward Ideal Presence, grounding the verse with analysis and empirical observation. On the other, the verse charges the scientific project with feeling and sensation, and stimulates the 'sentiment' of the ideal.

The lines on the sensitive plant nicely illustrate Darwin's sentimental style.

> Weak with nice sense, the chaste MIMOSA stands,
> From each rude touch withdraws her timid hands;
> Oft as light clouds o'erpass the Summer-glade,
> Alarmed she trembles at the moving shade;
> And feels, alive through all her tender form,
> The whisper'd murmurs of the gathering storm;
> Shuts her sweet eye-lids to approaching night;
> And hails with freshen'd charms the rising light.
> Veil'd, with gay decency and modest pride,
> Slow to the mosque she moves, an eastern bride;
> There her soft vows unceasing love record,
> Queen of the bright seraglio of her Lord.—
> So sinks or rises with the changeful hour
> The liquid silver in its glassy tower.
> So turns the needle to the pole it loves,
> With fine librations quivering, as it moves.
>
> (I.247–62)

Jones's idea—that we think of Creation as 'rather an *energy* than a *work*'—is fully realized in Darwin. This passage constructs an emblem for a vital and scientifically refigured Great Chain of Being. The two final images—the barometer and the compass—ask us to reimagine the plant as a vegetable instru-

ment that measures Nature's own (in this case, hydraulic) oper-
ations. The sensitive plant is (specifically) a natural barometer.
The compass image raises the level of the argument, however, by
suggesting that flowers, barometers, and compasses all registrate
fundamental natural law. This law, according to Darwin (and
Bernardin, and Wordsworth, and Goethe, etc.), is one, holy, and
(in an entirely secular sense) catholic. When Darwin here names
it love he echoes the sentimental chorus of his age.

But to speak in this (prose) fashion is exactly to translate Ideal
Presence into analytic terms. Darwin is most concerned with his
enlightened, scientific pursuits, but his philosophical papers (like
the prose parts of his poetical work) use the discourse of reason
and the empirical mind. Because his poetical MIMOSA comes to
us as a sentimental figure, she realizes Darwin's thought as an
energy rather than as a concept or 'work'. Her erotic vitality
replicates what Coleridge would famously call 'animated
nature'. That vitality, moreover, runs again *here*—in this text—
as the stimulating rhetoric of Darwin's verse. All his flowers,
male and female alike, grow in sentimental ground, which for
Darwin is a type of discourse apt for regenerating (not representing) Ideal Presence, that is, Creation as a self-sustaining
process of energy.

In this frame of reference we see that sentimental poetry is not
a defensive reaction against eighteenth-century empiricist philosophy but a reflection of its thought, and an effort to express
that thought in direct ways. The 'thought', however, requires
an 'expression' committed primarily to an affective rather than
a constative form of language. Seeing the universe (both human
and natural) as an energy field calls out a poem like Blake's
'The Lamb', which is nothing more (or less) than a perpetual-
motion machine of sympathetic energies. 'Lamb', 'Child',
and the unnamed Jesus are transformational terms. They do not
so much *reflect* each other, thus constructing a symbolic structure of meaning; they literally make and remake each other.
So the poem generates almost no statemental content, its 'idea'
is an embodied and literal act, a rhetorical dance of its own
terms.

Shelley, the master of this rhetoric, carries it to breathtaking
greatness in Act II scene 5 of *Prometheus Unbound*. It appears
as the revelation of Asia (the hydrogen cycle, Love, an alpine

dawn, the 'Life of Life')—ultimately, as the energetic translation of all these terms into and out of each other. The passage overwhelms because the transformations operate uniformly at all levels of the discourse, from the largest rhetorical units (the antiphon of responses) to the smallest lexical details and syntactic functions.

> Fair are others;—none beholds thee
>   But thy voice sounds low and tender
> Like the fairest, for it folds thee
>   From the sight, that liquid splendour,
> And all feel, yet see thee never
> As I feel now, lost forever.
>
>   (60–5)

Enjambed movement reinforces the synaesthetic dissolution of image into sound. Even the sharpest forms can but briefly shape themselves in this 'Sea profound, of ever-spreading sound' (84). So we only glimpse the figures playing through this exquisite sentimental rhetoric. The ambiguity of 'the sight, that liquid splendour', for example, does not stay for our intellectual consideration, even though it might well be used to define a conceptual order for the verse: for here are both 'the sight' of the sun rising through the mountain mists as well as the (material) organ of vision that half perceives and half creates that sight. But the passage moves on—inexorably, mercilessly—through its energetic intensities. Creation-as-energy is understood as an order of experience and feeling, not as an order of mind. Like Shelley's cloud, its perpetual arising is a process of ceaseless *un*building.

13

Sentimentalism as Consumption and Exchange

In this kind of rhetorical field, where feeling comes in aid of feeling, the private reader emerges as a decisive presence. Creation-as-energy and its social equivalent, sympathy, are 'proved' through a structure of emotional response. So the poets began to develop ways—verse conventions—for opening their texts to individual acts of (re)appropriation by a wide and diverse audience. Such poems do not ask for generalized translations or the valuative judgements that underlay such interpretations; they solicit processes of exchange very like what Marx describes in the opening of the first volume of *Capital*. The literary-critical equivalent for this kind of exchange, and this kind of poetry, is the 'appreciative' (or 'subjective') reading that climaxes in the work of Ruskin and especially Pater.

Consequently, the dynamic of this poetry gets clarified by one of its most characteristic answering forms—the personal reading, and in particular the private response articulated in marginalia. The nineteenth-century 'common reader''s marginalia, a vast record of this type of reading, explicates the conventions of sentimental poetry. Most useful are the marginalia generated by ordinary people in volumes of sentimental poets from their personal libraries. The subjectivity of this kind of commentary is its most distinctive and generic feature.

Take, for example, the copy of *The Poetical Works of Miss Landon* (Philadelphia, 1841) once owned by C. M. (and C. R.) Stenson.[1] The unrecorded character of the Stensons' lives marks

---

[1] I choose this copy for convenience (it is in my own library). Numerous reprints of Laetitia Elizabeth Landon's works (the famous L.E.L.) appeared after her death in 1838; this is a one-volume edition published by 'Carey and Hart, Chestnut Street'. It carries two signatures, one (C. R. Stenson) on the front flyleaf, the other (C. M.

the book and its marginalia in a salient way—as (as it were) mute inglorious Ruskins. In this case the marginal notations are few and, on the face of it, quite unspectacular. There are only three.

The first appears in 'The Zenana', a long narrative work that recapitulates a familiar romantic tale involving a warrior-hero (Murad) and his lover (Nadira). The poem opens with Nadira awaiting his return from the 'strife' heroes like Murad are fated to engage. He comes back and tells her about his battles ('Mine the fierce free existence spent/ 'Mid meeting ranks and armed tent', p. 63). Punctuating these struggles are Murad's brief meetings with Nadira ('which I steal/ At thy beloved feet to kneel') or the vision of her that he carries about with him:

> Ah! never is that cherish'd face
> Banish'd from its accustom'd place—

Annotating this couplet is the pencil note 'my heart'.

The second annotation appears in the brief lyric 'Pulo Penang' alongside the following lines.

> O, only those who part can know
> How dear the love that absence brings;
> O'er wind and wave my fancies go,
> As if my very heart had wings.

Pencilled in the margin is the word 'yes'.

Though we cannot be certain, the contexts argue that both of these annotations were made by a man. The final annotation is different. First of all, it is in ink—the only one in the book. Second, its context is a poem ('Can You Forget Me', p. 341) that is clearly gendered female. The annotation appears next to the last five lines:

> The happy hours that I have pass'd while kneeling
> Half slave, half child, to gaze upon thy face.
> —But what to thee this passionate appealing—

Stenson) on the title page. Both are in ink. Whether the marginalia are all by a single person, whether by a man or a woman, married or not, is uncertain. The context of the annotations suggests they were made by two different persons, one a man, the other a woman. Inside the front cover is the bookplate of the Baltimore Academy of the Visitation. Pencil marks alongside various passages appear throughout the book. Two of the marginal comments are in pencil, one is in ink.

> Let my heart break—it is a common case.
> You have forgotten me.

Here the note is placed next to the first line. It is a date: '1846 & 1847'.

A notable feature of this kind of commentary is its extreme privacy. The texts are being read as if their objective value had been translated into exchange value. Readers appropriate for their own use. The story of Murad and Nadira becomes an occasion for C. M. (or C. R.) Stenson's personal reflections. A passage in 'The Zenana' (just before the annotated passage), marked in pencil but with no marginal note, suggests this reader's awareness of the reading process he follows:

> What though our passing day but be
> A bubble on eternity;
> Small though the circle is, yet still
> 'Tis ours to colour at our will.

Stenson is responding to the sentimenal logic articulated by Murad in Landon's own text. When he marks this passage he is behaving (reading) in the same spirit that the author writ. When Murad narrates his adventures to Nadira, the same sympathetic logic is operating. 'Seated at his feet', as Murad later imagines himself at hers, Nadira

> For his sake feels the colour rise,
> His spirit kindle in her eyes,
> Till her heart beating joins the cry
> Of Murad and of victory.
>
> (p. 262)

Critics of such writing—most notably, early and mid-twentieth-century critics—deplore its formulaic procedures. These are pervasive, extending from the choice of certain (romantic) types of familiar story and subject to the deployment of equally familiar images and diction. A critical assumption can then be made that sentimental writers are simply deficient writers, lacking that poetic requirement (also assumed) 'the creative imagination' (an ideological formation equally assumed within most of the poetry as well). But what if we make other assumptions— for example, what if we assume that the style has been deliberately chosen, as it certainly was by many of its practitioners? It then will appear a style grounding itself in a commonplace, a style in which moves toward novelty might well be rare (or otherwise concealed) events, textual choices to be deliberated with great care and deployed with perhaps even greater circumspection.

This type of sentimental verse (so unlike the spectacular verse of Darwin and Jones) inclines to efface itself before the reader. Stenson's annotations to Landon's poems are clearly, in one sense, far more concrete and particular than Landon's formulaic 'originals'. But their particularity emerges as a direct function of the implicit invitation made to the reader through the verse. Seeing the annotations we suddenly encounter an intense yet cryptic emotional scene. Indeed, the annotated volume begins to generate its own emotional gravity, teasing us (its subsequent readers) into further ranges of sympathetic response (for instance, speculative reflections upon, or even active researches into, the 'meaning' of the annotations—perhaps starting with the identity of the Stensons). Landon's writing originates this process. It positively calls out the kind of personal responses whose remains are preserved in the margins of an old book. Landon's kind of poetry recalls nothing so much as Ahab's doubloon, whose worn lettering and figures activate a logic of suggestion, evoking the concealed thoughts and feelings of his crew.

This is the formal structure of the most widespread type of sentimental writing. We see it clearly elaborated in Helen Maria Williams's work, perhaps most dramatically in her translation of Bernardin's classic sentimental fiction *Paul et Virginie*. Williams's translation, first published in 1795, was reprinted often in the nineteenth century. It is by no means a 'literal' work. Not only does Williams leave out significant parts of Bernardin's tale, she makes even more significant additions to the original text. The most notable of these come with the series of original sonnets she introduces into Bernardin's story.

These sonnets, which punctuate the text at various points, comprise a running commentary on Bernardin's work. They are represented as the poems of one of the chief characters in the tale, Madame de la Tour, Virginia's mother. The first is a 'Sonnet to Love'.

Ah, Love! ere yet I knew thy fatal power,
Bright glow'd the colour of my youthful days,
As, on the sultry zone, the torrid rays
That paint the broad-leaved plantain's glossy bower:
Calm was my bosom at this silent hour,
When, o'er the deep, scarce heard, the zephyr strays,
'Midst the cool tam'rinds indolently plays,
Nor from the orange shakes the od'rous flower:
But, ah! since Love has all my heart possest,
That desolated heart what sorrows tear!
Disturb'd and wild as ocean's troubled breast,
When the hoarse tempest of the night is there!
Yet my complaining spirit asks no rest;
The bleeding bosom cherishes despair. (p. 15)[2]

An introductory prose paragraph (not in Bernardin) serves partly to connect poem to tale, and partly to construct a framework for the poem's meaning. Madame de la Tour 'Sometimes . . . poured forth the effusions of melancholy in the language of verse' that 'bear the marks of genuine sensibility'. Her poems are written, we are told, when she 'wandered out alone; and, amidst this sublime scenery, indulged that luxury of pensive sadness' which comforts the heartbroken (14). A sentimental mechanism begins to operate in natural solitudes, where human responses are forced to correspond at purely affective levels. Nature's language has no grammar or semantics.

But human language does, and Madame de la Tour's poetry is a linguistic response to nature's silence. The communication is optimal when the heart seems most desolated and empty. At those times, when worldly language is at a loss, the sentimental 'sublime'—a divine language—calls out to the soul sunk in its dark night. Madame de la Tour's sonnet is the result—the failed result. The logic of this kind of communication exposes the necessary emptiness of the verbal response. Human language cannot express its sense of the divine.

None the less, that language can reflect such divinity, even unbeknownst to itself. The sonnet 'to Love' speaks on two levels, though Madame de la Tour (like the reader) is immediately aware of just one. The latter expresses her grief at her

---

[2] My text of Williams's translation is an 1872 edition (London: T. Nelson and Sons).

human losses: the death of her husband, her rejection by her family, her exile from France to the island of Mauritius. This 'Love' seems, as Swinburne's Althaea will later say, 'one thing, an evil thing, and turns/ Choice words and wisdom into fire and air'. But to Williams Love is not *one* thing, its desolations conceal the secret ministry of a benevolent counter-spirit. The sonnet speaks beyond Madame de la Tour's consciousness, speaks with the voice of this spirit. So, concealed in the sonnet are a series of proleptic references to the climax and conclusion of Bernardin's tale, when Virginia will perish in the storm.

This (un)foreseen future may hardly appear benevolent since it brings only deeper sorrows. The 'zone' of the human is 'torrid' because—as the double-meaning of 'zone' suggests—it is the land of the heart's desires ('my bosom'). Its riches figure desolation, its zephyrs carry the promise of hurricanes. Madame de la Tour's past sorrows will be followed by further and worse, for to live (in the world, through the heart) is to be poured out and emptied. That traditional wisdom is here being translated into a psychic myth.

Retirement (to an island like Mauritius, to the solitude of nature, to the privacy of the sentimental poem) brings clarification through intensifying one's sense of the true nature of things. The benevolence of the counter-spirit comes as what Wordsworth called the 'thoughts that do often lie too deep for tears'. It comes as a consciousness that sees beyond the present, beyond even the seductive promises of a better future; it sees beyond the end.

That structure of thought—that 'world-view'—dictates the language of this sentimental sonnet. The words' signifiers and referents dissolve, like distant objects in a romantic landscape. The poem's unseen references (to the death of Virginia) do not fix the sonnet's meaning, they figure its sentimental transfiguration. The zone of despair consumes all meaning but the loss of meaning. The reader is therefore left in Madame de la Tour's (and Williams's) sym-pathetic position. We are moved by desire toward the ever-receding horizon of an ultimate meaning (whether particular or general). But all that one generates is translation, the extension of meaning defined through its continual loss.

The melancholy of the poem signals only a loss of meaning,

however, not a loss of vitality. The sonnet is finally not a work
but a field of energy revealed and maintained through processes
of conceptual loss and escape. Madame de la Tour can no more
comprehend the meaning of her words than Bernardin or
Williams can. All efforts at comprehension fail in the consuming
transaction of the verse, which is itself both indexed and replicated by Williams's (re)active translation. Like coral, or like the
'dead thoughts' Shelley celebrates in his great 'Ode to the West
Wind', the poetic field generates textual residues as part of its
vital process. Blake called these residues Golgonooza, the
Buildings of Los(s): dead, (in)human forms (words, images,
ideas) that reflect, by their own emptiness, the life they are for
ever losing.

14

Waking from Adam's Dream: L.E.L.'s Art of Disillusion

Like Poe in America, Laetitia Elizabeth Landon can scarcely be understood apart from a distinctive and shared literary context. Both writers established their reputations in the world of the 1820s and 1830s, that is to say, in a period when the institutions of literary production were undergoing drastic changes. We date the changes—for both countries—from two signal events: the founding of *Blackwood's Edinburgh Magazine* in 1817, and the publication of the *Forget Me Not* in 1823. These two works inaugurated an important shift in the way writing, especially poetry, essay, and short fiction, would be carried out for the rest of the century.

Mrs Hemans' poetry also gained its celebrity in this context. However, her style was formed earlier and under very different circumstances. She published three books of verse (one in 1808, two in 1812) before she was married (in 1812) and all were carefully prepared by and for a small coterie audience. Least of all were these books written for money. In this respect her early work follows the pattern of Byron's early work. Like Byron, however, she eventually became much interested in the monetary value of her poetry. She resumed her writing in 1816, and from 1818 she was well paid by a literary institution growing more and more conscious of its market character and interests.

The cultural change involved here is very great, and the poets (rather than the fiction writers) found it most difficult to manage; the tensions of the period appear most clearly in the poetry for that very reason. From Byron's clotted and mordant satire *The Age of Bronze* (1823) through Tennyson's obliquely troubled 'The Lady of Shalott' (1832), one observes a broad spectrum of conscious poetical reflection on the commerce of letters. In these events Hemans' work is central and runs a parallel course with the 'later Wordsworth'. Like Wordsworth, Hemans preserved a fastidious distance from the fast literary world that was emerging as the twilight of the romantic movement. That is to say, she did not locate herself in London or even in Edinburgh. Nevertheless, literary entrepreneurs like William Blackwood grasped and exploited the cultural arguments that are implicit in all of Hemans' monitory retirements. The power of her writing, especially in the 1820s, certainly comes in part from its ambiguous way of negotiating what it represents as an obscurely dangerous world. The contrast with the Wordsworth of the same period couldn't be greater: his later work suffers exactly from its reluctance to engage with 'the coming race'.

Landon's career and writing is at once very similar to Hemans' and very different. Her first published work was a poem titled 'Rome', which appeared (8 March 1820) in William Jerdan's *Literary Gazette*. Founded like *Blackwood's* in 1817, the *Literary Gazette* would remain the chief outlet for Landon's poetry for many years. It was, like *Blackwood's*, a compilation of verse, prose, and literary/cultural discussion (or gossip). It was also (like *Blackwood's*) determinedly *au courant*, but unlike the latter it avoided engaging controversial topics. It sought an aesthetic audience, though not the rather exclusive and intellectual readership imagined by the ill-fated *London Magazine* (1820–9). In this respect the founding of the *Literary Gazette* forecast the coming of the gift books and annuals, which were so important for the development of Landon's writing.

Like the young Felicia Browne (i.e., the later Mrs Hemans), Landon entered the literary world in protective custody. But unlike Browne, Landon was being ushered into a volatile cultural arena, the highly public and journalistic scene centred in London. Landon lived and worked in this world throughout her years of fame and she was swept up in many of its controversies. Hemans stayed away, and when her poems appeared in *Blackwood's*, as they often did in the 1820s, they signalled a region of cultivated domestic retirement by which to measure and judge the (imperial) controversies being played out in the other parts of the magazine. That removed domestic vantage became the mythic core of her writing—the feature of her work that her readers, both in and out of London, most wanted to experience.

The domestic and maternal love infusing so much of Hemans' work gets replaced in Landon with the subject of erotic love. By that choice of subject Landon gave an immediately provocative edge to her work. For one thing, it placed her writing in a direct relation to the problematic verse of the 1790s, i.e., to the poetry of the Della Cruscan line and its array of 'unsex'd females'. Landon's published volumes would only underscore the relation. Whereas the Della Cruscans' troubadour and *stil novist* conventions function in mostly non-explicit ways in their writing, Landon's book titles declare her allegiances: *The Troubador, The Improvisatrice, The Golden Violet*. In works like these, the subject of poetry and erotic love, and of the relation between the two, is being unequivocally announced.

The thirty years or so that separate the world of the Della Cruscans from the world of the magazines and gift books had brought irrevocable changes to the cultural scene. Most important was the establishment of imaginative writing as a commercial activity. The problematic character of this change comes into focus, as I have already suggested, when we reflect on the journalistic bent of 1820s writing, and especially on the equivocal reception of the gift books and annuals. Wordsworth's brief involvement with *The Keepsake* for 1829 dramatizes the great shift that was taking place, and exposes the difficulties that more traditional writers—even so clearly *professional* a writer as Wordsworth—were having with these changes.

The men involved in these events—De Quincey, Wilson, Hunt, Praed, Bulwer-Lytton, and so forth—were gender-licensed to engage the issues directly. But while women had now taken an important place in the profession of letters, the place remained sharply restricted. Erotic love was a topic to be handled very carefully; indeed, Landon's social difficulties stemmed in no small part from her determined pursuit of this subject. Furthermore, women were largely excluded from serious cultural controversy, which more than ever defined an 'unsex'd' condition. Hemans' fame and cultural significance is partly but certainly linked to the evident depth and breadth of her learning, on one hand, and her studious avoidance of controversy on the other.

Because Landon chose to work and publish in London, and to become intimately involved with its volatile life (both personally and professionally), her position as a writer was far more fragile and even perilous than, say, the position of Hemans. Landon had to negotiate her way with great care and deliberation. The consequence is a (socially) self-conscious style of writing that often—especially in the later work—comes inflected with a disturbing mood or tone of bad faith. Again and again the poetry seems oblique, or held in reserve, or self-censored. Its romantic subjects lack altogether the fresh and 'naïve' quality of the work of Burns, Wordsworth, and Coleridge, or even of disturbed and belated works like Byron's *The Giaour* or Keats's 'On First Looking Into Chapman's Homer'. In Landon there is little new under the sun, although there is much that is novel. Her poetry recreates a factitious world and she is shrewd enough (and cursed enough) to see that her own perceptions are part of that world, as is the language in which she can speak of it.

Like Poe, Landon is a second-order Byron. By this I mean that (as writers) both (*a*) inherit Byron's social self-consciousness, and (*b*) develop it to a higher level of abstraction. The case of Poe, which is better known, may be usefully recalled here to explain what happens in Landon's work. Poe's proto-Wildean aesthetic manifestos 'The Philosophy of Composition' and 'The Poetic Principle' are theoretically important exactly because they are parodic texts, and not least of all self-parodies. Poe not only knows how to write a *Blackwood* article, he writes 'How to Write a *Blackwood* Article'. Byron taught Poe and Landon that they lived in a world of signs and conventions, and they quickly realized that this knowledge came with its own arbitrary and conventional structure. 'The Fall of the House of Usher' is (explicitly) a comic rehearsal of Byron's life reconstructed from a reading of Thomas Moore's *Letters and Journals of Lord Byron* (1831–2).[1]

Landon approaches writing in the same spirit that Poe does. She rehearses established forms and ideas, she echoes and alludes to recognized authors and styles. Byronic tags and phrases (in particular) recur throughout her work because Byron's writing is well known; as such, its signs may be effectively deployed as second-order signs of the presence of a poetical discourse.

---

[1] See Katrina Bachinger, ' "The Sombre Madness of Sex": Byron's First and Last Gift to Poe', *The Byron Journal* 19 (1991), 128–40.

Organized in these terms, Landon's self-consciously quotational writing works to demystify the ancient authority of poetry. This result obtains because Landon, like Poe, implicitly argues that 'authority' and 'tradition' can only be, in an immediate frame of reference, what is more or less popular. In the end Landon replays the battle of the Ancients and the Moderns not to argue the case for one side or the other but to expose the struggle as a Blakean Orc Cycle of reciprocating engines. What emerges in her writing is not an 'Art of Allusion', as Reuben Brower once called the poetry of Pope, but an Art of Disillusion.

As in Poe's work, things are rarely what they appear to be in Landon's poetry of appearances. Printed in the 'Original Poetry' columns of Jerdan's *Literary Gazette*, the verse regularly ironizes the journal heading because it may at first appear so *un*original—indeed, so superficial. As Kingsley Amis shrewdly remarked of Hemans' poetry, however, such writing is more accurately seen as 'superficially superficial'. This description does not involve (as such) an evaluation of Hemans' or Landon's writing but a definition of its style and operating conventions.

The 10 November 1821 issue of the *Literary Gazette* supplies a typical instance. The 'Original Poetry' here is headed by L.E.L.'s 'Six Songs of Love, Constancy, Romance, Inconstancy, Truth, and Marriage'. These 'Songs' follow as the set of lyrics separated from each other by a thin hairline. Each is unheaded except the last, which is titled 'Matrimonial Creed' and which appears to represent the sixth of the songs, the 'Marriage' song. But reading problems arise throughout the sequence. A small but important one is located at the crucial intersection between the last and the penultimate song. A slightly abbreviated hairline separates what appears to be the final stanza of the fifth song ('Oh! would that love had power to raise') from the rest (the previous four stanzas). The event introduces an ambiguity into the sequence. Perhaps there are seven lyrics rather than 'Six Songs': i.e., 'Six Songs' (untitled) accompanied by the 'Matrimonial Creed', which would be serving as a coda to the others. The point is significant for two reasons. First, the titles of the poems are relevant as instructions for reading; uncertainty (or ambiguous titles) suggest different paths of meaning. Indeed, because titles are not actually supplied at the head of specific 'Songs', the

continuum of Landon's subject matter (love in the world) makes
the songs bleed into each other, as if here one might as easily
title a poem 'Constancy' or 'Inconstancy', 'Romance' or 'Truth'.
Second, because the poems present themselves as a sequence
with distinct (and even nameable) parts, one needs to 'know' (or
at any rate, to *decide*) what the parts are. Take the four lines
preceding the 'Matrimonial Creed', i.e., the lines whose place-
ment is rendered uncertain by the game with the hairlines:

> I thought thus of the flowers, the moon,
> This faery isle for you and me;
> And then I thought how very soon
> How very tired we should be.

Setting aside for the moment the question of these lines' semantic meaning, we also have to decide their rhetorical position. Is
this the whole of the 'Truth' or the conclusion of the 'Truth'?
Rhetorically considered, the problem is quite like the problem
posed at the end of Keats's 'Ode on a Grecian Urn'. In each case
a rhetorical strategy—an ambiguity of punctuation—makes a
representation about a crucial feature of any poetical contract:
that it awaits the decision of the reader, much as a musical score
invites an interpretive performance.

One might miss, or *dis*miss, these important problems of
reading but for Landon's dramatic, not to say melodramatic,
strategy at the end of the sequence. At this point a 'Marriage'
song coolly saps the preceding set of love/romance/pathos lyrics.
A commercial 'Creed' reflects on all that has gone before:

> He must be rich whom I could love,
> His fortune clear must be,
> Whether in land or in the funds,
> 'Tis all the same to me.

These lines open a poem that by itself makes a simple debunking
move on the superficialities of love and romance. As part of the
poetical sequence, however, the final poem forces one to reassess
the superficialities of the preceding texts—for example, the
second (whose subject is presumably 'Constancy'). The cunning
of that 'Song' demands full quotation:

> Oh! say not love was never made
> For hearts so light as mine;

Must love then seek the cypress shade,
Rear but a gloomy shrine.

Oh! say not, that for me more meet
The revelry of youth;
Or that my wild heart cannot beat
With deep devoted truth.

Tho' mirth may many changes ring,
'Tis but an outward show,
Even upon the fond dove's wing
Will varying colours glow.

Light smiles upon my lip may gleam
And sparkle o'er my brow,
'Tis but the glisten of the stream
That hides the gold below.

'Tis love that gilds the mirthful hour,
That lights the smile for me,
Those smiles would instant lose their power,
Did they not glance on thee.

'Gold'/'gilds'; 'light'/'lights'; 'smiles', 'love', 'truth': the words slip in suggestive ways all the more surely for coming to us under the (apparent) sign of 'Constancy'. For the convention of the poetic sequence establishes a fictive identity between the 'author' of the 'Matrimonial Creed' and the 'author' of this 'Song'. Such an identity can only be massively contradicted: loving and loveless, superficial and deep, fantasizing and self-conscious. Most troubling of all, perhaps, the poetry participates in that field of contradictions, for it makes only the most *superficial* efforts to disguise its superficialities.

If it is true, as has been said, that women have a special knowledge of imaginary worlds—having lived so long in mirrors and as visionary objects—one understands the source of Landon's poetic authority. An imagination like hers has few illusions about illusory worlds, and least of all about that supreme Land of Cockayne, the romantic imagination. Small wonder that her work, like her spectacular and mythic life, was banished from our high-minded cultural memories. For institutions committed to maintaining king's treasuries and queen's gardens, she is a dangerous writer, for she understands how they function, having put such long service into both.

15

The Loss of Sentimental Poetry

'For such loss . . . abundant recompence' ('Tintern Abbey', 88–9): this formula governs a view of elegy now, apparently, become normative. Something works to redeem the harrowing logic of ultimate loss, perhaps even—as in certain Christian and Marxian mythoi—to transform it into splendour. In its lowest common denominator the formula traces out a dismal science of balanced books or capitalist growth. More impressive and even thrilling is the cancellation of loss executed through a general economy of gift-giving or potlatch. Of course 'civilized' cultures—witness the historical evolution of Christianity—have always tried to restrict the economy of wholesale sacrifice, to bring order and a measure of reasonableness to the sad, ecstatic, or spectacular stories of the deaths of kings. To pagan philosophers of Rome the early Christian communities were lunatic. But then, of course, each of those worlds became what they beheld, until Rome itself grew a synonym for the once despised and rejected cult of Jesus. Centuries later Blake would sum up the logic of these events in a wonderful apothegm: 'Know that after Christs death, he became Jehovah.'[1]

In literary terms, the compensatory schemas of elegy develop a further, special argument whereby the elegy itself—the intercourse of its writing or its reading or both—carries out or embodies the logic of redemption. Here too one observes the double option of either a normative or an ecstatic line, a restrictive or a general economy. Because the former (restrictive

---

[1] For the normative line on elegy see Peter Sacks, *The English Elegy: Studies in the Genre from Spenser to Yeats* (Baltimore: Johns Hopkins University Press, 1985). My discussion of restrictive and general economies is of course taken from Georges Bataille. The Blake quotation is from *The Marriage of Heaven and Hell* (plate 6).

economy) has come to dominate our understanding of elegy, its structure is a familiar one. In the romantic period Wordsworth epitomizes its movement (although his greatest elegiac writings—for instance the 'Ode to Duty' and the 'Elegiac Stanzas'—do not conform to type). In his normative mood the poet 'would enshrine the spirit of the past/ For future restoration' (*The Prelude* 1805, XI.342–3) through the memorial act of writing. Such verse is

> Woven out of passion's sharpest agonies,
> Subdued, composed, and formalized by art,
> To fix a wiser sorrow in the heart.
> (Wordsworth, 'Stanzas Suggested in a Steamboat off
> Saint Bees' Heads . . .', 74–6)

This 'sorrow' feeds on the famous 'thoughts that do often lie too deep for tears'. Nor can we doubt the wisdom of such sorrow—grieving in its most exalted mood. On the other hand, one may well think another thought, more sapphic: 'But who, alas! can love and then be wise?' (*Don Juan* I, st. 117) In grief as in love—the two run together—wise thoughts may be found altogether wanting. May well be found.

Among presently canonical English romantic poets, Blake erects a general cosmic mythos for dealing with the destructive nature of nature. Because the romantic 'system of nature' takes so much of its inspiration from Christian tradition, its redemptive mechanism can easily be mistaken. Blake's response to its dismal economies is like Jesus' response to the (rich) young man who asked 'What shall I do to attain eternal life?' The answer he received was not a comforting one: to give to the poor all of his possessions, 'take up the cross and follow me' (Mark 10: 17–21). To follow Jesus, in Blake's translation of this text, is to 'go to Eternal Death'. Blake's 'Buildings of Los' are exactly that, buildings of loss.[2]

Blake's scheme of things does not accrue spiritual rewards. It entails, rather, complete expenditure—'Los[s]'—or what Blake also calls (sometimes) 'creation' and (sometimes) 'Eternal Death'. The process of visionary ecstasy is its own reward, self-generating, self-consuming. So he imagines the Last Judgement

---

[2] See *Milton*, book I, plate 14; *Jerusalem* ch. 1. plate 14.

as a dionysian feast in which all things are literally 'consumed': eaten up, drunk up, burned up, annihilated. *All* things, including the Buildings of Los themselves, the enginery that sustains this 'eternal' apocalypse: the winepress, the printing press, 'war on earth'.

> This winepress is called War on earth; it is the printing-press
> Of Los, and here he lays his words in order above the mortal
>   brain,
> As cogs are formed in a wheel to turn the cogs of the adverse
>   wheel.
>   (*Milton*, plate 25[27]: 8–10)

In the machinery of Blake's art the world is turned inside out, exposed. This *is* the great eucharist: 'Timbrels & violins sport round the winepresses' to accompany a dance of death, Agape visioned as the *Liebestod* of 'Luvah's daughters' and 'Luvah's sons':

> They dance around the dying, & they drink the howl and groan;
> They catch the shrieks in cups of gold, they hand them to one
>   another,
> These are the sports of love, & these the sweet delights of
>   amorous play—
>   (*Milton*, plate 25[27]: 36–8)

This is redemption in and as ecstasy, something quite different from the wisdom pursued through logics of compensation. Translated into a formally elegiac structure, it appears often in Shelley's work, and most famously in *Adonais*. The injunction of the poem—consummated in the overwhelming last four stanzas—is simple yet catastrophic, like Jesus' response to the young man:

> The One remains, the many change and pass;
> Heaven's light forever shines, earth's shadows fly;
> Life, like a dome of many-coloured glass,
> Stains the white radiance of Eternity,
> Until death tramples it to fragments.—Die,
> If thou would be with that which thou dost seek!
>   (stanza LII)

The imperative verb establishes the mission of Shelley's verse. This is not the poetry of epitaphs, where the experience of loss is replaced by the memorial tribute of a shrine of loving language. Shelley goes to Keats's grave in Rome, to the grave that is Rome herself, only to 'pause' briefly (st. LI) before 'The bones of Desolation's nakedness/ Pass' utterly away from his higher purpose (st. XLIX). The point is not to fix a memory of loss forever but to establish all things on a basis of present and immediate life.

The poem therefore concludes in a process of self-enactment. Shelley is no longer thinking to remember Keats but—in an exact Nietzschean sense—he is thinking to forget. Or rather, he is writing to forget, turning all things over to, and into, an eternal present.

> The breath whose might I have invoked in song
> Descends on me; my spirit's bark is driven,
> Far from the shore, far from the trembling throng
> Whose sails were never to the tempest given;
> The massy earth and sphered skies are riven!
> I am borne darkly, fearfully afar;
> Whilst, burning through the inmost veil of Heaven,
> The soul of Adonais, like a star,
> Beacons from the abode where the Eternals are.
>
> (st. LV)

'Burning through' itself, Shelley's words become 'One' with the 'beacon' they are imagining as Keats ('What Adonais is, why fear we to become?', st. LI). The poem ends by not ending, ends in a light and fire carried through its verbs: all turning, literally, to the present, indicative, active. It does not remember 'Keats', it becomes 'Adonais'.

Blake's and Shelley's ecstatic economies leave no room for compensatory elegy. They are, in this respect, the clear precursors of Swinburne, Ginsberg, Plath.[3] I mention these later poets, however, because their similarities to Blake and Shelley call attention to certain important differences. These differences are clearest in Plath, whose anger and resentment at the agencies of loss are neither mitigated, nor recompensed, nor ecstatically

---

[3] For a good survey of modern elegy see Jahan Ramazani, *Poetry of Mourning: The Modern Elegy from Hardy to Heaney* (Chicago: University of Chicago Press, 1994).

transformed. Among the canonical English romantics, Byron most clearly anticipates her superb intransigence.

But where Plath is hot, a spirit of fire, Byron is cold. It is for this that Baudelaire so much admired him.

> Then the mortal coldness of the soul like death itself comes
>   down;
> It cannot feel for others' woes, it dares not dream its own;
> That heavy chill has frozen o'er the fountain of our tears,
> And tho' the eye may sparkle still, 'tis where the ice appears.
>
> ('Stanzas for Music' ['There's not a joy'], 9–12)

Byron's satanism appears as an unwanted inheritance. Descending upon him like a fate, his imagination turns it to a badge of honour—indeed, to a 'joy', though the word in this poem has no Wordsworthian meanings at all. On the contrary:

> There's not a joy the world can give like that it takes away . . .

Elsewhere Byron calls this emotional condition 'vacancy absorbing space' ('The Prisoner of Chillon', 243). Here it emerges through the corrosive ambiguity in the wordplay with 'that', which operates both as a relative pronoun and a conjunction. The latter's more secret and insidious syntax disturbs the line's otherwise conventional surface, pointing to a new kind of joy beyond the dialectics of good and evil (joy and sorrow). This is a joy like none other, a joy that arrives with and as the removal of every imaginable worldly joy, including the possible pleasure that might have come from its own perverse and ironic pleasure.

Emptied out in this way, the poem finds nourishment in 'the knowledge of its own desert' (*Manfred* III.396):

> Oh could I feel as I have felt,—or be what I have been,
> Or weep as I could once have wept, o'er many a vanished scene:
> As springs in deserts found seem sweet, all brackish though they
>   be,
> So midst the wither'd waste of life, those tears would flow
>   to me.
>
> ('Stanzas for Music' ['There's not a joy'], 17–20)

Drinking from such a fountain yields the refreshment of a perfect disillusionment, beyond the more primitive needs of comfort and regret.

THE LOST SOUL OF WOMAN: BYRON, SMITH, HEMANS

Byron was much attracted to this image of the fountain in the desert. It appears early, in *The Giaour* for example, when the narrator describes the courtyard of Hassan's palace. There the domestic scene is presided over by Hassan's mother, who waits for the return of her son from the hostile desert world he rules. In the personal desert Byron discovered in 1816, the fountain recollects the 'home' from which he has been exiled. Once again its presiding spirit is a woman—in this case, Byron's sister.

> In the desert a fountain is springing,
> In the wide waste there still is a tree,
> And a bird in the solitude singing,
> Which speaks to my spirit of *thee*.
> ('Stanzas to [Augusta]', 45–8)

As in the 'Stanzas for Music', Byron values this fountain not for the purity of its waters but for their troth. He turns to Augusta because she is his kindred in every sense—a fallen soul who has felt the 'joy' and 'bitterness' of a shared 'passion' ('Stanzas for Music'—'I speak not—I trace not—I breathe not thy name') and who can share as well the knowledge of their situation. Byron's myth of their relationship is that he can speak to her with entire candour, that truth and faith ('troth') mark their relationship. Like the clear sky of the Swiss Alps, Augusta and Byron face each other 'without a mask' ('[Epistle to Augusta]', 85). In this relation she appears as the antithesis of Byron's wife, whom he projects as a mask of perfection, and hence as an emblem of illusions and self-deceptions (his illusions, and perhaps her own as well).

I have explicated this familiar Byronic mythos because it recollects an important cultural context within which his verse is operating. In seeking a kindred or tutelary spirit for his famous despair, he invariably turns to female figures—or to feminized male figures disguised with female names. The implicit argument in Byronic elegy is that his acquaintance with grief comes not from a man but from a woman of sorrows—indeed, comes from woman as the model of sorrow and suffering. Byron's greatest declaration of this view comes in Canto I of *Don Juan*,

when Julia plays Diotima to Juan's Socrates in her letter of
farewell.

Indurated Byronic sorrow signifies a loss from which there is
no redemption. The traditional figure for such a loss is Satan, to
whom, of course, Byron will turn often enough. But the contemporary equivalent of Satan, in Byron's imagination, is an arch-
angel fallen not through an excess of knowledge but through an
excess of love. To Byron such a figure is a woman—more
particularly, any woman who acquires human lineaments by
discovering (to herself and to the world alike) her imperfection,
as well as the (ironically virtuous) source of that imperfectness:
love (more especially, erotic love). When the Corsair leaves a
name 'linked with one virtue, and a thousand crimes'
(*The Corsair* III.695–6), he fulfils a mythic structure whose
prototype Byron clearly imagines to be feminine. As Julia tells
Juan, while the disasters suffered by men may be mitigated
by various resources, women are (as it were fatally) determined simply 'To love again, and be again undone' (*Don
Juan* I, st. 194). In a fallen world, love is not wisdom, it is
catastrophe.

Byron's imagination therefore sees woman as a figure of exquisite contradiction: at once emblem of perfection and byword
of faithlessness. This mythos of Woman gets established very
early—in *The Giaour*, for example, it is already completely
elaborated. In accepting the total structure of this ideological
formation, Byron discovers the model of his own despair. For
according to this myth, 'the woman once fallen forever must
fall' ('[To Lady Caroline Lamb]', 14), like Satan hurled from
heaven. In Byron's rendering, a cosmic myth yields up its social
ground: no woman can ever recover her reputation once it has
been lost. With that loss she henceforth stands beyond redemption. Entering this mythos, however, Byron discovers a new
(other)world where the rhythms of redemption no longer function. It is a region of perfect loss, a place where one may see that
'not in vain/ Even for its own sake do we purchase pain'
('[Epistle to Augusta]', 40): where one may see not necessarily
why, but certainly *that*.

This Byronic reading of women's cultural experience has its
immediate source, I believe, in eighteenth-century elegy. As the
case of Byron suggests, many of the most impressive practitioners of such writing were in fact women—writers like

Charlotte Smith and Mary Robinson. The latter's collection of sonnets *Sappho and Phaon* (1796) is important not merely for some of its excellent poems, but also because it clearly defines an elegiac tradition (sapphic) that veers from the more traditional and well-known line. Smith's work is interesting, on the other hand, just because she doesn't write out of the (bisexual) erotic myth that will prove so fruitful for so many women poets for the next two centuries. In the historical framework of English romanticism, Smith is to Robinson as Hemans will be to Landon.

The peculiar force of Smith's *Elegiac Sonnets* (first published in 1784) comes from the fact that they are *not* elegies for some particular person or persons. *Lacrymae rerum*, they meditate a general condition. Smith then deepens the gloom by arguing, as Plath would do much later, that poets serve a savage god. The opening sonnet of Smith's popular and influential book brings a cool report on the visible darknesses of a poetical vocation. It is no comfort that 'The partial Muse' has 'smil'd' on her chosen ones ('sonnet I', lines 1–2). Poetry brings the consciousness of suffering, and the sympathy that follows only exacerbates the situation:

> For still she bids soft Pity's melting eye
>   Stream o'er the ills she knows not to remove,
> Points every pang, and deepens every sigh . . .
>   (9–11)

As so often in Smith's verse, wordplay generates corrosive ironies: 'knows not to remove' suggests both 'knows better than to remove' and 'knows not how to remove'. So a knowledge comes through this poetry that is worse, in its way, than no knowledge at all, since it is (in Manfred's words) 'the knowledge of its own desert' (*Manfred* III.4.136). A dismal conclusion is foregone:

> Ah! then, how dear the Muse's favors cost,
>   *If those paint sorrow best—who feel it most!*

Echoing *Eloisa to Abelard* (366), the final line introduces a disturbing possibility into Pope's argument that 'well sung woes shall soothe' the suffering soul. What if it were otherwise, what if poets must be 'cradled into poetry by wrong', as Shelley's Maddalo (i.e., Byron) will soon argue ('Julian and Maddalo',

545)? Smith's verse is all the stronger, all the more disturbing, for its hypothetical rhetoric. The poem ends with no clear resort—not even the resort of those desperate last stands that Byron would shortly make famous.

The *Elegiac Sonnets* relentlessly pursue that dreary vision. Near the conclusion of the sequence, for example, Smith continues to discover new ways to fail. When she re-dedicates herself to 'Fancy' in sonnet 47, she has no illusions about the machinery of illusion:

> Thro' thy false medium then, no longer view'd,
> May fancied pain and fancied pleasure fly,
> And I, as from me all thy dreams depart,
> Be to my wayward destiny subdu'd;
> Nor seek perfection with a poet's eye,
> Nor suffer anguish with a poet's heart.

Uncannily adept at subtle wordplay—which is why she makes such good sonnets—Smith rebuilds the labyrinth she 'knows not to remove'. The key words are 'Thro'' and 'fly': the former carrying both a spatial and a causal/intellectual sense, the latter meaning both 'flee' and 'move through' or 'hover in'. Depending on how one takes those words, the sestet manages to find itself lost on both sides, that is, lost whether Smith, like Sappho, practises poetry or abandons it. A generation later, when Keats stumbled into this same 'purgatory blind', he wrote the 'Ode to a Nightingale' and dramatized the pathos of his disillusion. Beginning where Keats left off, Smith dramatizes the perfection of hers.

There is no doubt that Byron followed Smith's sentimental tradition, rather than Wordsworth's romantic one, when he began to explore his waste places. But neither is there any doubt that he raised her dark measures to a spectacular level—briefly, that he made them romantic. If the gloom of the forever failing and falling woman provides the model for Byron's satanism, he charges the model with grandeur. Sentimentalism turns meteoric in his hands:

> The hour arrived—and it became
> A wandering mass of shapeless flame,
> A pathless comet, and a curse,
> The menace of the universe;

> Still rolling on with innate force,
> Without a sphere, without a course,
> A bright deformity on high,
> The monster of the upper sky!
> *(Manfred* I.1.116–24)

This is the figure Byron and his poetry made. Again and again he seems struggling to break wholly free from his sentimental sufferings—ultimately, to break wholly free from the doomed poetry that expresses and discovers those sufferings. Starry fables repeatedly call to him as promises of resurrection and better rewards:

> Ye stars, which are the poetry of heaven . . .
> That fortune, fame, power, life, have named themselves a star.
> The starry fable of the milky way . . .
> She saw her glories star by star expire . . .
> *(Childe Harold* III, st. 88; IV, sts. 151, 80)

Figures all of an ultimate perfection, they stand for a sentimental ideal, as we see quite clearly in the famous stanza 14 of *Beppo*:

> One of those forms which flit by us, when we
>   Are young, and fix our eyes on every face;
> And oh! the loveliness at times we see
>   In momentary gliding, the soft grace,
> The youth, the bloom, the beauty which agree,
>   In many a nameless being we retrace,
> Whose course and home we knew not, nor shall know,
> Like the lost Pleiad seen no more below.

Here the thought is strictly sentimental: to make feeling, and in particular human love, the ground of an experience of perfection: to 'Blend a celestial with a human heart' (*Childe Harold* IV, st. 119). Numa and Egeria, Venus and Anchises, Manfred and Astarte: all consummate in 'the lost Pleiad', who suffered her eclipse from the starry heavens because she fell in love with a mortal man. But if the thought is sentimental, the attitude in the poem is romantic throughout. The whole point of *Beppo* is to rewrite and redeem the disaster threatened by Byron's own imagination. In *Beppo* romantic irony comes to the rescue, much as the spot of time would come in Wordsworth's poetry.

How different is the road taken by Felicia Hemans in 'The Lost Pleiad', whose memory fixates on loss and whose ironies do not flaunt or celebrate themselves. That the poem has been so long forgotten turns it to an index of its own key thoughts, and of the sentimental tradition it so splendidly represents. The point and force of the work depend upon its sympathetic recovery of the Byronic inheritance announced in the title.[4] And the date of the poem is crucial. Though she wrote it the year before he died, in 1823, its initial book publication came a year later, in 1825. That is to say, the poem's association with Byron's death was established very early. In fact, however, the poem isn't an elegy for his death but an elegiac meditation on the meaning of his life, and specifically on the diminishment his fame underwent in the last few years of his life. As such the poem is, like *Adonais* and the *Elegiac Sonnets*, a poem about the poetry of loss.

The historical context of the poem—the realities that feed lines like 'Though thou art exil'd thence' (8)—is the period from 1816, the year Byron left his homeland in a cloud of scandal, never to return. His own poetry of 1816–24 made much of his exilic situation, and Hemans—whose work's thematic centre is the ideology of home and country—strongly sympathized with Byron's imagination, as this poem among many others clearly demonstrates.[5] 'The Lost Pleiad' focusses specifically on another known feature of those years—the gradual decline in England of Byron's immense fame as a poet and cultural icon.[6]

---

[4] My reading differs slightly, I think, from one intimated to me by Nan Sweet, in a correspondence we have had. Sweet emphasizes both Shelley and Byron as important presences in the poem. I am grateful to her for sharing her knowledge of the poem with me, and in particular for important facts about its publication history. See also Sweet's essay 'History, Imperialism, and the Aesthetics of the Beautiful: Hemans and the Post-Napoleonic Moment', in *At the Limits of Romanticism: Essays in Cultural, Feminist, and Materialist Criticism*, eds. Mary A. Favret and Nicola J. Watson (Bloomington and Indianapolis: Indiana University Press, 1994), 170–84.

[5] See Tricia Lootens, 'Hemans and Home: Victorianism, Feminine "Internal Enemies," and the Domestication of National Identity', *PMLA* 109/2 (Mar. 1994), 238–53.

[6] The decline in Byron's reputation was explicitly commented upon at the time, and Byron himself was quite aware of it, as many scholars have noted. See for example Samuel C. Chew's *Byron in England* (London: John Murray, 1924): 'The Anti-Byronism that so quickly overtook the poet's posthumous reknown is here [in

Perhaps the most arresting feature of the poem is the ease with which Hemans genders her textual signs female. The move is all the more notable because the subject is Byron, whose symbolic status could not be more erotic or more male (whether in a homo- or a heterosexual frame of reference). In this poem the world, including the universe of poetry, is unequivocally feminine. The importance of Hemans' approach has nothing to do with sexual issues but everything to do with cultural ideals of poetry and art. From the opening stanza the subjects are fame and poetry:

> And is there glory from the heavens departed?
> —Oh! void unmark'd!—thy sisters of the sky
>   Still hold their place on high,
> Though from its rank thine orb so long hath started,
> Thou, that no more art seen of mortal eye.

Conflating 'the lost Pleiad' Merope with the exiled poet Byron, Hemans establishes poetical terms for an inquiry into the relation of poetry and the world. In this respect the poem distinctly anticipates Tennyson's 'The Lady of Shalott', although its view of the relation is more Byronic than Tennysonian—more bleak than oblique.[7]

In the centre of the poem (stanzas 2–4), Hemans seems to fix her gaze on the stellar universe to ponder obsessively one simple but terrible fact: that the loss of the Pleiad appears to make no difference whatsoever to the order of the stars or to their watchers. The night still 'wears her crown of old magnificence' (7), mariners still chart their voyages by the Pleiades, all 'the starry myriads burning' (11) continue in their courses: 'Unchang'd they rise, they have not mourn'd for thee' (15). Hemans is careful to preserve the Byronic character of this situation—for example, in lines like these:

1823] definitely beginning in his lifetime' (117). See also Herman M. Ward, *Byron and the Magazines, 1806–1824*, Salzburg Studies in English Literature: Romantic Reassessment 19 (Salzburg: Universität Salzburg, 1973), esp. ch. 5.

[7] In a letter to me Anne Mellor suggests that one ought to read 'Byron' as Merope's beloved, Cyrus, with the implication that Merope is Hemans' self-projection. And of course that structure of reading is also operating in the text. My point is that Hemans' identification with Merope comes 'through' a mythic structure that has been gendered from the outset in masculinist terms, and that she understands that structure and exploits it in her poem.

No desert seems to part those urns of light,
'Midst the far depth of purple gloom intense.
(9–10)

Byron's poetry had fairly mapped, for the romantic age, the
psychic territory of the desert, and of course he had become, like
his famous heroes, a byword of 'gloom intense'. Furthermore,
perhaps no living poet had ever acquired a fame like Byron's,
nor does Hemans' poem doubt the splendour of his work.
Indeed, that splendour underscores her new astonishment at his
fall and the disappearance of his glory. Recollecting Act I of
Manfred, where Byron/Manfred is represented as an erratic and
destroyed star, Hemans wonders in stanza 4 how such a figure
could have been 'shaken from thy radiant place' (16).

The eclipse of Byron thus becomes a lesson on a familiar
theme: *sic transit gloria mundi*. That is the moral of the final
stanza.

Why, who shall talk of thrones, of sceptres riven?
—Bow'd be our hearts to think of what *we* are,
    When from its height afar
A world sinks thus—and yon majestic heaven
Shines not the less for that one vanish'd star.
(21–5)

Although in one sense nothing could be more conventional, the
stanza gains a special force by exploiting the female perspective
the poem has adopted from the outset. These lines, Hemans'
entire poem, speak with a double consciousness. Hemans knows
very well that the heaven of poetry, like the world of thrones
and sceptres, is a place (and emblem) of male power. The figure
of Merope stands for Byron, and in this frame of reference—as
in Shelley's *Adonais*—all the signs stand for men. But because
here the sign is resolutely feminized, a fresh set of views work
themselves into the texture of the poem.

So Hemans is able to exploit Byron's notoriety, the scandal of
his erotic life, to underscore the meaning of Merope as yet
another figure of the fallen woman. More important, by placing
her in a context where the central subject is poetic fame, 'the lost
Pleiad' becomes a sign of the poet—including the male poet—as
woman. As Hemans' poem suggests, this feminine light-source
has never *not* been part of the 'starry myriads' even though it

has long been eclipsed, indeed mythically (eternally, ideologically) eclipsed.

We turn briefly to Mary Robinson to clarify what Hemans is insinuating here. Robinson's *Sappho and Phaon* is a crucial work of the period because its central points are so openly declared: that Homer need not be taken as the symbolic origin of western poetry, that another source—Sappho—might be assumed; and furthermore, that Sappho's fate, her eclipsed glory, should be read literally—as a betrayal (in every sense). Betrayed by love (the gods, Aphrodite), by her own passion, and finally by her male lover Phaon, Sappho and her mythic history become in Robinson's verse a modern myth of women's cultural inheritance.

From 1780 or so that myth becomes widespread in women's writing. The most modest and retiring of poets, Hemans writes out of its cultural perspective. But 'The Lost Pleiad' shows how the sapphic myth need not be treated with the kind of passionate extravagance that Robinson cultivated in her verse. The strength of Hemans' poem lies in its reserve. Recalling the cool indifference of Byron's aggressively measured lyrics, Hemans softens Byron's edges. Indeed, she explicitly displaces that coldness to the realm of the 'starry myriads', the familiar heavens of poetic tradition. In this sense Merope's is a fortunate fall since it removes her from that imaginative universe. Hemans' poem thereby fashions an alternative (feminine) aesthetic out of what now comes before us as an illusive spectacle of art. Her poem gives its allegiance to a sympathetic consciousness that is deliberately eclipsed when art commits itself to fame.

In this respect 'The Lost Pleiad' is a reading of Byron— literally, a *sympathetic* reading, one that points to what she takes to be its true genius and lost soul. Furthermore, in so far as Byron appears in her poem as the very symbol and index of 'the poetical', the reading amounts to a reading of the entire tradition of poetry as it descends to her age. What she comes to argue is no more and no less than this: 'he who would save his life must lose it'. Nursed in a long and deep experience of loss, 'The Lost Pleiad' proposes an aesthetic of absolute contradiction. Canonized saints inhabit the heavens of poetry, by which the world sets its course and measures magnificence. Those are the saints of culture, the figures known through great traditions.

To Hemans' view, however, there is another world 'no more seen . . . of mortal eye'. It is a world of absolute loss whose motto, in no Dantescan sense, is simply: *lasciate ogni speranza.* Hemans writes that sign not above the entrance to hell, but over this world, its culture, its poetry.

POETRY AS FAILURE: L.E.L.

Hemans' poetry lives and moves and has its being under that dark sign. In her work, as in Charlotte Smith's, poetic failure ceases to be simply an available subject or theme to be addressed; it becomes a textual event, a new foundational feature of imaginative work. Our customary framework for understanding this mordant turn in the history of poetry has been the emergence of enlightenment and the authority of science, which appeared to announce the supercession of poetry as a norm of culture. In that context, poets and their defenders were soon drawn into various rearguard actions, skirmishing to maintain whatever shreds of authority they could. Hemans' imagination of disaster, however, like the Russians before Napoleon, simply abandons all those traditional positions in order to follow the central insight of the sapphic myth of poetry as that myth gets developed through the emergent history of women's sentimental writing. The myth—a historical construction of the eighteenth century—is simple, eloquent, impossible: poetry is the discourse of failure. That is to say, it is the only discourse to preserve the theoretical power of absolute truth-telling. Through this poetry we become citizens of a scandalized world ('which is the world/ Of all of us': *The Prelude* [1850] XI.142–3): a kingdom divided against itself, a house built on sand.

It is no wonder, then, that high modernism set a face of flint against such endeavours. Thrones, principalities, powers, and dominions, religious as well as secular, build myths of perdurance and enlist figures of imagination to shore up their ruins and fragments. Sentimental writing tends to flee such projects, including—perhaps especially including—the projects that are most dear to itself. Hemans' work may be fairly defined in precisely those terms: witness, for example, a poem like 'The Homes of England'.

Landon's poetry executes the sapphic programme even more clearly. This happens for two principal reasons, I think. First, her predominant subject is erotic love. Second, she foregrounds the commercial context of poetry and art. Much more traditional in this respect, Hemans displaces the latter subject into the discourse of fame, as one sees in a poem like 'The Lost Pleiad'. By contrast, Landon's poetry rarely forgets the Distinction now being critically re-explored by Pierre Bourdieu:[8] the symbiotic relation of cultural fame and marketing, poetic creation and the social production of texts. From that vision comes a peculiar and telling erosion of the romantic 'I' and its historical substrate, the integral self.[9]

Like Smith and Hemans, Landon's writing is always tied to financial needs. If it is too much to say that all three 'wrote for money', they all did need the money that their writing produced and they measured their work in such terms. As with Hemans, Landon's success—both literary and financial—was greatest when she wrote for the gift books and annuals, which paid considerable sums for original work. These books emerged in the early twenties and they came to dominate the Victorian poetical scene. Like the three-decker novel, the gift book constitutes a kind of genre in itself. Landon's poetical career culminated in the mid-1830s, when she became a dominant presence in these publications.

One must understand the character of such books in order to appreciate their distinctive poetry. The books were primarily organized around their visual materials, in particular around the engravings they printed (sometimes original, sometimes from paintings or drawings). Texts, both prose and verse, were written in relation to the pictures rather than (as in illustrated

---

[8] Bourdieu's project has been elaborated through a whole series of books and essays; see in particular his decisive *Distinction: A Social Critique of the Judgement of Taste*, trans. Richard Nice (Cambridge: Harvard University Press, 1984).

[9] For useful discussions of Landon in this general frame of reference, see Anne Mellor (ed.), *Romanticism and Feminism* (Bloomington: Indiana University Press, 1988), 110–23; Glennis Stephenson's essay 'Poet Construction: Mrs Hemans, L.E.L., and the Image of the Nineteenth-Century Woman Poet', in Shirley Neuman and G. Stephenson (eds.), *Reimagining Women* (Toronto: University of Toronto Press, 1993), 61–73. See also Sonia Hofkosh's 'Disfiguring Economies: Mary Shelley's Short Stories', in Audrey Fisch, Anne Mellor, and Esther Schor (eds.), *The Other Mary Shelley* (New York: Oxford University Press, 1993), esp. 204–8, for a good succinct treatment of the aesthetic economies of the Gift Book.

editions of Scott or Dickens) the other way round. Furthermore—and this is crucial—the poets were not free to select their
pictorial subject; the volume editor would assemble the desired
engravings and then ask the writer to produce something on the
subject.

Landon addresses this situation directly in her 'Introduction'
to the 1832 volume of *Fisher's Drawing Room Scrap-Book*,
which she edited and for which she wrote all but two of the
volume's 'Poetical Illustrations'.

It is not an easy thing to write [poetical] illustrations to prints,
selected rather for their pictorial excellence than their poetic capabili-
ties; and mere description is certainly not the most popular species
of composition. I have endeavoured to give as much variety as
possible, by the selection of any legend, train of reflection, &c. which
the subject could possibly suggest; and, with the same view, have
inserted two poems marked 'C,' for which I am indebted to a friend.

(p. [i])

Early in her career Landon wrote a number of 'poems for
pictures', but in those cases she could choose her own subjects.
Here the situation is very different. The arbitrariness of the
subject all but necessitates the emergence of a peculiar type of
picture-poem: a free textual variation upon the pictorial subject,
a poem that might spring from almost any element connected
with the picture. The best poems of this kind exploit their own
disjunctures and arbitrariness. The 1832 *Fisher's* volume has a
nice example of the type in Landon's 'Skeleton Group in the
Rameswur, Caves of Ellora'. The poem takes its title directly
from the picture it 'illustrates'. The work is self-described as 'a
paraphrase of a translation from the Siva-Pooraun' (32), the
translation having originally appeared in the official journal of
the Asiatick Society, the *Asiatick Researches*, which Landon
could have known from any number of its numerous printings.[10]
In point of fact, Landon's poem and its occasioning picture are

---

[10] The long prose note accompanying the poem indicates Landon's dependence on
the publication of the Asiatick Society, *Asiatick Researches*, which began in 1789
and went through twenty volumes during the next fifty years. Landon was also
working with the *Memoirs* of the celebrated orientalist Thomas Maurice (published
in 2 vols. in 1819–20). She may have consulted as well John Benjamin Seely's *The
Wonders of Elora* (1824). Selections from the *Asiatick Researches* were published
frequently into the 1830s.

hardly related at all, other than through the connection Landon
arbitrarily solicits in the 1832 volume of *Fisher's*. If Landon's
poem treats the marriage of Siva and Parvati, as she acknowledges, that subject is only adventitiously related to the Skeleton
Group, which treats a completely different subject. (Another
wall of the Rameswur cave, unrelated to the Skeleton Group
wall, has carvings that represent Siva and Parvati, though not
their marriage.)

The Caves of Ellora were a favourite tourist attraction for the
English in India. Much was written about them, and Landon's
poem counts upon her reader's general acquaintance with the
celebrated caves, and with the Indian art and mythology they
embodied. Even the most ignorant would therefore notice the
odd and disturbing disjunction between the events elaborated in
the poem and the scene rendered in the picture. Here is fulfilled
Landon's promise of a 'selection of any legend . . . which the
subject could possibly suggest', and the consequence is a work
whose 'opposite and discordant qualities' are effectively unbalanced and unreconciled. The final work is therefore extremely
disorienting, even a touch surreal. (One might perhaps recall a
reversed type of disjunction that characterizes 'The Tyger' as
Blake decided to engrave it.) What needs to be emphasized are
the institutional (and ultimately economic) factors that work to
produce the odd and even shocking effect in a poem like this
one. Equally important is the awareness that Landon herself has
of the social terms in which her writing is executed. The superb
'Lines of Life' calculates its own pursuit of a zero-degree of
writing:

> I live among the cold, the false,
>   And I must seem like them;
> And such I am, for I am false
>   As those I most condemn.
>   (9–12)

Making this statement an emblem of itself, the poem devours its
cultural patrimony—in this case, its immediate romantic inheritance, which it seeks to capitalize in the long withdrawing drift of
its second part (lines 49–108). Brilliantly horrific, the sequence
drags the reluctant reader through a catalogue of poetic debase-
ments—a set of psycho-cultural clichés drawn out beyond any

possibility of endurance. When Landon at last brings her cruel (and self-lacerating) poem to a halt, the romantic poet-prophet is not a Homeric figure recalling greatness, she is Cassandra foretelling disaster:

> Let music make less terrible
> The silence of the dead;
> I care not, so my spirit last
> Long after life has fled.
>
> (105–8)

The point is, of course, that 'culture' and 'civilization' do not want such a 'spirit' to live on, it is too pitiless, too intransigent, too sapphic.

Such writing does not offer any hope at all, it can only pray darkly on its own behalf ('Let music make less terrible/ The silence of the dead'). It is fundamentally a poetry of and as failure, its silent and deathly music being an imitation of the ways of life it shares.

Drawing that equivalence between itself and its world became a major preoccupation of Landon's work. It appears explicitly in many of her poems—for example, in a piece she wrote for the 1829 *Keepsake*:[11] the untitled lines written after Landseer's portrait of *Georgiana, the Duchess of Bedford* ('Lady, thy face is very beautiful'). The central theme of this work is what the poem itself calls 'vague imagination' (21). The phrase—at once threadbare and self-conscious—is tellingly chosen to rust

---

[11] This is the volume of the *Keepsake* in which Wordsworth, Coleridge, Southey, and Moore, among other notables, were induced to publish by its editor (and friend of Wordsworth), Frederick Mansel Reynolds. Peter Manning's essay on Wordsworth's involvement with the 1829 volume is thorough and important, showing as it does the sharp difference between Landon's and Wordsworth's involvement in the book (see 'Wordsworth in the *Keepsake*, 1829', in *Literature in the Marketplace*, ed. John O. Jordan and Robert L. Patten (Cambridge: Cambridge University Press, 1995), 44–73). Whereas Landon's work is thoroughly integrated into the conventions of the annual, Wordsworth's is not—indeed, he had to be coaxed to participate (although he did so, like everyone else, for clear commercial motives). Unlike Landon, however, Wordsworth could not make the 'degradation and reward' of his work a thematic part of his writing. But this is exactly what Landon does. The aftermath of his involvement left Wordsworth with a sense that he had done something sordid by letting his work appear in the pages of the *Keepsake*. Interestingly, I think Coleridge's contributions to the annual are much more integrated to its conventions—especially that strange and neglected piece 'The Garden of Boccaccio', which Coleridge wrote to 'illustrate' an engraving given him by Reynolds.

through that bright new machine invented to turn out the pure products of romanticism.

As with so much of Landon's best writing, this work unfolds a kind of antipoem. The work self-consciously exploits its own factitiousness. Much could be said about its mannered poeticality, the work's false elegancies that startle and disturb the reader from the outset—as the word 'very' in the first line emphasizes. Here it is sufficient to see, and to say, that the poem properly exists in the closest kind of relation to the original picture, as Landon's socio-economic treatment of her subject emphasizes. Furthermore, in this case art's relation to the economics of class, so central to Landseer's painting, receives a full bourgeois reinscription.

The textual situation is subtle and complex. Proceeding from the semantic wordplay in line 19 ('But thou art of the Present'), we can observe the relationship that this work is fashioning, in every sense, between text and picture. For instance, at the semantic level the poem simultaneously reflects upon its nominal subject, the Duchess, and addresses its real subject, the 'art of the Present'.[12] For Landon's poem is not written on the duchess or the painting so much as on the relation of the two. In this case the relation is signalled through two correlative forms: on one hand Landon's own verses, and on the other the visible language in which her poetry gets articulated—*The Keepsake* and its (reproduced) engraving.

Here one wants to recall the fact that Landseer's fame as an artist was largely secured through engravings that broadcast his work rather than through his original oils. The 'Georgiana, the Duchess of Bedford' is 'of the Present' in several senses, all of which are important to Landon. But most important are the contemporary artistic representations of the Duchess— the painting, the engraving, and now Landon's poem, the last two being framed and represented in *The Keepsake for MDCCCXXIX*, which is how the title page reads. Signifiers of Beauty, each comes forward here in a self-conscious, perhaps even a shameless, state of artistic exhaustion. Completely inte-

---

[12] That kind of cross-grammatical aural wordplay is quite common in Landon's work. The most dramatic example, I suppose, is her characteristic triple pun 'eye/I/ aye', which recurs in her verse (see e.g. 'A Child Screening a Dove from a Hawk').

grated, the engraving, the poem, and the book correspond to what Marx would shortly explore as 'the commodity form', that is, value abstracted into a fetishized condition.[13] In Landon, the exponent of that structure of illusions is the work of art, which her poetry works to demystify.

In contrast to Marx, however, for whom critical analysis is a form of intellectual mastery, Landon demystifies through a process of sympathetic identification. As a rule, romantic writing tries to resist or escape the (shameful) condition that Landon's poem solicits. Wordsworth's reluctant and finally repudiated engagement with the same volume of *The Keepsake* measures a crucial difference between two otherwise closely related styles of poetry.[14] It equally measures the differential that romanticism sought to establish between itself and its feeding source, the discourse of sensibility and sentiment. Landon returns to that source via her immediate romantic inheritance. But her writing makes no effort to transcend its commercial circumstances. On the contrary, it becomes what it beholds, mortifying itself through its sympathetic involvement. Romanticism's faith in beauty and art—imagination as a means of grace—gets recovered by a paradoxical move. Through her writing romantic poetry regains authenticity by a profoundly sentimental act. Identifying itself as a commodified form, her poetry forecloses that final (romantic) illusion of art: that it lives in a world elsewhere.

DOOMED WRITING

Sentimental writing begins as a self-conscious appropriation of the wisdom of the body, the knowledge that comes through sympathetic understanding. It articulates 'the true voice of feeling'. Recall the differences between sentimental and romantic traditions of love poetry and their *stil novisti* and petrarchan precursors. The latter pursue a poetry of vision, an art tied to this world through an intimate relation with the highest and

---

[13] See the first volume of *Capital*, chs. 1–3, and esp. ch. 1 section 3, parts C and D, and section 4.
[14] See above, note 11.

most spiritual of the senses (or so it was believed). Love is a
vision of the beautiful. In sentimental writing, by contrast, the
emblem of love is the kiss, where the authority of feeling and the
lowest order of the senses asserts itself.

The real significance of poems like Charlotte Dacre's 'The
Kiss' lies in its literally senti-mental character. The poem turns
kissing to a philosophical event. From the 1780s the Paolo and
Francesca episode comes to obsess the poets exactly because of
the ethical and philosophical questions raised by the story and
its images. In the *Commedia* the pilgrim Dante collapses in
sympathy for the damned lovers, but the poet Dante means us to
see that such sympathy involves a failure of vision and understanding. Indeed, it is a sympathy that fails precisely because it
operates at the same level as the lovers' kiss, which sealed their
damnation. God's sympathy and love are more surely founded,
just as His view of these acts is different from the untutored
pilgrim's view. The *Commedia* is Dante's way of seeking to
approach that higher view.

How different are the ways of sentimental and romantic
poets. Not that they fail to grasp the ethical problems involved;
but the lovers' kiss now operates through a tradition complicated by the arguments and experiences of Rousseau, of
Sterne, of Goethe. Once again we encounter a failure of love,
only in this situation the failure is not a spiritual falling-off.
Now, in a wholly secular sense, 'the spirit is willing, but the flesh
is weak':

> For the sword outwears its sheath,
>   And the soul wears out the breast,
> And the heart must pause to breathe,
>   And love itself have rest.
>   (Byron, 'So We'll Go No More A-roving', 4–8)

In this famous passage the word 'soul' stands closer to our late
twentieth-century meaning than to Dante's. It is a meaning
Byron appropriated from writers like Smith and Robinson.

In sentimental writing sympathy is both of and with the body.
The *Songs of Innocence* take Jesus as a model of love just
because he appears so mortal and even helpless—in the figures
Blake took from sentimentalism itself, like a child or a woman.
Much romantic verse will seek to reimagine this fragility as

triumphant strength—witness *Prometheus Unbound*. What I am pointing to here, however, is a contrary spirit altogether, one committed to disempowerment, to the order of the losers and the death-devoted.

This way of writing finds poetry an inevitable resort from the grand illusions entered through enlightenment and science. In this respect it is a poetical theory and practice firmly located in history—indeed, its theory and practice make historicality, with all its non-transcendental features, a defining quality of the poetical. Romanticism feeds upon this theory, but only to raise up cries of resistance, or to build temples in excremental places. Sentimental poetry, by contrast, brings all of its illusions, including its lost illusions, down to earth.

One encounters this work most surely through the developing line of women's writing, in Great Britain particularly: beyond Hemans and Landon to Christina Rossetti, Charlotte Mew, Veronica Forrest-Thomson. But their names are legion. The continuity of sentimental verse, whether in its secular or its Christian modes, is unmistakable to anyone who has thought about it. One can scarcely *not* see the similarities between a postmodern writer like Forrest-Thomson, for example, and a post-romantic writer like Landon. Forrest-Thomson teases us into thought of these parallels throughout her work: her poem 'Strike', for example (which comes written *'for Bonnie, my first horse'*):

> Hail to thee, blithe horse, bird thou never wert!
> And breaking into a canter, I set off on the long road south
> Which was to take me to so many strange places,
> That room in Cambridge, that room in Cambridge, that room in
>   Cambridge,
> That room in Cambridge, this room in Cambridge . . .[15]

Like Landon, Forrest-Thomson sets out for poetry by going to the proper cultural places. Where Landon went to Byron and the other romantics, this Scots writer 'canters' south to England and university—again like Landon, playing fast and loose with the master language (canting, chanting):

---

[15] Veronica Forrest-Thomson, *Collected Poems and Translations*. Agneau 2 (London, Lewes, Berkeley: Allardyce, Barnett, 1990), 84.

I was on some sort of quest.
There was an I-have-been-here-before kind of feeling about it.
That hateful cripple with the twisted grin. But
Dauntless the slughorn to my ear I set.

The poem travesties the entire British tradition, travesties—like
Landon yet once more—the deadly (so far as poetry is concerned) concept of 'tradition' itself. What remains from such
grim and comical emptyings? Nothing but the poetry and the
human life it signs:

What there is now to celebrate:
The only art where failure is reknowned.

16

Literary History, Romanticism, and Felicia Hemans

A Conversation between A. Mack, J. J. Rome, and G. Mannejc

AM. How agreeably 'historical' we've all become these days. But has criticism 'returned to history' only to discover its ruins? Traditional historicism was difficult enough with 'all those proper names and dates' beneath which 'the contemporary mind staggers'.[1] These new historicisms are worse. The older forms at least prized thoroughness and coherence. But a generation of fierce scepticism has brought historicism, like the rest of literary studies, to scenes of fragmentation— Lovejoy's splendid project turned into the *disintegration* of romanticisms.

JJR. So we are in a crisis? How romantic! How opportune!

    Effort, and expectation, and desire,
    And something evermore about to be.[2]

GM. 'Endless play', in other words?

JJR. Georg, read some Oscar Wilde for a change. One needs critical distance to think clearly. Don't you think so, Anne? I mean, if you're interested in exploring the historical shape of romanticism in England, it won't help very much to approach the problem in a romantic attitude. Wasn't it Blake who said you become what you behold? Assume a crisis and you'll get one.

AM. But a crisis does exist. The traditional picture of the Romantic Period has been smashed beyond recognition.

JJR. So what if it has. Let a thousand flowers bloom. Besides, this splintering may have been a fortunate fall, leaving the

---

[1] See Geoffrey Hartman, 'The Culture of Criticism', *PMLA* 99 (May 1984), 371-2.

[2] Quoting Wordsworth's *Prelude* VI.607-8.

world all before us. 'The prospects for a coherent and all-encompassing history of literature . . . depend on a new politics of knowledge taking the place of the old belligerence of ideologies. Literary historians and critics must be willing to discover the limits as well as the power of their methods and must be open to the possibility of new linkages between their accounts of the literary past and the accounts of others.'[3]

'There are no master narratives', right? only stories told at different times, for different purposes. The most traditional story of English romanticism centres in *Lyrical Ballads*—that is to say, in a book published after the English reaction to the French Revolution had established itself. But suppose one were to emphasize the importance of a project like *The Florence Miscellany* (1785)? What a different picture of English romanticism emerges from that vantage.

AM. Suppose that, suppose whatever you like! I suppose anyone could suppose anything!

JJR. It's not an arbitrary choice, after all, just an unfamiliar one. Because we've forgotten some of our history. *The Florence Miscellany* launched a decisive and influential early form of romantic writing. The importance of the Della Cruscans is partly measured by the amount of hostility they drew from conservative circles, and partly by the impact of their work on later romantic writing. Keats is probably the greatest product of the movement, the supreme example of its stylistic inertias.

GM. A charmingly outrageous view that I can't believe you mean seriously. And among its greatest charms is the way it might draw our attention away from your agreeably pluralist ideas about literary history. Your Keats remark exposes the poverty of what you're saying. To construct a literary history—any literary history, even a revisionist one like yours—one must torture poetry with gross instruments of scholarly rationalization. Among the worst of these are the periodic structures that march one through an historical bureaucracy of culture. No true poem will abide the questions that are raised by structures of periodization. Trash will abide such

---

[3] Rome is quoting Walter L. Reed's concluding 'Commentary' in the special issue of *New Literary History* devoted to the topic 'On Writing Histories of Literature', 16 (spring 1985), 678.

questions—that is to say, writing like Della Cruscan verse—
but poetry will not. Keats will not.

AM. So we should abandon periodic categories altogether? Is
Keats not properly a Romantic poet? Are the historical conventions of Romanticism not apparent in his works?

GM. Those are just the kinds of question that literary history
wants one to ask, but they are completely *mis*leading questions—*so far as the work of poetry is concerned*. For 'Romanticism' as the term has come to be defined is nothing but an
abstraction covering—I should even say *creating*—a multi-
tude of critical sins. If Keats is a Romantic poet, so is (we all
agree, right?) Byron; and yet the work of each is utterly
different. We have been taught to think of Keats as a great
lyric poet and of Byron as a mediocre one at best. But the
judgement is incompetent because each writes a completely
different kind of lyric. What 'To Autumn' shares in common
with 'Fare Thee Well!'—in terms of stylistic procedures—is
minimal, yet the commonplace evaluative judgement I just
gave is licensed by drawing the two poems into an abstract
and prefabricated comparison.[4]

Or ask yourselves: What are the great *topoi* of Romanticism? Subjectivity, Nature, Imagination, Reflexive Consciousness? Take any of all of those rubrics to different writers, or
even to different works by the same writer, or even to the
same work, and you will end up, if you are reading well, only
with a mass of differences.

JJR. And yet the very existence of modern literary history argues
that it serves the needs of writers and poets. Or are you
arguing that the birth of a modern historical consciousness
signalled the twilight of the gods of poetry?

GM. That common nineteenth-century view still seems relevant.
Poetry entered its Age of Anxiety as much with Wordsworth
and Shelley and Mill—its enthusiasts—as it did with Bentham
and Peacock and Macaulay—its elegists.

JJR. What a paradox lies there! For the renewal of the arts in the
Romantic Movement was closely connected to that new his-

---

[4] For a relevant discussion of Byron's 'Fare Thee Well!' see Jerome J. McGann,
'What Difference Do the Circumstances of Publication Make to the Interpretation of
a Literary Work?', in Roger D. Sell (ed.), *Literary Pragmatics* (Routledge: London
and New York, 1991), 208–24.

torical consciousness. The *philosophes*, the antiquarians, and finally the critical philologists and historians all came to break open the treasure-houses of western and eastern cultures.

GM. You mean 'to invade, plunder, and exploit'. And the rape of the biblical inheritance by the historical imagination is the exemplary tale of what happened. When the Bible began to be read in referential terms, when its truth was enquired after by factive and empirical measures, the texts were utterly alienated from themselves. The historicist reconstruction of the past was largely founded in that scientism of the text we call hermeneutics: the editing and interpreting of a vast corpus of classical, biblical, and national scriptures. The ultimate meaning of this project would not be the revelation or the renewal of the texts; on the contrary, it would rather bring a revelation of the 'truth' of science, the establishment of science *at the ideological level*, as the fundamental myth of modern consciousness.[5]

Of course men like Bodmer, Lowth, Herder, and Wolf all thought that their hermeneutical projects would rescue poetry and even religion from modern rationalism and scepticism. Their faith, however, was already grounded in the myth they were struggling against. Their explications of the texts and cultures of more primitive worlds often seem anything but rationalist or abstract—so filled can they be with minute particulars and 'thick description'. Nevertheless, the details emerge through the re-deployment of the myth of objectivity, and they only function as signs for various conceptual categories (e.g., 'primitive' and 'modern', 'naïve' and 'sentimental', or the more complex historical and structural schemas erected by scholars like Eichhorn and Wolf).[6]

[5] This is very clear, for example, in Herbert Butterfield's account of the rise of modern historical scholarship. See his *Man on his Past: The Study of the History of Historical Scholarship* (Cambridge: Cambridge University Press, 1969), esp. 1–26, 44, 50.

[6] For particular discussions see Emery Neff, *The Poetry of History: The Contribution of Literature and Literary Scholarship to the Writing of History since Voltaire* (New York: Columbia University Press, 1947); Peter Hans Reill, *The German Enlightenment and the Rise of Historicism* (Berkeley and Los Angeles: University of California Press, 1975); Max Wehrli, *Johann Jakob Bodmer und die Geschichte der Literatur* (Frauenfeld: Huber, 1936); *F. A. Wolf: Prolegomena to Homer, 1795*, trans. and ed. Anthony Grafton, Glenn W. Most, and James E. G. Zetzel (Princeton: Princeton University Press, 1985).

This is a cultural world not merely turned upside down, but rent with contradiction. Out of the cooked comes the raw, out of the sentimental appears the naïve. The cool light of the scholars creates a superheated literal scene which their own prose works then replicate: not necessarily in a positive extravagance of style—though some, like Herder, were so inclined—as in texts where restraint and methodical pursuit become negative signs of enormous moment.

The eighteenth-century antiquarians, philologues, and orientalists thus supplied only a fragile second-order life to the ancient cultures and poetries they so loved. This fragility passed over into the poetry of romanticism, which plundered the philological tradition for many of its key theoretical ideas, generic forms, and tropic resources.[7] Indeed, the new philology was itself nothing more—and nothing less—than the orientalist's dream come true, a mechanism for appropriating alien forms of cultural life. The richness of the poetry of Keats, as Arnold was acute to see, was an ominous symptom of aesthetic disease. Is anyone surprised that the consumptive should have become an emblem of romantic imagination? The famous 'pale hectic' is the *figura* of an illusory life, a false image, a death-sign.

AM. Meaning?

GM. I am narrating a cautionary tale.

AM. It sounds like literary history to me.

GM. I'd call it literary anti-history. With the advent of modern philology all the poets, ancient as well as modern, stand in peril of their lives. And in their peril we observe a serious threat to culture at large. Orientalism, like Apartheid, is a fate that will not cease until its fruits, for good and for evil, are uniformly distributed.

AM. Meaning?

GM. That we want not to wind, but to *un*wind, as many stories as we can. This is what literary anti-history might do. The poems must be removed to a world elsewhere, alienated

---

[7] See especially Elinor Shaffer, *'Kubla Khan' and The Fall of Jerusalem* (Cambridge: Cambridge University Press, 1975) and Jerome McGann 'The Ancient Mariner: The Meaning of the Meanings', in *The Beauty of Inflections: Literary Investigations in Historical Method and Theory* (Oxford: Oxford University Press, 1985), 135–72.

from their original homes. Literary anti-history, like the poems themselves, will then tell us equally of origin and of alienation, and of the relations that the two keep with each other.

JJR. Taking that point of reference, what would you say about Roger Lonsdale's recent pair of anthologies of eighteenth-century poetry? Are they models of what literary anti-history might be aspiring towards?

GM. Yes, exactly that. Their very form—which is anti-narrative—shows us that these are anti-histories. Both anthologies urge us to reimagine an historical shape for eighteenth-century poetry.[8] And by foregrounding the poetry (rather than stories about the poetry) these books are committed to imagination, and to acts of critical reimagination. *Literary* history should seek the truth of imagination, not the truth of science and history (thoroughness, accuracy) or the truth of philosophy (theoretical rigour and completion). The truth of the imagination is reimagination.

JJR. Reimagination of what?

GM. The poetry, of course! What else are we concerned with?

JJR. Well, some of us are at least as concerned with *history*. And Lonsdale's anthologies leave all the historical questions to implication. By keeping our attention on the poems, Lonsdale tends to invisibilize the theatre of their eventualities. In the end those anthologies are committed to an 'imagination' that repudiates history for poetry and writing.

I'm not criticizing Lonsdale's work, I'm just suggesting that there are other things to be done—for instance, drawing out what his books leave only to implication. One starts by imagining an impossible object—let us call it 'the origins of English romanticism'. Every historian knows that even the simplest event is meshed in a complex network of relations that no one could hope to unravel. So the quest for 'the origins of English romanticism' is an imaginative and hypothetical journey from the start—a romance-quest which is, in that sense, also a kind of anti-history.

---

[8] See *The New Oxford Book of Eighteenth Century Verse*, chosen and edited by Roger Lonsdale (Oxford: Oxford University Press, 1984); *Eighteenth-Century Women Poets: An Oxford Anthology*, ed. Roger Lonsdale (Oxford: Oxford University Press, 1989).

But then why even bother, one might ask? And the answer is that the quest is undertaken not to discover 'the origins of English romanticism', but to clarify the various ways this imaginary object might be defined and interpreted. To reimagine 'the origins of English romanticism' through a recovery of *The Florence Miscellany* and Della Cruscan poetry in general is, as you were arguing, to suggest a whole new series of related reimaginings. And so the ultimate object of the immediate hypothetical project emerges. We would not only have to read and re-evaluate a considerable body of unfamiliar poetry and cultural materials, we would have to reread and re-evaluate the cultural deposits that have grown so familiar to us—perhaps, indeed, all too familiar. And we would have to reread and reimagine the instruments by which our received books of memory and forgetting were made.

GM. What for, a compendious treatment of the varieties of literary experience? Something like the fifteen-volume Cambridge History of English Literature, where we are given the materials to see (for example) 'the origins of English romanticism' in a variety of possible perspectives? The Cambridge History's encyclopaedic character—its mass of details and scholarly apparatus—undermines its inertia toward coherent explanatory narrative. It is history and anti-history at the same time.

JJR. But its anti-historical potential is too obedient to the (historian's) signs of accuracy and thoroughness. I want a history at once more energetic and imaginative—a history that assumes the past has not yet happened, that it remains to be seen. If a history is to reflect its subject back to us, then the ideal literary history will be a structure of hypothetical worlds.

These will have to be precisely designed. To stay with our possible topic 'the origins of English romanticism', I imagine a critical narrative unwinding from suppositions like this: If we suppose romanticism to be structured on the double helix of the naïve and the sentimental, what is the historical place, in English romanticism, of Burns's *Poems, chiefly in the Scottish Dialect* (1786)? Or of Sir William Jones's poetic reconstructions of Vedic imaginative thought published in the mid-1780s? Or of the Della Cruscans' poetry, Blake's *Songs*, or the *Lyrical Ballads*?

Then one might advance other suppositions altogether. The best history of this kind, to plagiarize Byron, will 'suppose this supposition' itself, exposing the hypothetical character of the historical constructions and thereby encouraging other hypotheses. The point is to reveal what can be and has been supposed, what might be imagined and why. It is to reveal, precisely, not the truth of fact or of reason, but the truth of imagination as it operates in history.

AM. This is madness, or lies in the way to madness. It's worse than Georg's 'literary history as cautionary tale'. He comes in the posture of the critic, warning of the historian's abstractions. But you seem to be arguing for a kind of positive literary anti-history—as if the past were something that could be invented.

JJR. Romanticism, like its many works, *is* an artistic and poetical invention. And because the writers could not stop for death, scholarship came and kindly stopped for them, and escorted them to Beulahland. It is a killing kindness. Scholarship preserves the poetry of the past, but threatens it with a night of the living dead. What I say is, let us reimagine what history can do—at least for those who live by imagination and who carry out its work.

AM. But you can't just *invent* the past according to your desire! History's devotion to accuracy and thoroughness are important exactly because of the limits they set to imagination.

JJR. Exactly, as you say. But what you forget is that the historian's tools are themselves inventions. We have to invent and continually reinvent the limits of imagination, along with the instruments that will define the limits. For we do not desire the unlimited. *Le goût de l'infini* is an emblem for a desire toward new limits, to have the shape of the world redefined. It is a form of desire that is, like all such forms, historically specific. The desire for the infinite is a finite—a human—desire.

GM. This is mere sophistical avoidance of the presence of the past and its eventualities. Of course we are always inventing new ways of seeing; but we don't invent what has been seen, what has been done. These things have an independent existence, and their value to us lies in that independence. If the desire for the infinite is—what did you say?—'an emblem for a desire toward new limits', then a 'stubborn fact' is an emblem of everything that lies beyond desire and imagination. It is not a 'limit of imagination', it is a stumbling block, the unaccountable. There are powers as great as the imagination—forbidding powers that put a limit on the truths we might want to imagine, for example, about John Keats on one hand and Charlotte Dacre on the other.

AM. Such powers exist and their emblems *are* those stubborn, difficult 'facts' you want to celebrate. But they are never 'unaccountable', those facts. We always fit them to our stories, if only by writing them out.

I suggest we look—right now—very closely at a few of those unaccountabilities. For instance: do we know (or remember) that Felicia Hemans was the most published English poet of the nineteenth century? Do we know, or even think we know, what that might mean? Do we remember any of her poems? And if we do, are we so certain that the Victorians' admiration for her work was misguided? What would it mean to reimagine a work like 'The Homes of England', once so celebrated—or are we to reimagine only the rightful inheritance, the works that come to us sanctioned by what is now taken for established authority? The fate of 'The Homes of England' might well serve as a lesson to all literary authorities. Where's the coward that would not dare to fight for such a poem?

THE HOMES OF ENGLAND

> Where's the coward that would not dare
> To fight for such a land?
>
> *Marmion*

The stately Homes of England,
　　How beautiful they stand!
Amidst their tall ancestral trees,
　　O'er all the pleasant land.
The deer across the greensward bound
　　Through shade and sunny gleam,
And the swan glides past them with the sound
　　Of some rejoicing stream.

The merry Homes of England!
　　Around their hearths by night,

What gladsome looks of household love
    Meet, in the ruddy light!
There woman's voice flows forth in song,
    Or childhood's tale is told,
Or lips move tunefully along
    Some glorious page of old.

The blessed Homes of England!
    How softly on their bowers
Is laid the holy quietness
    That breathes from Sabbath-hours!
Solemn, yet sweet, the church-bell's chime
    Floats through their woods at morn;
All other sounds, in that still time,
    Of breeze and leaf are born.

The Cottage Homes of England!
    By thousands on her plains,
They are smiling o'er the silvery brooks,
    And round the hamlet-fanes.
Through glowing orchards forth they peep,
    Each from its nook of leaves,
And fearless there the lowly sleep,
    As the bird beneath their eaves.

The free, fair Homes of England!
    Long, long, in hut and hall,
May hearts of native proof be rear'd
    To guard each hallow'd wall!
And green for ever be the groves,
    And bright the flowery sod,
Where first the child's glad spirit loves
    Its country and its God!

                      (1827)[9]

Hemans recurs to this fantastic scene again and again, in a rich variety of poetical transformations. Speaking of another of those transformations, Kingsley Amis has described Hemans' once equally famous 'The Graves of a Household' as a 'superficially superficial piece'.[10] The phrase is apt in either case, for it calls attention to this poetry's deep involvement in

[9] The poem was first published in 1827 in *Blackwood's Magazine*; Hemans printed it again the following year as the first of the 'Miscellaneous Pieces' in her book *Records of Women, with other poems.*
[10] *The Faber Popular Reciter*, ed. Kingsley Amis (London: Faber, 1978), 15.

the exposition of wealth and power as spectacle, ideology, *superficies*.

GM. Do you seriously mean to offer a troglodyte like Kingsley Amis as a voice of authority?! That spokesman, that *epitome*, of reaction.

AM. All the more reason to listen carefully to what he has to say. As I recall, Trotsky quoted liberally from the Tsar and Tsarina's papers, and from government police reports, when he constructed his *History of the Russian Revolution*. Every word uttered makes a commitment to the truth—even those which are mistaken or duplicitous, even those which are self-deceived. In Amis's case, his very historical backwardness gives him a privileged view of Hemans' poem.

GM. An interesting theory which would allow you to translate any text into anything you might want it to say. But there are no secret subversive meanings in the intense inanity of Hemans' 'The Homes of England', and I hardly think that Amis meant to suggest there were. In any case, Hemans' poem offers no resistance to its own superficialities. The bland verbal surface is the index of the poem's sentimental attachments to its subjects.

AM. Those are the judgements of a mind schooled in twentieth-century critical canons. But perhaps, by invoking them before this poem, you have merely made it impossible to see or read 'The Homes of England', which evidently works through conventions not favoured by classical modernist styles. Pound, Eliot, Yeats, Stevens, Auden: these are the wrong points of departure for an encounter with Hemans.

If we want to read her, we would do better to start from the expectations and conventions of an early postmodern style like that of John Ashbery or—Ashbery's precursor in these matters—Gertrude Stein.

Hemans' poetry covets an undisturbed appearance: 'bland', your word, is a fair description, just as it is a word one sees applied fairly often to Ashbery. Nineteenth-century readers of Hemans repeatedly remark upon this quality in her work when they praise its 'elegance', its 'purity', its 'taste' and 'harmony'. Jeffrey's once famous 1829 review of *Records of Women* and *The Forest Sanctuary* typifies this now forgotten tradition of reading. Hemans' poetry, he says, is regulated and harmonised by the most beautiful taste. It is singularly sweet, elegant, and tender—touching, perhaps, and contemplative, rather than vehement and overpowering; and . . . finished throughout with an exquisite delicacy, and even severity of execution.[11]

With due allowance made for the differences between a romantic and a modern dialect, this passage might easily be applied to the work of Gertrude Stein. The critical terms here all carry a double burden, in that they are addressing at once the aesthetic and the moral qualities of the verse. Jeffrey's commentary shows that he refuses to distinguish the two. In this respect the analysis rhymes with its poetical subject. Not only is there to be no apparent divorce between content and form in this work, that wedding is to be celebrated in an equally intimate relation with moral and spiritual values.

'The very essence of poetry,' Jeffrey observes (sounding not a little like Coleridge), 'consists in the fine perception and vivid expression of that subtle and mysterious Analogy which exists between the physical and the moral world'. Because Jeffrey finds this axiom perfectly illustrated in Hemans' work, he praises its harmony, regularity, and delicacy—the latter (its delicacy) because Hemans has managed not only to execute the Analogy, but to convey its 'subtle and mysterious' character as well. What Jeffrey calls her 'deep moral and pathetic impression'[12]—her elegiac tone, the emotional sign of a condition or experience of inveterate loss—places her work in the centre of the romantic tradition, which Hemans of course consciously appropriates.

GM. She sounds to me like a debased Wordsworth: 'Accomplishment without genius, and amiability without passion' is how I should characterize her writing. She 'expresses with the richest intensity the more superficial and transient elements of Romanticism. She is at the beck and call of whatever is touched with the pathos of the far away, the bygone. . . . Her imagination floats romantically aloof from actuality, but it

---

[11] From the *Edinburgh Review* 50 (1829), reprinted in *Contributions to the Edinburgh Review by Francis Jeffrey* (Boston, 1857), 474.
[12] Ibid. 475.

quite lacks the creative energy of the great Romantics, and her fabrics are neither real substance nor right dreams.'[13]

AM. That is not the Hemans Wordsworth elegized in his famous lines about her:

> Mourn rather for that holy Spirit,
> Sweet as the spring, as ocean deep;
> For Her who, ere her summer faded,
> Has sunk into a breathless sleep.
>
> ('Extempore Effusion Upon the Death of James Hogg', 37–40)

Besides, a work like 'The Homes of England' illustrates the special paradox of a style that seems at once so rich and so empty. The poem is a celebration, but an indirect celebration. A superficial reading will only see it as a piece of sentimental Burkean ideology, a hymn in praise of the values of vertical and horizontal social continuities, and a statement of their perduring strength. But the poem is actually a celebration not of those ideological reference points, but of the images and forms that the ideology requires for its sustenance.

'The Homes of England', that is to say, operates at two interconnected semiological levels: the linguistic level, on one hand, and the level of an iconic semiology of architecture on the other. This is another of Hemans' superficially superficial poems. It is a poem evoking the superficiality of those apparently substantial things (language and architecture), and the substantiality of those apparently intangible things (ideas and moral attitudes).

To say that 'her fabrics are neither real substance nor right dreams' seems to me exactly right, though in my view to say this is also to explain why the work is important rather than why it should be dismissed. Hemans' poetry does not respect the distinction between substance and shadow that is posited in those anomalous Keatsian terms 'real substance' and 'right dreams'. In her poetry what appears as substance is imagined

---

[13] Mannejc is quoting C. H. Hereford's judgement of Hemans set forth in *The Age of Wordsworth* (1897). See *English Poetry and Prose of the Romantic Movement*, ed. George Benjamin Woods (Chicago and New York: Scott Foresman and Co., 1916), 1271.

on the brink of its dissolution, just as what comes as shadow continually refuses to evaporate. This is why she says that she has 'a heart of home, though no home be for it here':[14] like the stately houses reimaged through her poem, Hemans' works understand that they are haunted by death and insubstantialities. And like Tennyson's *Idylls of the King*, her work is a vision of the doom of an order of values which it simultaneously, and paradoxically, celebrates as a solid and ascendant order of things.

Mrs Hemans herself commented on these paradoxical experiences of substantial apparitions and superficial superficialities in one of her notebooks:

Our home!—what images are brought before us by that one word! The meeting of cordial smiles, and the gathering round the evening hearth, and the interchange of thoughts and kindly words, and the glance of eyes to which our hearts lie open as the day;—there is the true 'City of Refuge;'—where are we to turn when it is shut from us or changed? Who ever thought his home could change? And yet those calm, and deep, and still delights, over which the world seems to have no breath of power, they too are like the beautiful summer clouds, tranquil as if fixed to sleep for ever in the pure azure of the skies, yet all the while melting from us, though imperceptibly 'passing away!'[15]

In a letter she commented upon her 'passion for intellectual beauty' as an ambiguous gift and compared it to a 'rainbow, made up of light and tears'. This evaporating imagination, so close to Shelley's, acquires an entirely different character when it is carried out in the tents of prosperity, in the stately homes of England:

I heard a beautiful remark made by the Chief Justice, when I met him at Kilfane. I think it was with regard to some of Canova's beautiful sculpture in the room, that he said—'Is not *perfection always affecting?*' I thought he was quite right; for the highest degree of beauty in art certainly always excites, if not tears, at least the inward feeling of tears.[16]

[14] *Memoir of the Life and Writings of Mrs. Hemans. By her Sister* (Philadelphia, 1839), 188.
[15] *Memoir*, 131.
[16] *Memoir*, 249. The quotations are from a letter of 1829.

Hemans' comments help to explain (and expand) the relation
Jeffrey and others have noticed between the melancholy of her
work and its exquisite surface. Hers is a 'finished' poetry, in
both senses—an imagining of ultimate loss through the presentation of ultimate forms of gain.

No one ever thinks her home can change until she escapes
the imagination of the home's substantiality. In *Brideshead
Revisited* Waugh's hero Charles Ryder loves the 'buildings
that grew silently with the centuries, catching and keeping the
best of each generation'. England once 'abounded' in such
forms of a stable and continuous social fabric, Charles thinks,
but now they seem so fragile that he must 'salute their
achievements at the moment of extinction'.[17]

Charles dates the period of dissolution in the Edwardian
age, but Hemans knows better. Her superior knowledge
comes from her understanding that the stately homes and all
that we associate with them are only signifying systems.
Hemans distances and reimagines the stately home by raising
it up again in the form of an ideological network, a system of
images and signs. In that condition the home as figure of
continuity and substance is already actively 'melting from us'.

This is the experience set forth in Hemans' poetry, and this
is why the stately homes of England are the perfect topic for
such an act of reimagination. Although those edifices were
always homes, they were also always emblematic forms, part
of a non-linguistic and widely dispersed system of social
signification. The great English houses 'were not
originally . . . just large houses in the country in which rich
people lived. Essentially they were power houses'. In this
respect they functioned at two related levels, one
adminstrative, the other ideological. The country house was
'the headquarters from which land was administered and
power used', of course, but it was also 'a show-case' and 'an
image-maker' through which to display the credentials of
power.[18]

From at least as early as the seventeenth century the discourse of the stately home and the country house was firmly

[17] *Brideshead Revisited* (Boston: Little, Brown & Co., 1945), 226–7.
[18] See Mark Girouard, *Life in the English Country House: A Social and Intellectual History* (New Haven: Yale University Press, 1978), 2–3.

in place. The contemporary tourist is no more than the latest
representative of a long tradition of people who would visit
such places not as guests but as spectators. Ladies and gentlemen regularly went on trips to celebrated and picturesque
country homes, as we know from Pepys and other diarists.
Dudley Ryder's diary for 1 June 1716 is the record of a picnic
to Dyrham Park in Gloucestershire by himself and a company
of his friends.[19]

But even the guests in a stately home behaved as observers,
judges, and interpreters. This happened because such places
were always on display—indeed, were conceived and constructed, from the very first, as demonstrative and signifying
forms. When Henry James describes his experience of
Compton Wynyates, in Warwickshire, he says 'It is impossible to imagine a more perfect picture'.[20] James is looking at
an aesthetic and symbolic object—something that is understood to have been imagined, and hence as a signifying thing.

GM. Are you arguing that Hemans' poetry is valuable because it
is clichéd and sentimental?

AM. No, I am arguing that Hemans' is a poetry of quotation, a
conscious elevation of various inherited and signifying signs.
I do not mean so much her language as the materials and
topics she handles. She favours the representation of legendary materials because what is legendary (whether ancient or
modern) is already seen to be quoted. Furthermore, to be able
to 'quote' from what appears to be real—which is what
happens not only in a poem like 'The Homes of England', but
in her many historical texts—is to erode the distinction between what is real and what is mediated, between referent and
sign, between acts and texts.

As for Hemans' language as such, it is not in fact clichéd
and conventional, it is rather a vision and prophecy of such
things, and of the significance of such things. It appears as a
poetry asking to be repeated, rewritten, recited. Her poetry is
not clichéd and sentimental, as many have charged, it is a
prolepsis of the ideas of cliché and sentimentality. In the
work's actual achievement, therefore, in its century of success

---

[19] See *The Country House*, compiled by James Lees-Milne (Oxford: Oxford
University Press, 1982), 97.
[20] From his *Portraits of Places*, quoted in Lees-Milne, *The Country House*, 9.

and imitation and repetition, Hemans executes a remarkable critique of the ideology of cultural endurance—a critique all the more stunning for its domesticity and lack of pretension. Modernism and its muscular academic spokesmen would labour to sweep away Hemans' poetry in order to preserve and re-establish the romance of art's power, and of Power's art— that is to say, in order to preserve the illusion of such things. These are not illusions that can endure—in either sense of that word—Hemans' cabinets of perfection and polished surfaces. They are not illusions that can endure her success, or the success which her own work prophesies for them.[21]

Hemans' work is not so elaborate an achievement as Tennyson's, nor so demonic as D. G. Rossetti's. But it is the same order of achievement, and coming at the beginning of the Victorian Age, it announces much of what the poetry of that age had to bring. Idolatries, monuments, and illusions: one of the great missions of Victorian poetry was to expend itself in the service of such things, and to leave, thereby, little room for reimagining them as anything but whited sepulchres, buildings of loss.

The poet of all that is admirable, exquisite, and celebrated, Hemans saw deeply into a (textual as well as human) condition governed by attributions and adjectives:

A moment's transient entertainment—scarcely even that at times, is the utmost effect of things that 'come like shadows, so depart'. Of all things, never may I become that despicable thing, a woman living upon admiration![22]

And yet this result would be, like that of her age, her fate. As her fame grew during that now forgotten decade, the

---

[21] Noel Coward's wonderful parody of 'The Homes of England', in his *Operette* (London, 1938), 53–6, is by no means simply a farcical destruction of the original poem. The parody travesties Hemans' work in order to resurrect the central ideas of the poem in another quarter, and on new terms. *Operette* is a celebration of the power, and necessity, of maintaining appearances. In Coward's play, however, the standard for a saving artificiality is located in the 'low' world of the stage and music hall, and not in the insignia of the aristocracy. By inverting the apparitional terms of Hemans' poem, this transformation gives an explicit form to (it 'explicates') what Hemans was doing in more indirect ways.

[22] *Memoir*, 188.

1820s, she came to lament 'the weary part of *femme célèbre*, which I am now enacting'. More and more, like some prescience of Emily Dickinson, she shrank from leaving the narrow confines of her house: 'my heart is with those home enjoyments, and there, however tried, excited, and wrung, it will ever remain'.[23] That last remark is particularly telling for the way it probes painfully for the truth of her own most cherished fiction, the fiction of the stable and love-founded hearth.

GM. An elegant reading, but also a sublimed and generalized reading—a reading, indeed, after the manner of Francis Jeffrey, or Arnold, or any number of other nineteenth-century critics. In avoiding a close examination of the poem's language you betray the illusion of your reading. 'The Homes of England' will not stay for a close critical exploration carried out in the manner of Brooks and Warren's *Understanding Poetry*.

AM. My commentary was not meant to be exhaustive. I was simply sketching a framework where the poem's more localized and particular details might be able to be reimagined. But a 'close' linguistic reading of the kind you want would not be difficult to develop.

One could begin, for instance, with the poem's determined resort to a certain kind of diction: words like 'greensward', 'gladsome', and 'hamlet-fanes', along with their equivalent syntactical units ('O'er all the pleasant land', 'Some glorious page of old'). The text comes before us as a careful reconstruction made from materials which in 1827 are not only 'legend laden', but *evidently* legend laden. Unlike Keats, Hemans does not strive after 'right dreams' or lament their loss; her poem accepts from the start that these kinds of social dreams are the constructions not of the unconsciousness but of the consciousness, even of the super-ego. Their conscious origin is the source of their extreme fragility.

In that context, lines like 'Or lips move tunefully along/ Some glorious page of old' begin to float free, like ghosts seeking their local habitations and their names. The 'glorious page of old' snatches vainly for a specific referent—in real

<hr>

[23] *Memoir*, 189; see also 169–70.

history (perhaps some act of public service in war); in some
book or record of the event itself, perhaps an old ballad; in the
text of Hemans' poem, which may be imagining its own
recitation, its setting to music by someone in the future. The
eternal present imagined by the poem calls out each of these
possibilities, but in doing so it pulls itself into its own imagining. 'The Homes of England' itself becomes one of the glorious pages of old, and the lips that move along its evanescent
surface are the lips of shades. The poem's eternal present is
what Keats earlier called a 'pleasant death', only in Hemans'
case we are left with no room for imagining that death as
anything but an unreality. The poem that begins 'The stately
Homes of England!/ How beautiful they stand' does not, as
Byron once put it, 'c[o]me like truth, and disappear . . . like
dreams'; it comes as a dream from the start, and what it
announces is the fading of the 'truth' of the dream, the emergence of the dream as a construct.

Who, then, is the 'God' referred to in the poem's last line?
The 'country' is named—it is 'England'—but that word, by
the end of the poem, has acquired the same kind of nominal
existence as everything else in the poem. The god of this work,
we might want to say, is Felicia Hemans—a mother-god
answering the calls of the children evoked in the poem's
penultimate line. That reading works because it is so conson-
ant with Hemans' fundamental myth of domesticity—and, of
course, because Hemans is this text's constructor. But in a
poem built up through citation and recitation, Hemans can
seem no more than a local deity in an odd kind of pantheistic
landscape—or I should say, 'textscape'. The god of 'The
Homes of England' is one whose centre is nowhere and whose
circumference is everywhere. Many would see him as a certain
set of social relations and social values—a god very like
Jehovah, with his chosen people, his favoured nation. In our
critical age, he is usually called Ideology.

The great tradition of Cynical philosophy held that one did
not philosophize in order to learn how to live, one had first to
live, and then come later to study and reflect upon that
condition of our human being. I am reminded of the Cynical
view here because I think one cannot begin a close study of
Hemans' work, or of the work of any poet for that matter,

until one enters into its life. And you cannot even hope for such an event if you come to Hemans forearmed with the knowledge and truth you think you have acquired.

JJR. I applaud you, Anne. What a splendid reading. Not merely inventive but perverse, not merely perverse but utterly resolute in its perversity. What you say is too good to be true. Which makes it, in a certain sense, even better than if it *were* true.

GM. Is Jay right, is this reading of yours just a critical game? If you're serious I simply say this: I have great difficulty imagining Felicia Hemans as essential reading, even in a radically reorganized canon.

AM. It might prove less difficult if we remembered what sort of values the received canon, from which she was expelled, has come to stand for—and perhaps has always stood for.

GM. Fair enough. But then you will have to make more clear, at least for me, what place *your* Felicia Hemans might occupy in a reimagined canon. You may think that I have appropriated too much of the traditional (masculine) framework for reading literary texts, but your own commentary is hardly innocent in this regard. It is in many ways little more than a classic example of Adornian negative dialectics. The sentimentality of Hemans' poem, in this reading, seems devoid of positive values. It serves merely as a stylistic device for critique and deconstruction. Are those the banners under which your feminist programme means to march?

AM. One of the most impressive things about Hemans' poetry is the difference it marks off from the conventions of most modernist styles in art. Stein, of course, is the great exception—and (of course) Stein is about as far removed from our canonical views of modernism as Hemans is from our literary histories of 1815–35. In 'The Homes of England' sentiment is revealed as a ghostly presence, like everything else; but if it comes only in apparitional forms, the poem has not, at any rate, abandoned its faith in what its own sentimentality stands for: an imagination of a communal world held together by sympathy.

GM. But in Hemans' poem it is a sympathy without an object—a kind of abstract sympathy.

AM. Yes, but that is not to be taken simply as a critique of the poetry. It comprises, rather, a definition of the world of Hemans' experience. From our vantage this experience may seem threadbare and limited—as if it were unable wholly to resist its own adverse experiences, the way we imagine Dickinson and Stein did. And so we would say of Hemans that she is not, perhaps, so great a writer as Dickinson or Stein, that she became too much of what she beheld. That is certainly my view. But it is also my view that what Hemans has to offer is distinctive and important.

GM. It can be had for the asking in the magazines and annuals of the nineteenth century.

AM. You are wrong. There is a great deal of what has been called 'sentimental verse' in those magazines and annuals, but if you read much of it—by the way, *have* you read it?—you may begin to see the work differently. It is by no means so uniform as (y)our literary histories suggest. In any case, the whole question of the sentimental in poetry needs to be rethought and the relevant texts reread.[24]

GM. And then what? I think then we shall see Hemans' poems sink back into their former 'breathless sleep'.

AM. We shall see.

---

[24] For some efforts in this direction see *Romanticism and Feminism*, ed. Anne K. Mellor (Bloomington: Indiana University Press, 1988); Marlon B. Ross, *The Contours of Masculine Desire: Romanticism and the Rise of Women's Poetry* (Oxford and New York: Oxford University Press, 1989); *Out of Bounds: Male Writers and Gender(ed) Criticism*, eds. Laura Claridge and Elizabeth Langland (Amherst: University of Massachusetts Press, 1990).

Conclusion: Starting from Death: The Poetry of Ann Batten Cristall

And thought . . . is at the limit of this conflagration, like a candle blown out at the limit of a flame.

Georges Bataille

She published only one volume of verse, *Poetical Sketches* (1795). The title recalls Blake's first book, especially since Cristall associated with Blake's London circle. And because her book was published by Joseph Johnson. But we know little about her.[1]

I have seen only one copy of this volume—the British Library copy. Not many could have been printed. The single copy recorded in an American archive, at Columbia University, has been lost. The book was issued by subscription, with 234 named subscribers (including George Dyer, Samuel Rogers, and Mary Wollstonecraft).

But we know little about her. And her loss to us, her life as well as her work, measures the subject of this study. I want to conclude with Anne Batten Cristall not for any historical reasons, but because her work—what we have *not* made of it—passes a clear judgement on our visions of judgement.

For Cristall was a remarkable talent. Of course she deprecated her learning and her technical skills, as she would have been expected to do. We observe the correctness of her demeanour in the opening words of the preface she wrote for her book of poems:

These light effusions of a youthful imagination, written at various times for the entertainment of my idle hours, I now present to such

---

[1] See Roger Lonsdale's brief biographical notice, and his references, in his *Eighteenth-Century Women Poets: An Oxford Anthology* (Oxford: Oxford University Press, 1989).

Readers whose minds are not too seriously engaged; and should they afford any degree of amusement, my most sanguine expectations will be answered. To attempt any more in an age like this, enlightened by authors, whose lives have been devoted to the study of metaphysical and moral truth, would be presumptuous; and my experience does not justify such efforts. Most of my days have been passed in solitude, and the little knowledge I have acquired cannot boast the authority of much experience; my opinions, therefore, would carry little weight; for although the dictates of Nature may be sometimes more just than conclusions drawn from a partial knowledge of the world, yet even the most settled convictions are never, perhaps, unbiassed by prejudice, or uninfluenced by affection.

From among my juvenile productions I have principally selected for the volume some poetical tales and unconnected sketches, which a love for the beauties of nature inspired. The versification is wild, and still incorrect, though I have taken much pains to reduce it to some degree of order; they were written without the knowledge of any rules; of which their irregularity is the natural consequence. (p. ix)

This is no more disingenuous than any of those other admissions of 'incorrectness' so commonly made by women writers from 'The Amorous Lady' to Mary Robinson and beyond. Like her foremothers, Cristall understands the privilege that comes with what she calls her 'spontaneous and involuntary' (ix) methods. Her comments about the influence of 'prejudice' and 'affection' on 'settled convictions' are subtle and very self-aware. They undercut the 'authority' of worldly 'experience', on one hand, and they intimate the 'metaphysical and moral' importance of natural feelings on the other.

Cristall's oblique critical reflection implicitly asks us to reconsider the commonplace distinctions between 'nature' and 'experience', between writing from impulse and writing from rules, between poetries of pleasure and poetries of instruction. Her work, she says, is a poetry of pleasure: the 'light effusions' of her book hardly deserve notice or attention 'in an age like this, enlightened by' so many bright or weighty intelligences. Yet here, in her candid and modest address, we may well be struck by the more serious pretension of her work that comes through a (poetical? accidental?) play of language: the oblique rhyme between the 'light effusions' of imagination and the 'enlightened' study of philosophical truth.[2]

---

[2] One should also note the subtle gravity-field set up by the cognate terms 'Nature', 'nature', and 'natural'.

The accidental appearance of this effect is surely a deliberated poetical move, as we realize in the opening poem of the book, 'Before Twilight. Eyezion'. Exactly like *Prometheus Unbound*, the poem is a synaesthetic dialogue (between the lovers Eyezion and Viza) on the life and the light of sympathetic vision. The poem generates a changeful dance of 'light': the idea(s) of it, its phenomenal appearances, its verbal forms.

> DAWN had not streak'd the spacious veil of night,
> When EYEZION, the light poet of the spring,
> Hied from his restless bed, to sing,
> Impatient for the promis'd beams of light:
> Sweetly his voice through woods and vallies rang
> While fleeting o'er the hills these anxious notes he sang.
> Swift, swift, ye lingering hours,
> And wake the morning star;
> Rouse from the dew-fraught flowers
> The shades, and drive them far.
> Quick on the wing of morning,
> Dart the young glimmering light . . .
>
> (1–12)

What has roused Eyezion is not the dawn but, paradoxically, certain darknesses—'The shades' he glimpses on the flowers whose dew glimmers under a star-illumined light. This is the light that the poem associates with Eyezion's beloved Viza, whose eyes are 'star-like' (44) and who is explicitly identified with the morning star Venus.

The poem centres in a complex set of interchanges between its two poetical creatures. Their purely imaginative character is important, for the day they bring forth—the apparitionally natural events that illustrate or represent their love—is not at all quotidian. That day and its epiphenomena constitute a particular form assumed by the 'current of creative mind' (53) that sustains the Cristall world. Forms of light proliferate.

> Rise, Phoebus, from yon fountain,
> Your saffron robes display;
> Warm every lake and fountain,
> And kindle up the day.
> My soul, fledg'd with desires,
> Flutters, and pants for morn,
> To catch the orient fires

> Light trembling o'er the lawn.
>
> (15–22)

This is a song of light and fire calling up an imagination of the natural world. It is literally a 'light effusion', as Cristall's preface had promised. Here its 'Light trembling' appearance discloses as well the tactile status of its transformative potential: dawn is a warming and an upkindling as well as a visible event.

But most of all dawn is the mental dawning of aesthetic consciousness itself, Intellectual Beauty. Eyezion sings his song and 'VIZA unfolds her charms' (32):

> Midst rills she laves her tresses,
>   And blooming beams delight;
> Swift—love my soul oppresses—
>   Why's thought more quick than light?
>
> (35–8)

Here all moves as a play of language, as the excellent rhyme delight/light suggests. Do the lines reveal more of Eyezion or more of Viza? We cannot say, anymore than we should assign a determinate meaning to the word 'light'.

The startling wit of 'Before Twilight. Eyezion' incarnates that form of 'creative mind' celebrated through the poem. It is Thoreau's dawning form, and is characterized by words like 'delight', 'fertile fancy' (55), 'Love's light wings' (69), and 'Young joy' (77). Eyezion (like Viza) embodies this form:

> A current of creative mind,
> Wild as the wandering gusts of wind,
> 'Mid fertile fancy's visions train'd,
> Unzon'd I shot, and o'er each limit strain'd;
> Around in airy circles whirl'd
>   By a genius infinite,
> While Love in wanton ringlets curl'd
>   My tresses, passion to excite.
>
> (53–60)

The passage shows that Cristall has fully assimilated the speculative philosophical and aesthetic thought of her age. The text gives her version of Jones's 'Hymn to Na'ra'yena' and Blake's 'Song of Los'. But the distinctiveness of Cristall's verse comes through perhaps most clearly in the final pair of lines, where enjambment generates a moment of arresting and delightful

wordplay through the manipulation of the syntactic function of
the word 'curl'd'. Here is the lightest of touches, a figure
flaunting its purely decorative status. The anacreontic image is a
second-order sign for the style she has chosen, the discourse of
the 'feeling mind' ('Evening. Gertrude', 162).

Eyezion's explanation of the action of 'creative mind' finishes
reflexively. What Dante called 'intelletto d'Amore' informs the
current of Cristall's verse.

> Thus skimming o'er the tracts of life,
>   Borne on light elements I bound;
> Free from rage and coarser strife,
>   I catch new beauties all around . . .
>   Upon poetic spells I fly
> Wafted afar from black Despair;
>   And, as I sing,
>   Am rais'd on high:
> Young joy with pleasure smoothes the scene,
> Of mortal eyes unseen;
>   With these I fleet,
> Amid the Loves and Smiles sweet flowrets wreathe;
> And every sigh I waft, and every joy I breathe,
>   Mix'd with seraphic airs, fly on poetic feet.
>   (65–8, 73–82)

Two things should be said about this splendid and important
passage. The first is technical. We must guard against a reading
that would filter these lines through the stylistic conventions of
romantic writing. The argument about poetic diction in
Wordsworth's great Preface to *Lyrical Ballads* has gained such
authority—at any rate until the coming of the decorative styles
of postmodern writing—that we can easily lose our ability to
read verse written according to other conventions. The entirety
of Cristall's work is built upon a commitment to 'poetical diction', which Cristall (like Darwin and Jones) uses to construct
images that are explicitly cartoon-like and fragile. That quality
of the Cristalline world is fundamental. When Blake later names
it 'a Vision of the lamentation of Beulah over Ololon' (in
Milton, plate 31), he replicates one of Cristall's central preoccupations: that 'every human bosom starts from death' ('Written
When the Mind was Oppressed', 36). Here the wordplay with
'starts from' is doubly significant: as an index of her style, on

one hand, and as a locus of key philosophical preoccupations, on the other.

The technical features of Cristall's verse characteristically involve important 'metaphysical and moral' issues, as we see once again in this climactic sequence of the book's opening work. 'Before Twilight. Eyezion' initiates a five-poem sequence whose principal subject is poetry itself, and in particular the poetry licensed through eighteenth-century sensationalist philosophy. The final couplet of the passage at hand underscores the philosophical authority being assumed in the poetic method, that is, in an argument by images and poetical devices.

The massively assonantal character of Cristall's verse is both typical and telling. 'Before Twilight. Eyezion', for example, is in an obvious sense a celebration of the morphemic and phonemic possibilities of the 'i' form. The aural substructure founds the work's powerful synaesthesia, which itself embodies the argument about the intellectual authority of feeling. At once agent, medium, and receptor, Eyezion's poetical discourse discovers figures for its 'light effusions'. His words are themselves theophanies—literal forms of the creative mind he celebrates. So the text fills itself with the earth and 'airs' of its own imaginings, it creates beings of pure sound who then 'fly' through these worlds on their evanescent 'poetic feet'.

But 'Before Twilight. Eyezion' by no means discovers the whole truth about the 'creative mind' it calls to our attention. Cristall deploys a five-part sequence of poems to complete her presentation. The 'Loves and Smiles' of the first poem define a special experience Blake called 'Infant Joy'. As this twilight world turns to its morning, noon, and evening—to the poems 'Morning. Rosamonde', 'Noon. Lysander', 'Evening. Gertrude'—engines of Loss discover the torments of love and jealousy. When Rosamonde enters the 'glowing' world announced by Viza ('Before Twilight. Eyezion', 105–8), 'Nature's wild harmony,/ Breath'd love, and sang delight' ('Morning. Rosamonde', 11–12).

These harmonies, this love and its delights, bring surprising difficulties ('surprising', that is, when initially encountered in the perspective of the first poem's 'Young Joy'):

> Fresh ROSAMONDE the glowing scene surveys,
> Her youthful bosom inly stung with pain;

> Early amid the shadowy trees she strays,
>   Her shining eyes the starting tears restrain;
>   While tyrant Love within her pulses plays
>   (13–17)

'Morning. Rosamonde' deconstructs the 'i' world created *ex nihilo* through the opening poem's delights of love: VIZA gets a new name, ROSAMONDE, EYEZION turns to URBAN. 'Starting tears' are re-straining the poetical instruments, we hear the world in different tones. Words like 'glowing' and 'bosom' find new sounds echoing to their senses: 'shadowy', 'pulses': 'Love' (!). The familiar becomes quickly estranged from itself, and words—those apparently firm self-identities—acquire altogether new meanings, new feelings. The 'Love' articulated in the second poem appears very different from the 'Love' we met in the first.

So the changes unroll through the sequence. The climax of these transfigurations comes at the end of the fourth poem, 'Evening. Gertrude', where the heroine's final reflections echo and complete Eyezion's earlier discourse on poetry and the currents of creative mind. All along the desires of love are equated with the poetic impulse. Before the coming of the 'Night'—the final text—Gertrude has a critical vision of a pastoral feast of the poets:

> Gay wicked wit amid the circle spread,
>   And wanton round the lively sallies sped;
>   Each neat-trimm'd maiden laugh'd with playful glee,
>   Whom whispering swains divert with mimicry.
>   Fair ROSAMONDE, whose rival bosom burn'd,
>   With taunting mirth directs young URBAN's eyes;
>   He, with mischievous archness, smiles return'd,
>   Amid whose circles wounding satires rise;
>   Their sportive feet still beat the flowery ground,
>   While wicked looks, and jests, and jeers went round.
>   (135–44)

Here Gertrude attends to the love-play—the poetry—of all the couples named earlier in the poem. These couples define her own identity, for they represent her 'wandering' desires. Gertrude's vision establishes the ground of her anti-poetics. Consequently, she flees the illusions generated through her own desire:

> With shame she burns, and blushes at her woe,
> And wonders at her weakness and her pain.
>
> (151–2)

The definitive figure of Gertrude's flight comes as the termination of this poem, where the emblems of sensibility begin to undergo their final set of transmutations. In the end we are turned over to the culminant text of the sequence, Cristall's 'Night Thoughts'.

The title form of this last text in the sequence—it is not bifurcated like the previous four titles—signals the poem's commitment to a firm Truth. 'Night' dismisses all the apparitions and transformations we know and cherish:

> SOLEMN is night, when Silence holds her reign,
> And the hush'd winds die on the heaving main;
> When no short gleam of scatter'd light appears,
> Nor lunar beams make faint the nobler stars . . .
>
> (1–4)

Earlier Eyezion set us 'skimming o'er the tracts of life'. Now a final figure, Henry, rediscovers the underlying truth of those tracts.

> O! how sublime this tract, for man design'd!
> Vast the perceptions of his rapid mind!
> Strongly to earth his young affections cling,
> While fancy waves her bright and various wing;
> But soon each hope of earthly bliss is cross'd,
> Nipt in the bud, or in possession lost;
> Blushing, our empty wishes we survey,
> When we our passions with our motives weigh.
>
> (31–8)

The lines bring a kind of Final or Last Judgement to the visionary history that here ends in 'Night', and this climactic event is brilliantly signalled by the second coming of the word 'tract'. The effect of this verbal refiguring is startling and even uncanny. Cristall's dismissal of poetry—the verse argues nothing less— comes in a classical poetic form, a wordplay that demands an end to wordplay, that calls for moral truth and clear ideas.

The most important of those ideas calls up paradoxical thoughts like: 'he who would save his life must lose it'. But Cristall is not preaching an art of renunciation. Her Night

Thoughts make no discounts from either the pleasures or the pains of mortal experience. The argument is grounded in a commitment to (not a mere belief in) expenditure and ecstasy.

> Deeply I feel this still and solemn hour,
> Impress'd with GOD's immeasurable power;
> While worlds unnumber'd 'mid yon ether burn,
> And thoughts immense pour in where'er I turn.
> How much man errs, whose soul, with thought sublime,
> Looks on tow'rds endless bliss thro' boundless time!
> When he to earthly passions gives dire sway,
> Or mourns those joys which of themselves decay!
>
> (39–46)

Here the current of creative mind continues to operate, perpetuating itself under the sign of Energy. As they pass through Cristall's 'thought sublime', errors are passing beyond their commonplace apparitions. The soul may err if its eyes are fixed too near or too far, or if it cedes power to *earthly* passions, or if it *mourns* the expenditures of its own intensities.

Once again we may recall the benevolent double-meaning insinuated through the night thought 'And every human bosom starts from death'. The unenlightened are figures of fear, the thoughtful are figures stepping westward. Cristall typically sees the latter in forms of deprivation. 'A Fragment. The Blind Man' foretells the argument we know best through Wordsworth's 'Resolution and Independence'. A 'Rash youth' (4) encounters a blind old man—at once a figure of Lear and of Homer—wandering allegorically on a dark and stormy night. He is rash because his sympathies, while quick, see neither out far nor in deep. The old man has a third eye lit with 'a ray of sacred light' (5). He understands the agencies at work around and within him.

> Hark! 'tis GOD's voice which urges on the storm;
> He to this world of elements gave form.
> From them he moulded all, yet gave not peace,
>   But broke the harmony, and bade them rage;
> He meant not happiness should join with ease,
>   But varied joys and pains should all the world engage.
>
> (24–9)

The fragment is yet another 'tract' on the 'metaphysical and moral' function of poetry. The old man's words distinctly recall Cristall's discussion of poetical incorrectness and her own 'wild'

harmonies. The storm is another figure of 'creative mind', and
so is the 'Blind Man' of the poem, and so is the text's 'Fragment'
genre.

For all its Wordsworthian form, this fine little poem makes a
move rarely taken by Cristall's romantic successor. The rash
youth's effort to protect the old man from 'this horrid scene'
(21) is accepted by Cristall's old man, who 'yields' to the 'fear'
driving the youth's benevolence (23). Like Wordsworth in so
many of the poems we know and admire, the blind old man
might well have chosen a more grand gesture. For all his modesty, the leech-gatherer is a *figura* of romantic self-reliance,
whose features recur throughout Wordsworth's writing:

> And this huge Castle, standing here sublime,
> I love to see the look with which it braves,
> Cased in the unfeeling armour of old time,
> The light'ning, the fierce wind, and trampling waves.
> ('Elegiac Stanzas . . . ', 29–32)

That is not the gesture Cristall either makes or needs. The power
of her old man lies as much in his fortitude as in his weakness,
in what he can give as in what he should receive. Or so at least
one might frame the situation in moral terms.

In sensational terms, her old man's body must possess more
Blakean 'inlets of soul' than could be fulfilled on dark and
barren heaths. 'Tis better to give than to receive? Not necessarily—at least not in the dynamics of sensibility and sentiment.
Eyezion and Viza, Rosamonde and Urban, all (like Ahab) have
their humanities. They are also some of the names we might give
to this blind old man, whose names (in poetic fact) are legion.

Legion and evanescent. Unlike Wordsworth's leech-gatherer,
Cristall's old man follows the Song of the Spirits in Shelley's
Prometheus Unbound, who urge Asia to 'Resist not the weak-
ness/ Such strength is in meekness' (II.3.93–4). The old man is
one current of creative mind, borne along a larger flood. What
he does not seek is precisely an 'unfeeling armour' that would
protect him from 'The storm whereon [he] ride[s], to sink at last'
(*Childe Harold*, III, st. 44).

That commitment to life as energy and expenditure—to a
God who is the totality of their eternal recurrence—defines
the verse style that Cristall practises. In this respect her single

volume of work, and the single surviving copy known to us, are alike emblems of her mortalized and unworldly aesthetics. For her poetry should not be defined by measures of fame or endurance. A thing of beauty is not a joy for ever, it is a joy for now.

Though not a sentimental writer like Hemans, Cristall's sensibility none the less forecasts the lament for the lost Pleiad:

> They rise in joy, the starry myriads burning—
>   The shepherd greets them on his mountains free;
>   And from the silvery sea
> To them the sailor's wakeful eye is turning—
> Unchanged they rise, they have not mourned for thee.
>
>   (11–15)

Indeed, for what should they mourn? The Lost Pleiad fairly defines the character of all these starry myriads, whose triumph comes through the 'old magnificence' (7) of their 'burning' and eventual death. Starting from that death, the Lost Pleiad alone founds the transpersonal abundance written in the stars.

> Why, who shall talk of thrones, or sceptres riven?
>   —Bow'd be our hearts to think of what we are,
>   When from its height afar
> A world sinks thus—and yon majestic heaven
> Shines not the less for that one vanish'd star.
>
>   (21–5)

Like the sentimentality of Hemans, Cristall's sensibility measures the fame so desperately sought by Keats and found by Byron. Beside the 'vanish'd star' of her life and single volume of poems, they and their works seem curiously humbled. Her writing possesses a clear generosity that gets regularly sacrificed to the high cultural ambitions pursued by the poets and dispensed by their critics.

Indeed, her writing is engaged exactly in defiance of those palpable cultural designs. But 'defiance' is perhaps too strong a term, too 'palpable'. For Cristall's writing doesn't defy the brilliant cultural illusions of those whose names are written, if not in the book of life, then in the annals of literature. Her work celebrates the losses that poets like to imagine they might save. In this she recollects the truth about all the dancers whose 'sportive feet still beat the flowery ground' ('Evening.

Gertrude', 144): that they live through illusions that cannot be sustained.

In Cristall we see that the One Life within us and abroad is exactly that, just one life. It is a life that spends itself in living. If written down it comprises only one book, however many volumes it may accumulate. And that one book might just as easily vanish as not since it was written, like L.E.L.'s love letter, to be burned up.

Bibliography

AKENSIDE, MARK, *The Poetical Works of Mark Akenside*, ed. Rev. Alexander Dyce (Boston: Little, Brown & Co., 1854).

AMIS, KINGSLEY (ed.), *The Faber Popular Reciter* (London: Faber, 1978).

Asiatick Researches Publications of the Asiatick Society. (Calcutta; repr. London for Vernor and Hood, . . .). 1798–[1809].

BACHINGER, KATRINA, '"The Sombre Madness of Sex": Byron's First and Last Gift to Poe'. *The Byron Journal* 19 (1991), 128–40.

BARFIELD, OWEN, *What Coleridge Thought* (Middletown: Wesleyan University Press, 1971).

BARKER-BENFIELD, G. J., *The Culture of Sensibility: Sex and Society in Eighteenth-Century Britain* (Chicago: University of Chicago Press, 1992).

BEER, JOHN, *Coleridge's Poetic Intelligence* (London and Basingstoke: Macmillan, 1977).

BLAKE, WILLIAM, *The Complete Poetry and Prose*, ed. David V. Erdman, commentary by Harold Bloom. New and rev. edn. (Berkeley: University of California Press, 1982).

BOSCOVICH, RUDJER, *A Theory of Natural Philosophy*, trans. James M. Child (Chicago: Open Court Publishing Co, 1922).

BOURDIEU, PIERRE, *Distinction: A Social Critique of the Judgement of Taste*, trans. Richard Nice (Cambridge, Mass.: Harvard University Press, 1984).

BOYLE, ANDREW, *An Index to the Annuals* (Worchester: Andrew Boyle, 1967).

BREDVOLD, LOUIS I., *The Natural History of Sensibility* (Detroit: Wayne State University Press, 1962).

BRETT, R. L. and JONES, A. R. (eds.), *Lyrical Ballads: Wordsworth and Coleridge* (London: Methuen, 1965).

The British Album, in two vols. (London: John Bell, 1790).

BROOKS, CLEANTH, *Modern Poetry and the Tradition* (Chapel Hill: University of North Carolina Press, 1939).

BUTTERFIELD, HERBERT, *Man on his Past. The Study of the History of Historical Scholarship* (Cambridge: Cambridge University Press, 1969).

BYRON, GEORGE GORDON, LORD, *The Complete Poetical Works*, ed. Jerome J. McGann, 7 vols. (Oxford: Clarendon Press, 1980–93).

——*Letters and Journals*, ed. Leslie A. Marchand, 12 vols. (Cambridge, Mass.: Belknap Press, Harvard University Press, 1973–82).

CHEW, SAMUEL C., *Byron in England* (London: John Murray, 1924).

CLARIDGE, LAURA and LANGLAND, ELIZABETH (eds.), *Out of Bounds: Male Writers and Gender(ed) Criticism* (Amherst: University of Massachusetts Press, 1990).

CLARK, S. H., ' "Pendet Homo Incertus": Gray's Response to Locke', in *Eighteenth-Century Studies* 24/3, 4 (spring–summer 1991), 273–91, 484–503.

COLERIDGE, SAMUEL TAYLOR, *Collected Letters*, ed. E. L. Griggs, 4 vols. (Oxford: Clarendon Press, 1956–9).

——*Biographia Literaria*, eds. James Engell and W. Jackson Bate, 2 vols (Princeton: Princeton University Press, 1983).

——*The Poems*, ed. Ernest Hartley Coleridge (Oxford: Oxford University Press, 1912).

CONGER, SYNDY McMILLEN and CONROY, PETER V., Jr., 'Sensibility: A Select Bibliography of Secondary Sources,' in J. H. Hagstrum, *Eros and Vision* (Evanston: Northwestern University Press, 1989).

CRISTALL, ANN BATTEN, *Poetical Sketches* (London: J. Johnson, 1795).

DACRE, CHARLOTTE, *Hours of Solitude* (London: D. N. Shury, 1805).

DARWIN, ERASMUS, *The Botanic Garden 1791* (Menston: The Scholar Press, 1973).

DEJEAN, JOAN, *Fictions of Sappho 1546–1937* (Chicago: University of Chicago Press, 1989).

DOODY, MARGARET ANNE, *A Natural Passion* (Oxford: Clarendon Press, 1974).

DWYER, JOHN, 'The Melancholy Savage: Text and Context in the *Poems of Ossian*', in Howard Gaskell (ed.), *Ossian Revisited* (Edinburgh: Edinburgh University Press, 1991), 164–206.

ELIOT, T. S., 'Charleston, Hey! Hey!', *The Nation and Athenaeum* (29 Jan. 1927), 595.

——*Selected Essays: A New Edition* (New York: Harcourt Brace and Co., 1950).

ELLISON, JULIE, 'Redoubled Feeling: Politics, Sentiment, and the Sublime in Williams and Wollstonecraft', *Studies in Eighteenth Century Culture*, 20 (1990), 197–215.

ERHARDT-SIEBOLD, ERIKA VON, 'Some Inventions of the Pre-Romantic Period and their Influence upon Literature', *Englische Studien*, 66 (1931–2), 347–63.

FAVRET, MARY A. and WATSON, NICOLA J. (eds.), *At the Limits of Romanticism: Essays in Cultural, Feminist, and Materialist Criticism* (Bloomington: Indiana University Press, 1994).

FAXON, FREDERICK W., *Literary Annuals and Gift Books—A Biblio-graphy 1823–1903* (Middlesex: PLA, 1973).

FAY, ELIZABETH, *Becoming Wordsworthian: A Performative Aesthet-ics* (Amherst: University of Massachusetts Press, 1995).

FISCH, AUDREY A., MELLOR, ANNE K., and SCHOR, ESTHER (eds.), *The Other Mary Shelley: Beyond Frankenstein* (New York: Oxford Uni-versity Press, 1993).

Fisher's Drawing Room Scrap-Book, with Poetical Illustrations by L.E.L. (London: Fisher, Son, and Jackson, 1832).

The Florence Miscellany (Florence, privately printed, 1785).

FORREST-THOMSON, VERONICA, *Collected Poems and Translations*. Agneau Books 2 (London, Lewes, Berkeley: Allardyce, Barnett, 1990).

GIFFORD, WILLIAM, *The Baviad and Maeviad*, A New Edition Revised (London, Philadelphia: Reprinted for William Cobbett, 1799).

GIROUARD, MARK, *Life in the English Country House: A Social and Intellectual History* (New Haven: Yale University Press, 1978).

GRAY, THOMAS, *Letters*, selected and ed. by H. Milford (Oxford: Oxford University Press, 1925).

——*The Complete Poems*, eds. H. W. Starr and J. R. Hendrickson (Oxford: Clarendon Press, 1966).

GUILLAMET, LEON, *The Sincere Ideal: Studies in Sincerity in Eight-eenth-Century English Literature* (Montreal and London: McGill-Queens University Press, 1974).

HAGSTRUM, JEAN H., *Sex and Sensibility: Ideal and Erotic Love from Milton to Mozart* (Chicago: University of Chicago Press, 1980).

——*Eros and Vision: The Restoration to Romanticism* (Evanston: Northwestern University Press, 1989).

HEJINIAN, LYN, *A Thought is the Bride of What Thinking* (Berkeley: Tuumba no. 1, 1977).

HEMANS, FELICIA, *The Works of Mrs. Hemans, with a Memoir of her Life by her Sister*. 7 vols. (Edinburgh: William Blackwood and Sons, 1844).

JEFFREY, FRANCIS, *Contributions to the Edinburgh Review by Francis Jeffrey* (Boston, 1857).

JONES, CHRIS, *Radical Sensibility: Literature and Ideas in the 1790s* (New York: Routledge, 1993).

KEATS, JOHN, *The Letters of John Keats*, ed. Hyder E. Rollins. 2 vols. (Cambridge, Mass.: Harvard University Press, 1958).

——*The Poems of John Keats*, ed. Jack Stillinger (Cambridge, Mass.: Belknap Press, 1978).

The Keepsake for MDCCCXXIX, ed. Frederick Mansel Reynolds (London: Hurst, Chance, and Co., 1829).

LAKOFF, GEORGE, *Women, Fire, and Dangerous Things: What Categories Reveal About the Mind* (Chicago: University of Chicago Press, 1987).

LANDON, LAETITIA ELIZABETH, (L.E.L.), *The Poetical Works of Miss Landon* (Philadelphia: Carey and Hart, 1841).

——*Poetical Works*. 2 vols. (London: Longman, Brown, Greene, and Longmans, 1855).

LAWRENCE, CHRISTOPHER, 'The Nervous System and Society in the Scottish Enlightenment', in B. Barnes and S. Shapin (eds.), *Natural Order: Historical Studies of Scientific Culture* (London, 1979).

LEES-MILNE, JAMES (ed.), *The Country House* (Oxford: Oxford University Press, 1982).

LEIGHTON, ANGELA, *Victorian Women Poets: Writing Against the Heart* (Charlottesville: University Press of Virginia, 1992).

LEVINSON, MARJORIE, *Keats's Life of Allegory: The Origins of a Style* (Oxford: Blackwell, 1988).

LOCKE, JOHN, *An Essay Concerning Human Understanding*, ed. John W. Yolton. 2 vols. (London: J. M. Dent, 1961, rev. 1965).

LONSDALE, ROGER (ed.), *The New Oxford Book of Eighteenth Century Verse* (Oxford: Oxford University Press, 1984).

——(ed.), *Eighteenth-Century Women Poets: An Oxford Anthology* (Oxford: Oxford University Press, 1989).

LOOTENS, TRICIA, 'Hemans and Home: Victorianism, Feminine "Internal Enemies", and the Domestication of National Identity', *PMLA*, 109/2 (Mar. 1994), 238–53.

MACPHERSON, JAMES, *The Poems of Ossian*, intro. William Sharp (Edinburgh: John Grant, 1926).

——*Fragments of Ancient Poetry*, intro. John Dunn. Augustan Reprint Society no. 122 (Los Angeles: William Andrews Clark Memorial Library, University of California, 1966).

MAGNUSON, PAUL, ' "The Eolian Harp" in Context', *Studies in Romanticism*, 24 (1985), 3–20.

MANNING, PETER, 'Wordsworth in the *Keepsake*, 1829', in *Literature in the Marketplace*, ed. John O'Jordan and Robert L. Patten (Cambridge: Cambridge University Press, 1995), 44–73.

MARX, KARL, *Capital*, ed. Frederick Engels (New York: International Publishers, 1967).

MAURICE, THOMAS, *Memoirs of the Author of the Indian Antiquities* (London: privately printed for the author, 1819–20).

MCGANN, JEROME (ed.), *The New Oxford Book of Romantic Period Verse* (Oxford and New York: Oxford University Press, 1993).

MELLOR, ANNE K. (ed.), *Romanticism and Feminism* (Bloomington: Indiana University Press, 1988).

——*Romanticism and Gender* (New York: Routledge, 1993).

MORE, HANNAH, *The Complete Works of Hannah More*. 2 vols. (New York: J. C. Derby, 1854).

MULLAN, JOHN, *Sentiment and Sociability: The Language of Feeling in the Eighteenth Century* (Oxford: Clarendon Press, 1988).

NEFF, EMERY, *The Poetry of History: The Contribution of Literature and Literary Scholarship to the Writing of History since Voltaire* (New York: Columbia University Press, 1947).

NEUMAN, SHIRLEY and STEPHENSON, GLENNIS (eds.), *Reimagining Women: Representations of Women and Culture* (Toronto: University of Toronto Press, 1993).

OVID (P. Ovidius Naso), *Amores, Epistulae, De Medicamine, Artis Amatoriae, Remediorum Amoris*, ed. Rudolphi Merkelii (Lipsiae: G. Teubneri, 1852).

PALEY, MORTON, 'Coleridge and the Annuals', *Huntington Library Quarterly*, 57 (1994), 1–26.

PATEY, DOUGLAS LANE, ' "Aesthetics" and the Rise of Lyric in the Eighteenth Century', *Studies in English Literature*, 33 (1993), 587–608.

PERELLA, JAMES, *The Kiss Sacred and Profane* (Berkeley and Los Angeles: University of California Press, 1969).

POPE, ALEXANDER, *An Essay on Man*, ed. Maynard Mack (London: Methuen & Co., 1950).

POLWHELE, RICHARD, *The Unsex'd Females; a Poem, addressed to the Author of the Pursuits of Literature . . .*, ed. Peter Byrnes, *et al.* A Hypermedia edition. *British Poetry 1780–1900: A Hypertext Archive of Scholarly Editions*, gen. ed. Jerome McGann. (Charlottesville: University of Virginia, the Electronic Text Center, Alderman Library, 1994) (email: etext@virginia.edu).

POOVEY, MARY, *The Proper Lady and the Woman Writer: Ideology as Style in the Works of Mary Wollstonecraft, Mary Shelley, and Jane Austen* (Chicago: University of Chicago Press, 1984).

POPE, ALEXANDER, *An Essay on Man*, ed. Maynard Mack (London: Methuen and Co. Ltd., 1950).

POUND, EZRA, *Pavannes and Divisions* (New York: Alfred A. Knopf, 1918).

PRIESTLEY, JOSEPH, *Disquisitions relating to Matter and Spirit . . .* (London: J. Johnson, 1777).

RAMAZANI, JAHAN, *Poetry of Mourning: The Modern Elegy from Hardy to Heaney* (Chicago: University of Chicago Press, 1994).

REILL, PETER HANS, *The German Enlightenment and the Rise of Historicism* (Berkeley and Los Angeles: University of California Press, 1975).

RICKS, CHRISTOPHER, *Keats and Embarrassment* (Oxford: Clarendon Press, 1974).

ROBINSON, MARY, *Poems* (London: J. Bell, 1791).

——*Sappho and Phaon: In a Series of Legitimate Sonnets, With Thoughts on Poetical Subjects and Anecdotes of the Greek Poetess*, ed. Christopher Nagle, *et al.* A Hypermedia Edition. *British Poetry 1780–1900: A Hypertext Archive of Scholarly Editions*, gen. ed. Jerome McGann (Charlottesville: University of Virginia, the Electronic Text Center, Alderman Library, 1994) (email: etext@virginia.edu).

ROSS, MARLON B., *The Contours of Masculine Desire. Romanticism and the Rise of Women's Poetry* (Oxford and New York: Oxford University Press, 1989).

SACKS, PETER, *The English Elegy: Studies in the Genre from Spenser to Yeats* (Baltimore: The Johns Hopkins University Press, 1985).

SAINT-PIERRE, JACQUES-HENRI-BERNARDIN DE, *Etudes de la nature*. 4 vols. (Paris: Didot, 1788).

——*Paul and Virginia*, trans. Helen Maria Williams (London: T. Nelson and Sons, 1872).

SCHILLER, FRIEDRICH, *Uber naive und sentimentalische Dichtung* (Oxford: Oxford University Press, 1950).

——*Naïve and Sentimental Poetry and On the Sublime; two essays* (New York: F. Ungar Publishing Co., 1967).

SCHOFIELD, ROBERT E., *Mechanism and Materialism: British Natural Philosophy in an Age of Reason* (Princeton: Princeton University Press, 1970).

SEELY, JOHN BENJAMIN, *The Wonders of Ellora* (London: G. & W. B. Whittaker, 1824).

SELL, ROGER D. (ed.), *Literary Pragmatics* (London and New York: Routledge, 1991).

SHAFFER, ELINOR, *'Kubla Khan' and The Fall of Jerusalem* (Cambridge: Cambridge University Press, 1975).

SHELLEY, MARY, *Frankenstein*, eds. D. L. Macdonald and Kathleen Scherf (Peterborough, Ontario: Broadview, 1994).

SHELLEY, PERCY BYSSHE, *Shelley's Poetry and Prose*, eds. Donald H. Reiman and Sharon B. Powers (New York: W. W. Norton and Co., 1977).

SHERBO, ARTHUR, *English Poetic Diction from Chaucer to Wordsworth* (East Lansing: Michigan State University Press, 1975).

SITTER, JOHN, *Literary Loneliness in Mid-Eighteenth-Century England* (Ithaca: Cornell University Press, 1982).

SMITH, CHARLOTTE, *The Poems of Charlotte Smith*, ed. Stuart Curran. *Women Writers in English 1350–1850*, gen. ed. Susanne Woods (New York: Oxford University Press, 1993).

SPACKS, PATRICIA, *The Female Imagination* (New York: Alfred Knopf, 1975).

STEWART, DUGALD, *The Collected Works*, ed. Sir William Hamilton. 10 vols. (Edinburgh: T. Constable and Co., 1854).

TODD, JANET, *Sensibility: An Introduction* (London and New York: Methuen, 1986).

WARD, HERMAN M., *Byron and the Magazines, 1806–1824*. Salzburg Studies in English Literature, Romantic Reassessment 19 (Salzburg: Universität Salzburg, 1973).

WEHRLI, MAX, *Johann Jakob Bodmer und die Geschichte der Literatur* (Frauenfeld: Huber, 1936).

WELLEK, RENÉ, *Kant in England, 1793–1838* (Princeton: Princeton University Press, 1931).

WILLIAMS, HELEN MARIA, *Poems*. 2 vols. (London: A. Rivington and J. Marshall, for Thomas Cadell, 1786).

WOLF, F. A., *F. A. Wolf: Prolegomena to Homer. 1795*, trans. and eds. Anthony Grafton, Glenn W. Most, and James E. G. Zetzel (Princeton: Princeton University Press, 1985).

WOLLSTONECRAFT, MARY, *The Works of Mary Wollstonecraft*, eds. Janet Todd and Marilyn Butler (London: William Pickering, 1989).

WORDSWORTH, WILLIAM, *William Wordsworth: The Literary Criticism*, ed. Paul M. Zall (Lincoln: University of Nebraska Press, 1966).

——*The Poems*, ed. John O. Hayden. 2 vols. (Harmondsworth: Penguin Books, 1977).

——*The Prelude 1799, 1805, 1850*, eds. Jonathan Wordsworth, M. H. Abrams, and Stephen Gill (New York: W. W. Norton & Co., 1979).

YEARSLEY, ANN, *Poems on Several Occasions* (London: T. Cadell, 1785).

——*Poems on Various Subjects* (London: G. G. J. and J. Robinson, 1787).

——*The Rural Lyre* (London: G. G. J. and J. Robinson, 1796).

YOLTON, JOHN W., *Thinking Matter: Materialism in Eighteenth-Century Britain* (Minneapolis: University of Minnesota Press, 1983).

YOUNG, EDWARD, *The Complete Works, Poetry and Prose*. 2 vols. (1854; repr. by G. Olms, London, 1968).

Index